THE CULTURES OF CITIES

ADVANCE PRAISE FOR *THE CULTURES OF CITIES:*

"*The Cultures of Cities* gives a tremendous boost to urban cultural analysis. Full of fresh details and original ideas, it should significantly influence the whole discourse on cities and culture." – Harvey Molotch, co-author of *Urban Fortunes*

"Sharon Zukin has written a penetrating and nuanced portrait of the displacement of planning by marketing in our cities, of the ways in which they extend and increasingly depend on the spurious automations of culture that have become America's most important product. What makes her book especially rare, though, are her recordings of the ways these cultural superpositions reverberate in the life of the street, the negotiations and compromises forced on the real lives of people harried by this symbolic economy and its seemingly inexorable cooptation of the spaces of public life." – Michael Sorkin, architect, editor of *Variations on a Theme Park*

BLACKWELL PUBLISHING
350 Main Street, Malden, MA 02148-5020, USA
9600 Garsington Road, Oxford OX4 2DQ, UK
550 Swanston Street, Carlton, Victoria 3053, Australia

First published 1995

10   2006

Library of Congress Cataloging-in-Publication Data

Zukin, Sharon
  The cultures of cities / Sharon Zukin
    p.   cm.
  Includes bibliographical references (p.) and index.
  ISBN 1-55786-436-5 (hbk. : alk. paper)—ISBN 1-55786-437-3 (pbk. : alk. paper)
  1. Cities and towns. 2. City and town life. 3. Urban sociology. I. Title.
HT109.Z85   1995
307.76—dc20   95–7534
                                                            CIP

ISBN-13: 978-1-55786-437-6 (pbk. : alk. paper)

A catalogue record for this title is available from the British Library.

Set by AM Marketing

The publisher's policy is to use permanent paper from mills that operate a sustainable
forestry policy, and which has been manufactured from pulp processed using
acid-free and elementary chlorine-free practices. Furthermore, the publisher
ensures that the text paper and cover board used have met acceptable
environmental accreditation standards.

For further information on
Blackwell Publishing, visit our website:
www.blackwellpublishing.com

THE CULTURES OF CITIES

Sharon Zukin

BLACKWELL
Publishers

FOR ELISABETH RACHEL ZUKIN ROSEN

CONTENTS

Preface vii

1 Whose Culture? Whose City? 1
   The Symbolic Economy ◆ *Culture as an Economic
   Base* ◆ *Culture as a Means of Framing Space*
   ◆ *Public Space* ◆ *Security, Ethnicity, and Culture*

2 Learning From Disney World 49
   Real Theme Parks ◆ *A Shared Public Culture* ◆
   The Spatial Reality of Virtual Reality ◆ *Disney
   World as a Service Industry* ◆ *Disney's Symbolic
   Economy*

3 A Museum In The Berkshires
   with Philip Kasinitz 79
   Trouble in the Berkshires ◆ *Global Art Worlds* ◆
   The Conceptual Museum ◆ *Cultural Politics* ◆
   Museums and Metropolitan Culture

4 High Culture And Wild Commerce
   In New York City 109
   Measuring the Arts Economy ◆ *High Culture as
   Space and Symbol* ◆ *Landmarks* ◆ *Museums*
   ◆ *Times Square* ◆ *Jobs and Money* ◆ *A Culture
   Capital?*

5   Artists And Immigrants In New York City
     Restaurants
     with Louis Amdur, Janet Baus, Philana Cho,
     Dalton Conley, Stephen Duncombe, Herman
     Joseph, Daniel Kessler, Jennifer Parker, and
     Huaishi Song   153
     *Restaurants as a Cultural Site ◆ Immigrants and
     Global Trends ◆ New York Restaurants ◆
     Restaurant Employees ◆ The Social Division of
     Labor ◆ The Ethnic Division of Labor ◆
     Restaurant Owners ◆ Symbolic Economy and
     World Economy*

6   While The City Shops   187
     *A Child's Cartography ◆ Ghetto Shopping
     Centers ◆ Downtown Brooklyn ◆ 125th Street
     ◆ Indoor Flea Markets ◆ Remembering Walter
     Benjamin*

7   The Mystique Of Public Culture   259
     *The Meanings of Culture ◆ Cultural Strategies ◆
     Seeing Visions ◆ A Word About Theory*

     References   295

     Index   313

PREFACE

This book has both a personal history and an intellectual history. It is the first book I have written since my daughter was born four years ago. Unlike me, Elisabeth is a native New Yorker. Everything about the city is self-evident to her. So I have tried to explain to her all the little truths that took me so long to figure out – why cities are great as well as fearsome – as well as a lot of smaller, related mysteries. Why do I prefer buses to subways? Why do we never sit in the last car of the subway train? Why do art museums build sculpture gardens but do not let you touch the statues? Like all parents' stories, mine are full of contradictions. Sometimes there are even glaring contradictions between what I teach or write, as an observer of cities, and what I do as a mother.

For instance, the very week I discussed with graduate students Donna Haraway's article on "Teddy Bear Patriarchy," in which Haraway scathingly deconstructs the arrogant worldview embodied in the stuffed-animal dioramas and original wildlife program of the founders of the American Museum of Natural History, I took Elisabeth to the zoo. The fact that its name has been changed to the *wildlife conservation center* and its visual presentations brought up to date with ecological concerns did not make me feel more at ease with the contradictions between my various roles. In part, I have tried to write my way through them. So the book has some of the defects of parental stories that want to explain too much and manage to explain too little.

Some of the contradictions, however, arise in the changed meanings of culture in cities today. In the last few years, culture has become a much more explicit part of urban politics and policies. *Multiculturalism* has become a code word for social inclusion or exclusion, depending on your point of view, and has sparked long-running battles over what is taught in the public schools and which books are bought by public libraries. The atmosphere of tolerance that city people historically claim has been charged with the lightning rods of social and cultural "diversity." Accepting diversity implies sharing public space – the streets, buses, parks, and schools – with people who visibly, and quite possibly vehemently, live lives you do not approve of. Cultural institutions, such as art museums, which were assumed to enhance a city's reputation for civility, have been challenged as "elitist" and are in the process of being "democratized" or redefined. At the same time, the wealth of these institutions is praised by public officials for strengthening a city's competitive position in relation to other cities. When we look at a painting by Van Gogh and see tourist dollars, when we think of social class differences in terms of "cultures," when we design a downtown shopping center as Disney World – we are walking through the contradictions of the cultures of cities.

The Cultures of Cities also grows out of my fascination with the material side of cultural production and cultural representations. When I wrote *Loft Living* a number of years ago, I tried to make clear the seductive influence of the arts on urban redevelopment. Using artists' studios or lofts to stimulate housing markets and raise property values was an unanticipated effect of encouraging artistic careers – yet in its connections with an ever-expanding tide of cultural consumption in the city's art galleries, restaurants, and gourmet food stores, it was a first step toward gentrification. The response to *Loft Living* by urbanists and artists alike encouraged me to emphasize the symbolic importance of the arts in urban political economy. With a continued displacement of manufacturing and development of the financial and nonprofit sectors of the economy, cultural production seemed to be more and more what cities were about.

By the time I wrote *Landscapes of Power: From Detroit to Disney World,* North American cities had shifted even farther from traditional manufacturing of material things toward more abstract kinds of products: stocks and bonds, real estate, and the experiences of cultural tourism. Redevelopment in both cities and suburbs was based on control of visual images of social homogeneity, from the rolling hills of corporate suburbs to the gentrified restaurants of nouvelle cuisine. What I saw all around me moved me to make the radical argument that the way consumption was organized – in spaces, in jobs, in television shows and literary images – had become at least as important in people's lives as the organization of production. Cultural capital was as "real" as investment capital in its effects on society.

Using the concept "landscape" enabled me to focus attention on social communities, from factory towns to postmodern cities, as both material and symbolic constructions. As I continued to think about cities, I began to think of their economies as based increasingly on symbolic production. The growth of restaurants, museums, and culture industries pointed toward a symbolic economy whose material effects – on jobs, ethnic and social divisions, and cultural images – could scarcely be imagined.

Before I conceived of *The Cultures of Cities* as a book, I gave a series of lectures that implicitly developed the theme of a symbolic economy. In 1991, in a paper I wrote for a conference at the University of Bremen, the symbolic economy took on the shape of the New York art market in the 1980s and early 1990s – its inflated expansion and underbelly of social fears. In 1992, I spoke at Syracuse University about the plan to develop a Massachusetts Museum of Contemporary Art in North Adams, a town suffering from deindustrialization and high unemployment. Around the same time, I gave another lecture, at a conference at the State University of New York at Binghamton, on how public spaces – from empty storefronts to neighborhood shopping streets – are changed by conditions of economic decline. I also continued to write and think about Disney World as an emblem of the service economy and a flagship of a certain kind of urban growth – orderly, well-mannered, placing individual desire under corporate control. I spoke about these issues at a conference at the University of California at Davis. Working with my graduate students, I developed a research project on restaurants as a space of cultural production and consumption. This work was published as an article on artists and immigrants in New York City restaurants. Eventually, I thought about representations of culture in public space – in parks, art museums, and city streets – and saw how public culture is defined by competition in these spaces for the right to experience, conceptualize, and control them. The design transformation of Bryant Park crystallized these issues, which I spoke about at conferences at Stanford, Oxford, and the City University of New York. I finally wrote the chapter on autobiography and hegemony in shopping streets in 1994.

These are very different concerns from those that animated Lewis Mumford's classic work *The Culture of Cities,* whose title inspired mine. Though his book and mine are both concerned with urban design, democracy, and the market economy, for me the very concept of culture has become more explicit and problematic.

So much for this book's origins. Although thinking through the book has been an individual journey, I have had lots of good companionship along the way.

I owe a great acknowledgment to my coauthors on Chapters 3 and 5. While I bear the major responsibility for conceptualizing and writing both chapters, Philip Kasinitz, associate professor of sociology at Hunter College and the City University Graduate School, carried out an essential part of both the research and writing of preliminary drafts of the chapter on MASS MoCA, and my graduate students in a seminar on urban sociology at the City University of New York did all the research for, and much of the preliminary writing of, the chapter on restaurants. It was a joy to work with such good collaborators.

I am also grateful to a series of dedicated research assistants: Jenn Parker, Danny Kessler, and Alex Vitale. Not only did they share my interests in putting this book together, they cheered me by their continued ability to be convinced of its importance.

After the book was written, I benefited from a careful reading of the whole manuscript by my friend Harvey Molotch. Few scholars in the urban field combine such broad knowledge with such discriminating aesthetic taste. Harvey undoubtedly saved me from committing the worst errors; the lesser ones remain my own.

Nor could the book have been written without the readiness of colleagues to listen to my hesitant questions and rambling conjectures, to read a few pages I was unsure of, to offer encouragement. I have learned from Setha Low, my co-conspirator in teaching an interdisciplinary course on "Objects, Space, and Vision"; Priscilla Ferguson, my faithful collaborator in research on cuisine; and Janet Wolff, Tony King, Rolf Meyersohn, Steve Steinberg, Bill Kornblum, George Cunningham, and Bob Viscusi. Herbert Gans, Peter Marcuse, and Tony Schumann offered helpful comments on a presentation I made at Columbia University. For my colleagues and students at the City University Graduate School, who thought I must be writing great things when they continually passed the open door to my darkened office and saw me typing away on the computer to the light of a 60-watt bulb, I hope this book has not turned out to be an anticlimax. I am sorry I cannot celebrate its publication with my colleague Vernon Boggs, who died after the manuscript was completed. He was a constant friendly presence in the corridor as I wrote.

The idea of writing "a book of essays" came from Chris Rojek, formerly of Routledge and now returned to university teaching. Anyone who has embraced such an idea knows the time and effort involved in developing the coherent themes and style of a book. My editor at Blackwell, Simon Prosser, has the skill and tact that should, but so rarely do, go with the calling. He has shown both courage and forebearance in waiting for the book to take shape. The final product has also benefitted from the care of Jan Leahy, Blackwell's production manager, who spent endless telephone conversations talking with me about layout, type styles, and whether Kmart gets a hyphen.

My greatest gratitude must be expressed, of course, to Elisabeth and to Richard Rosen. They are with me wherever I go. When Elisabeth arranges her postcards and toys on the dining room floor and says she is "playing museum" or lays out her toy dishes and plastic foods to "play café," I think there must be some consistency to my life.

New York City
October 1994

THIS FALL, TOUR THE WORLD OF ART.
OR THE MUSEUMS OF NEW YORK.
SAME DIFFERENCE.

Subway advertisement, New York City, 1994

WE GOING
BE OPEN
SON
　　RAY' PIZZA

Sign outside restaurant, New York City, 1993

■ The restoration of Bryant Park: Domestication by cappuccino.

Photo by Alex Vitale.

1

WHOSE CULTURE? WHOSE CITY?

Cities are often criticized because they represent the basest instincts of human society. They are built versions of Leviathan and Mammon, mapping the power of the bureaucratic machine or the social pressures of money. We who live in cities like to think of "culture" as the antidote to this crass vision. The Acropolis of the urban art museum or concert hall, the trendy art gallery and café, restaurants that fuse ethnic traditions into culinary logos – cultural activities are supposed to lift us out of the mire of our everyday lives and into the sacred spaces of ritualized pleasures.[1]

Yet culture is also a powerful means of controlling cities. As a source of images and memories, it symbolizes "who belongs" in specific places. As a set of architectural themes, it plays a leading role in urban redevelopment strategies based on historic preservation or local "heritage." With the disappearance of local manufacturing industries and periodic crises

---

1. Over the past few years, I have presented parts of this chapter at conferences or lectures at Oxford, Stanford, Columbia, Georgia State, Harvard, and Temple Universities and the City University of New York Graduate Center. The discussion of Bryant Park always gets a buzz of recognition from the audience because the privatization of public space is such an important issue everywhere. I am grateful to City University graduate students Jeffrey Hochman and Andrea Kanapell for their research on BIDS and Bryant Park, respectively.

in government and finance, culture is more and more the business of cities – the basis of their tourist attractions and their unique, competitive edge. The growth of cultural consumption (of art, food, fashion, music, tourism) and the industries that cater to it fuels the city's symbolic economy, its visible ability to produce both symbols and space.

In recent years, culture has also become a more explicit site of conflicts over social differences and urban fears. Large numbers of new immigrants and ethnic minorities have put pressure on public institutions, from schools to political parties, to deal with their individual demands. Such high culture institutions as art museums and symphony orchestras have been driven to expand and diversify their offerings to appeal to a broader public. These pressures, broadly speaking, are both ethnic and aesthetic. By creating policies and ideologies of "multiculturalism," they have forced public institutions to change.

On a different level, city boosters increasingly compete for tourist dollars and financial investments by bolstering the city's image as a center of cultural innovation, including restaurants, avant garde performances, and architectural design. These cultural strategies of redevelopment have fewer critics than multiculturalism. But they often pit the self-interest of real estate developers, politicians, and expansion-minded cultural institutions against grassroots pressures from local communities.

At the same time, strangers mingling in public space and fears of violent crime have inspired the growth of private police forces, gated and barred communities, and a movement to design public spaces for maximum surveillance. These, too, are a source of contemporary urban culture. If one way of dealing with the material inequalities of city life has been to aestheticize diversity, another way has been to aestheticize fear.

Controlling the various cultures of cities suggests the possibility of controlling all sorts of urban ills, from violence and hate crime to economic decline. That this is an illusion has been amply shown by battles over multiculturalism and its warring factions – ethnic politics and urban riots. Yet the cultural power to create an image, to frame a vision, of the city has become more important as publics have become more mobile and diverse, and traditional institutions – both social classes and political parties – have become less relevant mechanisms of expressing identity. Those who create images stamp a collective identity. Whether they are media corporations like the Disney Company, art museums, or politicians, they are developing new spaces for public cultures. Significant public spaces of the late 19th and early 20th century – such as Central Park, the Broadway theater district, and the top of the Empire State Building – have been joined by Disney World, Bryant Park, and the entertainment-based retail shops of Sony Plaza. By accepting these spaces without questioning their representations of urban life, we risk succumbing to a visually seductive, privatized public culture.

▓ The Symbolic Economy

Anyone who walks through midtown Manhattan comes face to face with the symbolic economy (see map of Manhattan). A significant number of new public spaces owe their particular shape and form to the intertwining of cultural symbols and entrepreneurial capital.

◆ The AT&T Building, whose Chippendale roof was a much
   criticized icon of postmodern architecture, has been sold to
   the Japanese entertainment giant Sony; the formerly open public
   areas at street level have been enclosed as retail stores and
   transformed into Sony Plaza. Each store sells Sony products:
   video cameras in one shop, clothes and accessories related
   to performers under contract to Sony's music or film division in
   another. Sony's interactive science museum features the
   opportunity to get hands-on experience with Sony video
   equipment. Sony had to get the city government's approval
   both to enclose these stores and set them up for retail shopping,
   for the original agreement to build the office tower had
   depended on providing *public* space. Critics charged that retail
   stores are not public space, and even the city planning
   commissioners admitted they were perplexed by the question
   (AIA Forum, "Sony Plaza: Public Space or Corporate Face,"
   May 1994). "In return for the retail space," the chairman of the
   local community board said, "we would like to hold Sony to
   the original understanding to create a peaceful refuge, which
   certainly didn't include corporate banners and a television
   monitor." "We like it," the president of Sony Plaza replied. The

■ Sony Plaza: Retail stores as public space.

Photo by Richard Rosen.

banners "are seen as art and bring warmth and color to the space" (*New York Times,* January 30, 1994).

◆ Two blocks away, André Emmerich, a leading contemporary art dealer, rented an empty storefront in a former bank branch to show three huge abstract canvases by the painter Al Held. Entitled *Harry, If I Told You, Would You Know?* the group of paintings was exhibited in raw space, amid falling plaster, peeling paint, exposed wires, and unfinished floors, and

▓ A selective view of Manhattan's symbolic economy: Downtown financial district, parks, art museums, midtown business improvement districts and African market.

▓ Culture as a means of framing space: Second installation of paintings by Al Held in vacant storefront at 650 Madison Avenue, October 1992-January 1994.

Photo by Kevin Ryan, courtesy of André Emmerich Gallery.

passersby viewed the exhibit from the street through large plate glass windows. The work of art was certainly for sale, yet it was displayed as if it were a free, public good; and it would never have been there had the storefront been rented by a more usual commercial tenant.

◆ On 42nd Street, across from my office, Bryant Park is considered one of the most successful public spaces to be created in New York City in recent years. After a period of decline, disuse, and daily occupation by vagrants and drug dealers, the park was taken over by a not-for-profit business association of local property owners and their major corporate tenants, called the Bryant Park Restoration Corporation. This group redesigned the park and organized daylong programs of cultural events; they renovated the kiosks and installed new food services; they hired a phalanx of private security guards. All this attracted nearby office workers, both women and men, who make the park

▓ Prêt-à-porter in public space: Twice a year, huge white tents are erected in Bryant Park to show the fashion collections of New York City designers.

Photo courtesy of Patrick McMullan and 7th on Sixth.

a lively midday gathering place, as it had been prior to the mid 1970s – a public park under private control.

Building a city depends on how people combine the traditional economic factors of land, labor, and capital. But it also depends on how they manipulate symbolic languages of exclusion and entitlement. The look and feel of cities reflect decisions about what – and who – should be visible and what should not, on concepts of order and disorder, and on uses of aesthetic power. In this primal sense, the city has always had a symbolic economy. Modern cities also owe their existence to a second, more abstract symbolic economy devised by "place entrepreneurs" (Molotch 1976), officials and investors whose ability to deal with the symbols of growth yields "real" results in real estate development, new businesses, and jobs.

Related to this entrepreneurial activity is a third, traditional symbolic economy of city advocates and business elites who, through a combination of philanthropy, civic pride, and desire to establish their identity as a patrician class, build the majestic art museums, parks, and architectural complexes that represent a world-class city. What is new about the symbolic economy since the 1970s is its symbiosis of image and product, the scope and scale of selling images on a national and even a global level, and the role of the symbolic economy in speaking for, or representing, the city.

In the 1970s and 1980s, the symbolic economy rose to prominence against a background of industrial decline and financial speculation. The metamorphosis of American-made products into Mexican blue jeans, Japanese autos, and East Asian computers emptied the factories where those goods had been made. Companies that were the largest employers in their communities went out of business or were bought and restructured by takeover artists.

The entrepreneurial edge of the economy shifted toward deal making and selling investments and toward those creative products that could not easily be reproduced elsewhere. Product design – creating the look of a thing – was said to show economic genius. Hollywood film studios and media empires were bought and sold and bought again. In the 1990s, with the harnessing of new computer-based technologies to marketing campaigns, the "information superhighway" promised to join companies to consumers in a Manichean embrace of technology and entertainment. "The entertainment industry is now the driving force for new technology, as defense used to be," the CEO of a U.S. software company said ("Entertainment Economy" 1994, p. 60).

The growth of the symbolic economy in finance, media, and entertainment may not change the way entrepreneurs do business. But it has already forced the growth of towns and cities, created a vast new work force, and changed the way consumers and employees think. In the early 1990s, employment in "entertainment and recreation" in the United States grew slightly more than in health care and six times more than in the auto industry ("Entertainment Economy" 1994, p. 61). The facilities where these employees work – hotels, restaurants, expanses of new construction and undeveloped land – are more than just workplaces. They reshape geography and ecology; they are places of creation and transformation.

The Disney Company, for example, makes films and distributes them from Hollywood. It runs a television channel and sells commercial spinoffs, such as toys, books, and videos, from a national network of stores. Disney is also a real estate developer in Anaheim, Orlando, France, and Japan and the proposed developer of a theme park in Virginia and a hotel and theme park in Times Square. Moreover, as an employer, Disney has redefined work roles. Proposing a model for change in the emerging service economy, Disney has shifted from the white-collar worker described by C. Wright Mills in the 1950s to a new chameleon of "flexible" tasks. The planners at its corporate headquarters are "imagineers"; the costumed crowd-handlers at its theme parks are "cast members." Disney suggests that the symbolic economy is more than just the sum of the services it provides. The symbolic economy unifies material practices of finance, labor, art, performance, and design.

The prominence of culture industries also inspires a new language dealing with difference (see Ewen 1988). It offers a coded means of discrimination, an undertone to the dominant discourse of democratization. Styles that develop on the streets are cycled through mass media, especially fashion and "urban music" magazines and MTV, where, divorced from their social context, they become images of cool. On urban billboards advertising designer perfumes or jeans, they are recycled to the streets, where they become a provocation, breeding imitation and even violence. The beachheads of designer stores, from Armani to A/X, from Ralph Lauren to Polo, are fiercely parodied for the "props" of fashion-conscious teenagers in inner city ghettos. The cacophany of demands for justice is translated into a coherent demand for jeans. Claims for public space by culture industries inspire the count-erpolitics of display in late 20th century urban riots.

The symbolic economy recycles real estate as it does designer clothes. Visual display matters in American and European cities today, because the identities of places are established by sites of delectation. The sensual display of fruit at an urban farmers' market or gourmet food store puts a neighborhood "on the map" of visual delights and reclaims it for gentrification. A sidewalk cafe takes back the street from casual workers and homeless people. In Bryant Park, enor-mous white tents and a canopied walkway set the scene for spring and fall showings of New York fashion designers. Twice a year, the park is filled by the fashion media, paparazzi, store buyers, and supermodels doing the business of culture and reclaiming Bryant Park as a vital, important place. We New Yorkers become willing participants in the drama of the fashion business. As cultural consumers, we are drawn into the interrelated production of symbols and space.

Mass suburbanization since the 1950s has made it unreasonable to expect that most middle-class men and women will want to live in cities. But developing small places within the city as sites of visual delectation creates urban oases where everyone *appears* to be middle class. In the fronts of the restaurants or stores, at least, consumers are strolling, looking, eating, drinking, sometimes speaking English and sometimes not. In the back regions, an ethnic division of labor guarantees that immigrant workers are preparing food and cleaning up. This is not just a game of representations: developing the city's symbolic economy involves recycling workers, sorting people in housing markets, luring investment, and negotiating political claims for public goods and ethnic promotion. Cities from New York to Los Angeles and Miami seem to thrive by developing small districts around specific themes. Whether it is Times Square or el Calle Ocho, a commercial or an "ethnic" district, the narrative web spun by the symbolic economy around a specific place relies on a vision of cultural consumption and a social and an ethnic division of labor.

As cities and societies place greater emphasis on visualization, the Disney Company and art museums play more prominent roles in defining public culture. I am speaking, first, of public culture as a process of negotiating images that are accepted by large numbers of people. In this sense, culture industries and cultural institutions have stepped into the vacuum left by government. At least since the 1970s debacles of Watergate and the Vietnam War, through Irangate in the 1980s and the confessions of politicians in the 1990s, government has lacked the basic credibility to define the core values of a common culture. On the local level, most mayors and other elected officials have been too busy clearing budget deficits and dealing with constituents' complaints about crime and schools to project a common image. The "vision thing," as George Bush called it, has been supplied by religious leaders from Jerry Falwell to Jesse Jackson and by those institutions whose visual resources permit or even require them to capitalize on culture.

I also see public culture as socially constructed on the micro-level. It is produced by the many social encounters that make up daily life in the streets, shops, and parks – the spaces in which we experience public life in cities. The right to be in these spaces, to use them in certain ways, to invest them with a sense of our selves and our communities – to claim them as ours and to be claimed in turn by them – make up a constantly changing public culture. People with economic and political power have the greatest opportunity to shape public culture by controlling the building of the city's public spaces in stone and concrete. Yet public space is inherently democratic. The question of who can occupy public space, and so define an image of the city, is open-ended.

Talking about the cultures of cities in purely visual terms does not do justice to the material practices of politics and economics that create a symbolic economy. But neither does a strictly political-economic approach suggest the subtle powers of visual and spatial strategies of social differentiation. As I suggested in *Landscapes of Power* (1991), the rise of the cities' symbolic economy is rooted in two long-term changes – the economic decline of cities compared to suburban and nonurban spaces and the expansion of abstract financial speculation – and in such short-term factors, dating from the 1970s and 1980s, as new mass immigration, the growth of cultural consumption, and the marketing of identity politics. This is an inclusive, structural, and materialist view. If I am right, we cannot speak about cities today without understanding:

- how cities use culture as an economic base,
- how capitalizing on culture spills over into the privatization and militarization of public space, and
- how the power of culture is related to the aesthetics of fear.

Culture as an Economic Base

Suppose we turn the old Marxist relation between a society's base and its superstructure on its head and think of culture as a way of producing basic goods. In fact, culture supplies the basic information – including symbols, patterns, and meaning – for nearly all the service industries. In our debased contemporary vocabulary, the word *culture* has become an abstraction for any economic activity that does not create material products like steel, cars, or computers. Stretching the term is a legacy of the advertising revolution of the early 20th century and the more recent escalation in political image making. Because culture is a system for producing symbols, every attempt to get people to buy a product becomes a culture industry. The sociologist Daniel Bell used to tell a joke about a circus employee whose job it was to follow the elephant and clean up after it; when asked, she said her job was in "the entertainment business." Today, she might say she was in "the culture industry." Culture is intertwined with capital and identity in the city's production systems.

From one point of view, cultural institutions establish a competitive advantage over other cities for attracting new businesses and corporate elites. Culture suggests the coherence and consistency of a brand name product. Like any commodity, "cultural" landscape has the possibility of generating other commodities. Historically, of course, the arrow of causality goes the other way. Only an economic surplus – sufficient to fund sacrifices for the temple, Michelangelos for the chapel, and bequests to art museums in the wills of robber barons – generates culture. But in American and European cities during the 1970s, culture became more of an instrument in the entrepreneurial strategies of local governments and business alliances. In the shift to a post-postwar economy, who could build the biggest modern art museum suggested the vitality of the financial sector. Who could turn the waterfront from docklands rubble to parks and marinas suggested the possibilities for expansion of the managerial and professional corps. This was probably as rational a response as any to the unbeatable isolationist challenge of suburban industrial parks and office campuses. The city, such planners and developers as James Rouse believed, would counter the visual homogeneity of the suburbs by playing the card of aesthetic diversity.

Yet culture also suggests a labor force that is well suited to the revolution of diminished expectations that began in the 1960s (Zukin, 1989 [1982]). In contrast to high-rolling rappers and rockers, "high" cultural producers are supposed to live on the margins; and the incomes of most visual artists, art curators, actors, writers, and musicians suggest they must be used to deprivation. A widespread appreciation of culture does not really temper the work force's demands. But, in contrast to workers in other industries, artists are flexible on job tasks and work hours, do not always join labor unions, and present a docile or even "cultured" persona. These qualities make them, like immigrants, desirable employees in service industries (see Waldinger 1992, 107–8). Dissatisfaction with menial and dead-end jobs does not boil over into protest because their "real" identity comes from an activity outside the job.

Cultural work has a larger economic role than the reduced expectations of cultural workers might suggest. Culture industries feed both products and innovative ideas throughout an economy, providing "software," as Sony calls television programs, compact discs, and laser discs, for TV sets and VCRs produced around the world. When companies locate innovation centers, corporate headquarters, and marketing agencies in the same city, whether Los Angeles, London, or Tokyo, it has an energizing effect on the entire urban economy (see Molotch forthcoming). Interpersonally, in terms of providing a social context for face-to-face relations, culture aids the transactions of highly mobile, sophisticated business elites, and facilitates communication among them across genders and sexual persuasions.

Art museums, boutiques, restaurants, and other specialized sites of consumption create a social space for the exchange of ideas on which businesses thrive. While these can never be as private as a corporate dining room, urban consumption spaces allow for more social interaction among business elites. They are more democratic, accessible spaces than old-time businessmen's clubs. They open a window to the city – at least, to a rarified view of the city – and, to the extent they are written up in "lifestyle" magazines and consumer columns of the daily newspapers, they make ordinary people more aware of the elites' cultural consumption. Through the media, the elites' cultural preferences change what many ordinary people know about the city.

The high visibility of spokespersons, stars, and stylists for culture industries underlines the "sexy" quality of culture as a motor of economic growth. Not just in New York, Los Angeles, or Chicago, business leaders in a variety of low-profile, midsize cities are actively involved on the boards of trustees of cultural institutions because they believe that investing in the arts leads to more growth in other areas of the urban economy (Whitt 1987; Whitt and Lammers 1991). They think a tourist economy develops the subjective image of place that "sells" a city to other corporate executives. Las Vegas, Los Angeles, and Miami have shown the way to an economic development strategy based on the ethnographic "gaze" (Urry 1990b), the "sale and consumption of pleasure" (Mullins 1991, 331), the location of objects in space by a singular, coherent vision.

Whether there is a singular, coherent vision no longer depends on the power of a single elite group. Constant political pressures by interest groups and complex interwoven networks of community groups, corporations, and public officials signal multiple visions. The ability to arrange these visions artfully, to orchestrate and choreograph images of diversity to speak for a larger whole, has been claimed by major nonprofit cultural institutions. This is especially true of art museums.

Since the 1980s, museums have fallen victim to their own market pressures. Reduced government funding and cutbacks in corporate support have made them more dependent than ever on attracting paying visitors ("gate"). They rely on their gift shops to contribute a larger share of their operating expenses. They try out new display techniques and seek crowd-pleasing exhibit ideas. In an attempt to reach a broader public, the Metropolitan Museum of Art and the Museum of Modern Art in New York have upgraded their restaurants and offer jazz performances on weekend evenings. Yet financial pressures have also led museums to capitalize on their visual holdings. By their marketing of cultural consumption, great art has become a *public* treasure, a tourist attraction, and a representation – divorced from the social context in which the art was produced – of public culture. Like Calvin Klein jeans on a bus stop billboard, the work of art and the museum itself have become icons of the city's symbolic economy.

Conflicts over representation have made organizing exhibitions a deeply and explicitly political activity (e.g., Karp and Lavine 1991). Who would speak for the Indians at the National Museum of the American Indian that the Smithsonian Institution opened in New York in 1994 and whether the museum has the right to exhibit certain objects outside the time and space of the appropriate rituals – these issues gave rise to much criticism while the museum was being planned. Several years earlier, the Guerrilla Girls, a group of female artists who appear in masks and costumes, protested the lack of works by female artists in the opening exhibit at the Guggenheim Museum's downtown branch. Whether the Whitney Museum's biannual exhibit of contemporary American art should be a "political" rather than an aesthetic statement about sexism, racism, and freedom of expression is fought out every two years in the art columns of the New York newspapers.

Not only are political battles fought over the exhibits, struggles also erupt around the location and importance of museums in a city's political economy. Museums are supported, in general, by local elected officials and public-private coalitions. But the big museums, the high culture institutions with deep endowments, get more public support than the fledgling, populist institutions. The big museums, moreover, are always battling for more public resources. They want more space on public land, more money from the city's department of cultural affairs, more flexibility in profit-making activities, such as the right to sell the air rights above their buildings to real estate developers. Why should they get more public support? Because art confers money and power.

As William Luers, the president of the Metropolitan Museum of Art and co-chairman of a New York City promotion, Arts and Culture Week, says, "By featuring our cultural institutions in promotions such as NY93, we show one of our city's finest faces, and stand to reap the proven economic gain that culture also brings" (*New York Observer,* May 24, 1993). Philippe de Montebello, the Metropolitan's director, says about a patron's gift of Van Gogh's *Wheat Field with Cypresses,* "It is pictures such as these that a visitor never forgets and always wishes to return to, and that are the measure of a great museum" (*New York Times,* May 25, 1993). If visible culture is wealth, the ability to frame the vision brings power.

▓ Culture as a Means of Framing Space

For several hundred years, visual representations of cities have "sold" urban growth. Images, from early maps to picture

■ Art as a means to power: Vincent Van Gogh's *Wheat Field with Cypresses* (1889) at the Metropolitan Museum of Art.

The Metropolitan Museum of Art, Purchase, The Annenberg Foundation Gift, 1993 (1993.132). Photograph © The Metropolitan Museum of Art. All Rights Reserved.

postcards, have not simply reflected real city spaces; instead, they have been imaginative reconstructions – from specific points of view – of a city's monumentality. The development of visual media in the 20th century made photography and movies the most important cultural means of framing urban space, at least until the 1970s. Since then, as the surrealism of *King Kong* shifted to that of *Blade Runner* and redevelopment came to focus on consumption activities, the material landscape itself – the buildings, parks, and streets – has become the city's most important visual representation. Indeed, in *Blade Runner,* the modern urban landscape is used as a cult object. Far more than King Kong's perch on the Empire State Building, *Blade Runner*'s use of the Bradbury Building, an early 20th century office building in downtown Los Angeles that has been preserved and lovingly restored, emphasizes the city's material landscape as a visual backdrop for a new high-tech, global society. Historic preservation has been very important in this re-presentation. Preserving old buildings and small sections of the city re-presents the scarce "monopoly" of the city's visible past. Such a monopoly has economic value in terms of tourist revenues and property values. Just an image of historic preservation, when taken out of context, has economic value. In Syracuse, New York, a crankshaft taken from a long-gone salt works was mounted as public sculpture to enhance a redevelopment project (Roberts and Schein 1993; see also S. Watson 1991).

Harry, If I Told You, Would You Know? is an even more surreal example of culture framing space to project an image of urban growth. In 1991, the André Emmerich Gallery, which represents the abstract painter Al Held, rented a vacant ground floor retail space in the upscale commercial district at 58th Street and Madison Avenue to show a group of Held's large-scale canvases. Emmerich thought of renting the store to show the paintings because they did not fit into the elevator to the gallery, which is on 57th Street. In the old days – the growing art market of the 1970s and 1980s – Emmerich might have shown these paintings at their SoHo branch, which was opened in 1971 in a loft building configured for wide loads. But that gallery was closed several years ago, and the storefront on Madison Avenue was vacated by the consolidation, in 1991, of two of the largest New York City banks, Chemical and Manufacturers' Hanover. The sight of the store, bare except for Held's bright paintings, with makeshift lighting on cement floors and thick columns, recalls the success of SoHo in upgrading property through cultural gentrification. Or else it suggests a scenario of continued economic recession, with empty spaces taken up by the symbolic economy.

As recession lasted through 1993, the gallery continued to use the empty bank as temporary exhibition space. But this was not just an isolated phenomenon. Emmerich's eccentric idea became taken up as public policy. When the long-delayed project to replace Times Square movie theaters and peep shows with office towers coincided with a real estate recession, the public redevelopment authorities worked with nonprofit arts organizations on an "interim" plan featuring renovation and re-creation of restaurants, night clubs, and stores, all preceded by an effort to "reanimate" 42nd Street by an extended, site-specific art installation (*New York Times,* June 27, 1993, sec. 10, p. 1; see also July 5 and July 7, 1993). Stores that were emptied by the state's right of eminent domain became a sculptor's casting studio, sites for video installations, and exhibition spaces. Movie marquees and bill-

■ Art as a redevelopment strategy: First on-site art installation in Times Square, 1993.

Photo by Danny Kessler.

boards advertising real movies and products were indistinguishable from Jenny Holzer's caustic aphorisms ("Men Don't Protect You Any More").

The on-site art installation drew so much favorable attention it was repeated the following year. The re-presentation of Times Square as both a populist and an avant-garde cultural attraction – helped by continued public subsidies for hotel construction and office relocation – attracted corporate cultural industries. The Disney Company decided to open a theater for live stage shows on 42nd Street; and MTV, whose corporate offices are already in the area, decided to open a new production studio.

More common forms of visual re-presentation in all cities connect cultural activities and populist images in festivals, sports stadiums, and shopping centers. While these may simply be minimized as "loss leaders" supporting new office construction (Harvey 1989a, 12–14), they should also be understood as producing space for a symbolic economy. In the 1960s, new or restored urban shopping centers from Boston to Seattle copied suburban shopping malls by developing clean space according to a visually coherent theme. To the surprise of some urban planners, they actually thrived (Frieden and Sagalyn 1989, 72–77). No longer did the city's dream world of commercial culture relate to the bourgeois culture of the old downtown or the patrician culture of art museums and public buildings. Instead, urban commercial culture became "entertainment," aimed at attracting a mobile public of cultural consumers. This altered the public culture of the city.

Linking public culture to commercial cultures has important implications for social identity and social control. Preserving an ecology of images often takes a connoisseur's view of the past, re-reading the legible practices of social class discrimination and financial speculation by reshaping the city's collective memory (see Boyer 1992; Sontag 1977, 180). Boston's Faneuil Hall, South Street Seaport in New York, Harborplace in Baltimore, and London's Tobacco Wharf make the waterfront of older cities into a consumers' playground, far safer for tourists and cultural consumers than the closed worlds of wholesale fish and vegetable dealers and longshoremen. In such newer cities as Los Angeles or San Antonio, reclaiming the historic core, or the fictitious historic core, of the city for the middle classes puts the pueblo or the Alamo into an entirely different landscape from that of the surrounding inner city. On one level, there is a loss of authenticity, that is compensated for by a re-created historical narrative and a commodification of images; on another, men and women are simply displaced from public spaces they once considered theirs.

Consider Taos and Santa Fe, New Mexico, where residents of "native" cultural enclaves were replaced early in the 20th century by affluent homebuyers of Anglo ethnicity. Between 1900 and World War II, East Coast artists moved to these cities and founded artists' colonies. Rebelling against the dominance of European art and seeking to develop a "native" – i.e., American – representation of nature and culture, the artists capitalized on the economic marginality of Indians and Mexicans, hired them as servants and models, and eventually built their folk cultures into a tourist industry (Rodriguez 1989). Even then, culture was used to legitimize the unequal benefits of economic growth, including higher property values, jobs in construction, hotels, and restaurants, and displacement of locals by a cosmopolitan population.

But incorporating new images into visual representations of the city can be democratic. It can integrate rather than segregate social and ethnic groups, and it can also help negotiate new group identities. In New York City, there is a big annual event organized by Caribbean immigrants, the West Indian–American Day Carnival parade, which is held every Labor Day on Eastern Parkway in Brooklyn. The parade has been instrumental in creating a pan-Caribbean identity among immigrants from the many small countries of that region. The parade also legitimizes the "gorgeous mosaic" of the ethnic population described by Mayor David N. Dinkins in 1989. The use of Eastern Parkway for a Caribbean festival reflects a geographical redistribution of ethnic groups – the Africanization of Brooklyn, the Caribbeanization of Crown Heights – and a social transformation of leisure, similar to that of Central Park, but far "distant from [Frederick Law] Olmsted's stately vision" (Kasinitz 1992, 142). More problematically, however, this cultural appropriation of public space supports the growing political identity of the Caribbean community and challenges the Lubavitcher Hassidim's appropria-

▓ From indigenous people to sellers of crafts: The Indian Market,
Santa Fe.

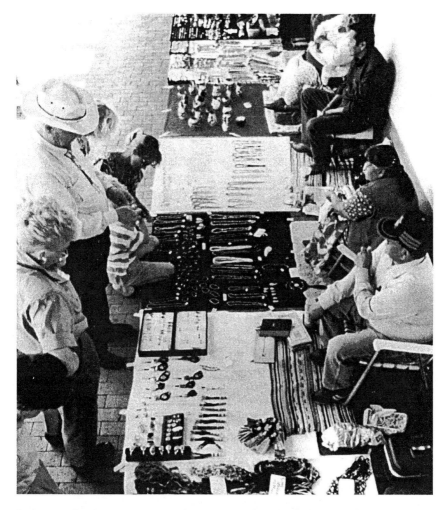

Indians selling their wares under the portal of the Palace of Governors,
Santa Fe © Mark Nohl, New Mexico Magazine.

tion of the same neighborhood. In Pasadena, California,
African-American organizations have demanded representation on the nine-person commission that manages the annual
Rose Parade, that city's big New Year's Day event. These
cultural models of inclusion differ from the paradigm of legally
imposed racial integration that eliminated segregated festivals and other symbolic activities in the 1950s and 1960s (see
Gates 1994). By giving distinctive cultural groups access to

■ From immigrants to New Yorkers: West Indian-American Day
Carnival Parade, Eastern Parkway, Brooklyn.

Photo by Ernest Brown.

the same public space, they incorporate separate visual
images and cultural practices into the same public cultures.

Culture can also be used to frame, and humanize, the
space of real estate development. Cultural producers who supply art (and sell "interpretation") are sought because they
legitimize the appropriation of space (Deutsche 1988). Office
buildings are not just monumentalized by height and facades,
they are given a human face by video artists' screen installations and public concerts. Every well-designed downtown has
a mixed-use shopping center and a nearby artists' quarter.
Sometimes it seems that every derelict factory district or
waterfront has been converted into one of those sites of visual
delectation – a themed shopping space for seasonal produce,
cooking equipment, restaurants, art galleries, and an aquarium. Urban redevelopment plans, from Lowell, Massachusetts, to downtown Philadelphia, San Francisco, and Los
Angeles, focus on museums. Unsuccessful attempts to use
cultural districts or aquariums to stop economic decline in
Flint, Michigan, and Camden, New Jersey – cities where there

is no major employer – only emphasize the appeal of framing a space with a cultural institution when all other strategies of economic development fail.

Artists themselves have become a cultural means of framing space. They confirm the city's claim of continued cultural hegemony, in contrast to the suburbs and exurbs. Their presence – in studios, lofts, and galleries – puts a neighborhood on the road to gentrification (Zukin 1989 [1982]; Deutsche 1988). Ironically, this has happened since artists have become more self-conscious defenders of their own interests as artists and more involved in political organizations. Often they have been co-opted into property redevelopment projects as beneficiaries, both developers of an aesthetic mode of producing space (in public art, for example) and investors in a symbolic economy. There are, moreover, special connections between artists and corporate patrons. In such cities as New York and Los Angeles, the presence of artists documents a claim to these cities' status in the global hierarchy. The display of art, for public improvement or private gain, represents an abstraction of economic and social power. Among business elites, those from finance, insurance, and real estate are generally great patrons of both art museums and public art, as if to emphasize their prominence in the city's symbolic economy.

The financial boom that lasted for most of the 1980s influenced sharp price rises in the real estate and art markets where leading investment bankers, stock traders, and developers were so active. Regardless of aesthetics, investment in art, for prestige or speculation, represented a collective means of social mobility. At the same time, a collective belief in the growth of the symbolic economy of art represented belief in the growth of the city's economy. Visual representation became a means of financially re-presenting the city. By the 1990s, it seemed to be official policy that making a place for art in the city went along with establishing a marketable identity for the city as a whole. No matter how restricted the definition of art that is implied, or how few artists are included, or how little the benefits extend to all social groups, the visibility and viability of a city's symbolic economy play an important role in the creation of place.

So the symbolic economy features two parallel production systems that are crucial to a city's material life: the *production of space,* with its synergy of capital investment and cultural meanings, and the *production of symbols,* which constructs both a currency of commercial exchange and a language of social identity. Every effort to rearrange space in the city is also an attempt at visual re-presentation. Raising property values, which remains a goal of most urban elites, requires imposing a new point of view. But negotiating whose point of view and the costs of imposing it create problems for public culture.

Creating a public culture involves both shaping public space for social interaction and constructing a visual representation of the city. Who occupies public space is often decided by negotiations over physical security, cultural identity, and social and geographical community. These issues have been at the core of urban anxieties for hundreds of years. They are significant today, however, because of the complexity and diversity of urban populations. Today the stakes of cultural reorganization are most visible in three basic shifts in the sources of cultural identity:

♦ from local to global images,

♦ from public to private institutions, and

♦ from ethnically and racially homogeneous communities to those that are more diverse.

These rather abstract concepts have a concrete impact on framing urban public space (see drawing).

■ Public Space

The fastest growing kind of public space in America is prisons. More jails are being built than housing, hospitals, or schools. No matter how well designed or brightly painted they may be, prisons are still closely guarded, built as cheaply as possible, and designed for surveillance. I can think of more pleasant public spaces, especially parks that I use in New York City. But is the Hudson River Park, near Battery Park City, or Bryant Park, on 42nd Street, less secure or exclusive than a prison? They share with the new wave of prison building several characteristics symptomatic of the times. Built or rebuilt as the city is in severe financial distress, they confirm the withdrawal of the public sector, and its replacement by the

■ The framing of public space

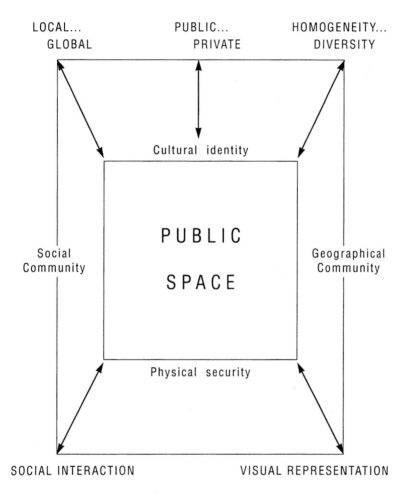

private sector, in defining public space. Reacting to previous failures of public space – due to crime, a perceived lower-class and minority-group presence, and disrepair – the new parks use design as an implicit code of inclusion and exclusion. Explicit rules of park use are posted in the parks and enforced by large numbers of sanitation workers and security guards, both public and private. By cleaning up public space, nearby property owners restore the attractiveness of their holdings and reconstruct the image of the city as well.

It is important to understand the histories of these symbolically central public spaces. The history of Central Park,

■ The aestheticization of fear: New landscape design and a uniformed police officer restore civility to Bryant Park.

Photo by Alex Vitale.

for example (Rosenzweig and Blackmar 1992), shows how, as definitions of who should have access to public space have changed, public cultures have steadily become more inclusive and democratic. From 1860 to 1880, the first uses of the park – for horseback riders and carriages – rapidly yielded to sports activities and promenades for the mainly immigrant working class. Over the next 100 years, continued democratization of access to the park developed together with a language of political equality. In the whole country, it became more difficult to enforce outright segregation by race, sex, or age.

By the late 1950s, when Arkansas Governor Orville Faubus failed to prevent the racial integration of Central High School in Little Rock, public parks, public swimming pools, and public housing were legally opened to all of a city's residents. During the 1970s, public space, especially in cities, began to show the effects of movements to "deinstitutionalize" patients of mental hospitals without creating sufficient community facilities to support and house them. Streets became crowded with "others," some of whom clearly suffered from sickness and disorientation. By the early 1980s, the destruction of cheap housing in the centers of cities, particularly single-room-occupancy hotels, and the drastic decline in producing public housing, dramatically expanded the problem of homelessness. Public space, such as Central Park, became unintended public shelter. As had been true historically, the democratization of public space was entangled with the question of fear for physical security.

Streets and parks became camping grounds for mental patients, released from hospitals without access to alternative residential and treatment facilities. Sleeping on the sidewalks alongside them were increasing numbers of drug abusers who had drifted away from their families but were also cut off from other possible support systems. A growing population of homeless families begged for apartments in public housing. A series of lawsuits in various cities made it all but impossible to treat any of these people as criminals. In New York City, a jerry-built system of public shelters offered inadequate, often unsafe beds for a night, hotel rooms for a longer period, and subsidized apartments for persistently homeless families. No government initiatives have yet penetrated the sources of homelessness in poverty and unemployment, hospitals and drug treatment centers, and lack of cheap housing. But homeless people remain a visible presence in public spaces: on the streets, in the parks, on plazas in front of expensive apartment houses, in office building atrium lobbies, in subway cars and stations, in bus stations, in railroad terminals, under bridge and highway entrances.

New York City parks have removed and redistributed the homeless by creating the "defensible spaces" that Oscar Newman wrote about in the 1960s, using the design guidelines prescribed by William H. Whyte in the 1980s. Playgrounds are fenced in for children and their guardians, and parks are closed at night. Tompkins Square Park in lower Manhattan, site of violent confrontations in 1988 and 1991 between the police and neighborhood homeowners, punk activists, and homeless men sleeping in the park – all of whom, or some of whom, opposed gentrification – was closed for two years for extensive landscaping. When the park was reopened, open sight lines permitted children, ballplayers, and elderly bench sitters to keep an eye on each other while using their own spaces.

In 1989, a private organization that manages Central Park, the Central Park Conservancy, demanded demolition of the Naumberg Bandshell, site of popular concerts from the 1930s to the 1950s, where homeless people gathered. Similarly, the Bryant Park Restoration Corporation started cleaning up the midtown business district by adopting the social design principles developed by Whyte. Whyte's basic idea is that public spaces are made safe by attracting lots of "normal" users. The more normal users there are, the less space there will be for vagrants and criminals to maneuver. The Bryant Park Restoration Corporation intended their work to set a prototype for urban public space. They completely reorganized the landscape design of the park, opening it up to women, who tended to avoid the park even during daylight (see Cranz 1982), and selling certain kinds of buffet food. They established a model of pacification by cappuccino.

Central Park, Bryant Park, and the Hudson River Park show how public spaces are becoming progressively less public: they are, in certain ways, more exclusive than at any time in the past 100 years. Each of these areas is governed, and largely or entirely financed, by a private organization, often working as a quasi-public authority. These private groups are much better funded than the corresponding public organization. Design in each park features a purposeful vision of urban leisure. A heightened concern for security inspires the most remarkable visible features: gates, private security guards, and eyes keeping the space under surveillance. The underlying assumption is that of a paying public, a public that values public space as an object of visual consumption. Yet it has become inconceivable in public discussions that control of the parks be left in public hands. When the *New York Times* praised plans to require developers to provide public access to the city's extensive waterfront, the newspaper said that only a public-private partnership could raise the funds to maintain such a significant public space (editorial, October 14, 1993).

A major reason for privatization of some public parks is that city governments cannot pay for taking care of them. Since the 1960s, while groups of all sorts have requested more use of the parks, the New York City Parks Department has been starved of government funds. Half the funding for Central Park is now raised privately by the Central Park Conservancy, which enjoys a corresponding influence on parks policy. Founded by private donors in 1980, the conservancy's original mission was to raise funds in the private sector to offset the park's physical deterioration. But it soon developed an authoritative cultural voice. The conservancy publicly defends the intentions of Olmsted and Vaux, the park's original designers, to create a "natural" landscape for contemplation. Most often, they beautify the park by restoring its 19th century buildings and bridges or setting up a nature program or skating facilities on one of its landscaped ponds. The conservancy has also become an arbiter between groups that want to use the park for sports or demonstrations, thus mediating between the homeless and the joggers, between athletes who come to the park from all over the city and those who come from low-income neighborhoods on the park's northern borders. The conservancy, moreover, has spoken loudly and often in favor of hiring nonunion labor. While Roy Rosenzweig and Betsy Blackmar (1992) show that, historically, the unionization of park employees was an important means of democratizing access to Central Park, the park's public administrator (who is also the conservancy's director) argues that nonunion labor is more efficient and less costly than unionized public employees. By being able to implement its viewpoint on this most central of public spaces, the conservancy has become a more important guardian of public culture than the city's Parks Department.

In midtown, Bryant Park is an even more aggressive example of privatization. Declared a New York City landmark in 1975, the nine-acre park is essentially run by the Bryant Park Restoration Corporation, whose biggest corporate members are Home Box Office (HBO), a cable television network, and NYNEX, a regional telecommunications company. Like the Central Park Conservancy, the Bryant Park Restoration

Corporation raises most of the park's budget, supervises maintenance, and decides on design and amenities.

The design of Bryant Park, in 1934, was based on an Olmstedian separation of a rural space of contemplation from the noisy city. By the late 1970s, this was determined to have the effect of walling off the park's intended public of office workers outside from drug dealers and loiterers inside. When the restoration corporation was formed, it took as its major challenge the development of a new design that would visually and spatially ensure security. The wall around the park was lowered, and the ground leveled to bring it closer to the surrounding streets. The restoration corporation bought movable chairs and painted them green, as in Parisian parks, responding to William H. Whyte's suggestion (1980; 1988, 119–23) that park users like to create their own small spaces. Whyte recommended keeping "the undesirables" out by making a park *attractive*. Victorian kiosks selling cappuccino and sandwiches were built and painted, paths were repaved and covered with pebbles, a central lawn was opened up, and performers were enlisted to offer free entertainment in the afternoons. The restoration corporation hired its own security guards and pressured the New York City Police Department to supply uniformed officers. Four uniformed New York City police officers and four uniformed private security guards are on duty all day.

Plainclothes private security guards are also on patrol. A list posted at all entrances prohibits drug use, picking flowers, and drinking alcohol except for beverages bought at park concessions, which are limited to certain seating areas. It states the park's hours, 9 a.m. to 7 p.m., coinciding roughly with the business day. The rules specify that only homeless people connected to a particular shelter in the neighborhood have the right to rummage through the garbage cans for returnable bottles and cans. Unlike Parks Department workers, Bryant Park maintenance workers do not belong to a labor union. Starting salary for a maintenance worker is $6 an hour, half the starting rate of unionized workers in other city parks.

On a sunny summer day at noon, Bryant Park is full of office workers out to lunch – between 1,500 and 6,000 of them. The movable chairs and benches are filled; many people are sitting on the grass, on the edge of the fountain, even on the pebbled paths. Men and women eat picnic lunches singly, in couples, and in groups. Some traditional social hierarchies are subverted. Women feel free to glance at men passing by. Most men do not ogle the women. The dominant complexion of park users is white, with minority group members clustered outside the central green. Few people listen to the subsidized entertainment, an HBO comedian shouting into a microphone; no one notices when she finishes the show. A large sculpture by Alexander Calder stands in the middle of the lawn, on loan from an art gallery, both an icon and a benediction on the space. At sunset in the summer, HBO shows free movies from their stock of old films, a "take back the night" activity similar to those now being tried in other cities. This is a very deliberate exception to the rule of closing the park at night. During lunchtime, at least, the park visually represents an urban middle class: men and women who work in offices, jackets off, sleeves rolled up, mainly white. On the same day, at the same hour, another public space a block away – the tellers' line at Citibank – attracts a group that is not so well dressed, with more minority group members. The cultural strategies that have been chosen to revitalize Bryant Park carry with them the implication of controlling diversity while re-creating a consumable vision of civility.

The problem of controlling Bryant Park is not new (Biederman and Nager 1981). In 1932, when the park was filled with unemployed people during the Great Depression, private entrepreneurs built a replica of Federal Hall, charged an entrance fee of 25 cents, and installed turnstiles to control access to the park – an early Magic Kingdom until a public boycott forced it to be shut down. In 1944, Mayor Fiorello LaGuardia decreed that anyone caught loitering in the park after 10 p.m. would be arrested.

Since its renovation, Bryant Park has changed character. It has become a place for people to be with others, to see others, a place of public sociability. John Berger (1985) once criticized New Yorkers for eating while walking alone on the street, alienating a social ritual from its proper context. Yet now, in the park, eating becomes a public ritual, a way of trusting strangers while maintaining private identities. Because of the police and security guards, the design, and the food, the park has become a visual and spatial representation of a middle-class public culture. The finishing touch will be a privately owned, expensive restaurant, whose rent payments will help finance the park's maintenance. This, however, is a degree of privatization that has stirred prolonged controversy. First envisioned in the 1980s, the restaurant remained the subject of public approvals processes until 1994.

The disadvantage of creating public space this way is that it owes so much to private-sector elites, both individual philanthropists and big corporations. This is especially the case for centrally located public spaces, the ones with the most potential for raising property values and with the greatest claim to be symbolic spaces for the city as a whole. Handing such spaces over to corporate executives and private investors means giving them carte blanche to remake public culture. It marks the erosion of public space in terms of its two basic principles: public stewardship and open access.

The Central Park Conservancy, a group of 30 private citizens who choose their own replacements, represents large corporations with headquarters in the city, major financial institutions, and public officials. The membership echoes both the new (the nonelected, tripartite Emergency Financial Control Board that has overseen New York City's budget since the fiscal crisis of 1975) and the old (the board of "gentlemen" trustees that originally guided the planning of Central Park in the 1860s). The idea of governing public space in Central Park by a board of trustees was periodically resurrected until the 1930s and again in the 1970s (Rosenzweig and Blackmar 1992, 507). The fiscal crisis of the 1970s, however, inspired a wider institutionalization of local elite control. Overlapping the Carter and Reagan administrations in Washington, D.C., the New York City Parks Commissioner encouraged the formation of private groups to oversee public parks from 1978 to 1983. He also named special administrators for the largest parks, Central Park and Prospect Park. For more than 10 years, the Central Park adminstrator has also been the president of the Central Park Conservancy. Significantly, while she is one of several people in the Parks Department, including the commissioner, who earn $106,000 a year, her salary is paid by the conservancy. In addition to paying the administrator's salary and expenses, the conservancy raised $64 million during the 1980s (Siegel 1992, 38). According to two political scientists who act as watchdogs over the city's parlous economy, private parks conservancies are one of the few "bright spots" in the Parks Department's budget (Brecher and Horton 1993, 308, 311 ff.).

The Bryant Park Restoration Corporation, a subsidiary of the Bryant Park Business Improvement District, follows a fairly new model in New York State, and in smaller cities around the United States, that allows business and property owners in commercial districts to tax themselves voluntarily for maintenance and improvement of public areas and take these areas under their control. The concept originated in the 1970s as special assessment districts; in the 1980s, the name was changed to a more upbeat acronym, business improvement districts (BIDs). A BID can be incorporated in any commercial area. Because the city government has steadily reduced street cleaning and trash pickups in commercial streets since the fiscal crisis of 1975, there is a real incentive for business and property owners to take up the slack. A new law was required for such initiatives: unlike shopping malls, commercial streets are publicly owned, and local governments are responsible for their upkeep. BIDs were created by the New York State Legislature in 1983; by 1993, 26 were up and running in New York City: 10 in Brooklyn, 9 in Manhattan, 5 in Queens, and 1 each in the Bronx and Staten Island. In 1994, as new BIDs were still being formed, a super-BID was established for an area of lower Manhattan from City Hall to the Battery. One of its "public" functions will be to enhance the area surrounding the World Financial Center and Battery Park City, which are publicly owned but leased to private developers. At the same time, private schools and apartment buildings on the affluent Upper East Side have discussed forming a BID to fight street crime in their area with neighborhood security guards. BIDs have also spread to other states. There are 400 of them in New Jersey.

In New York City, Manhattan BIDs are the richest, reflecting higher property values and business volume. While the entire sum of all special assessments in the 10 Brooklyn BIDs in fiscal year 1993 was a little less than $4 million, 3 BIDs in Manhattan *each* had an assessment over $4 million. These unequal resources enable rich BIDs to do more. A BID

in a neighborhood shopping strip in Queens may just be able
to buy street cleaning services and put up Christmas lights,
but a midtown BID can undertake public works. The Grand
Central Partnership, a 53-block organization whose center is
on 42nd Street near Bryant Park, employs uniformed street
cleaners and security guards, runs a tourist information booth,
refashions the illumination of Grand Central Terminal, closes
a street in front of the terminal to make a new outdoor eating
space, and hires lobbyists to ask the state legislature for sup-
plemental funds from the state budget. Also, while the staffs
of BIDs in the outer boroughs worry about working without
health benefits and pensions, the executive director of the
Grand Central Partnership, who also oversees the Bryant
Park Restoration Corporation and the 34th Street BID, earns
$315,000 a year – more than double the mayor's salary.

What kind of public culture is created under these conditions? Do urban BIDs create a Disney World in the streets,
take the law into their own hands, and reward their entrepreneurial managers as richly as property values will allow? If
elected public officials continue to urge the destruction of
corrupt and bankrupt public institutions, I imagine a scenario
of drastic privatization, with BIDs replacing the city government. As Republican Mayor Rudolph Giuliani said enthusias-
tically at the second annual NYC BIDs Association Conference
in 1994, "This is a difficult time for the city and the country
as we redefine ourselves. BIDs are one of the true success
stories in the city. It's a tailor-made form of local government"
(*Daily News,* November 16, 1994).

The Grand Central Partnership, a midtown BID established in 1988, assumed a key governmental function four
years later by issuing its own bonds. At that time, the BID
sold $32.3 million worth of 30-year bonds with an A1 rating
from Moody's Investors Service Inc. and Standard & Poor's
Corp.; this was a higher rating than that of New York City
bonds. In contrast to municipal bonds, which are backed by
tax rolls, the BID's bonds are backed by the special property
assessment building owners pay annually to the BID. With
the proceeds of its bond sales, the Grand Central Partnership
plans to rebuild public space in its domain, taking on projects
that the city government has neither the will nor the means
to accomplish. Traffic is banned from the Park Avenue viaduct

while the partnership, acting as a nonprofit developer, creates new space and leases it to a restaurant. Another area across the street will be redesigned as a demonstration district for new lighting, signage, landscaping, street furniture, kiosks, and traffic grids.

We know who defines this image of the city, but who will occupy it? City government agencies have approved the BID's plans, not least because the property owners (including the Philip Morris Corporation) are powerful and their projects promise to create revenue. But the local community board, representing a wide variety of business interests, has challenged the BID's plans because they make traffic more crowded and alter the somewhat rakish, small business character of the area around Grand Central Terminal (Feiden 1992; Wolfson 1992; Slatin 1993). (Creating a pedestrian mall here also makes a taxi ride from Grand Central Terminal to my house more expensive, since cars can no longer turn straight into Park Avenue to drive downtown.) The community board has raised questions about the effectiveness of the BID's "services" for the homeless and the brusqueness of their removal by the BID's security guards (*New York Observer,* January 17, 1994; Community Board 6, March, 1994). These issues were dramatized when the Coalition for the Homeless, an advocacy group, sued the partnership for hiring out the homeless as security guards at below the minimum wage. The partnership was also accused of failing to give homeless people job training and hiring some of them, itself, as low-wage employees (Drucker, 1994). "For years," the coalition stated in a complaint filed February 1, 1995, with the U.S. District Court, Southern District of New York, the Grand Central Partnership and 34th Street Partnership

have victimized the homeless . . . by tantalizing them with their alluringly named 'Pathways to Employment' ('PET') program, which promises job training and meaningful employment. In fact, the PET program provides neither meaningful job training nor meaningful jobs. Rather, it is bait that lures the homeless to Defendants at illegal, subminimum wages. . . . This cheap, and largely defenseless, labor pool has enabled Defendants to land significant contracts because Defendants' use of a captive, underpaid homeless labor force enables them to underbid competitors who compensate their own employees at lawful rates.

When, in January 1995, the partnership proposed expanding its jurisdiction up Madison Avenue as far as 56th Street, including Sony Plaza, the Coalition for the Homeless offered the only principled opposition.

In their own way, under the guise of improving public spaces, BIDs nurture a visible social stratification. Like the Central Park Conservancy, they channel investment into a central space, a space with both real and symbolic meaning for elites as well as other groups. Like the Central Park Conservancy, the resources of the rich Manhattan BIDs far outstrip those even potentially available in other areas of the city, even if those areas set up BIDs. The rich BIDs' opportunity to exceed the constraints of the city's financial system confirms the fear that the prosperity of a few central spaces will stand in contrast to the impoverishment of the entire city.

BIDs can be equated with a return to civility, "an attempt to reclaim public space from the sense of menace that drives shoppers, and eventually store owners and citizens, to the suburbs" (Siegel 1992, 43–44). But rich BIDs can be criticized on the grounds of control, accountability, and vision. Public space that is no longer controlled by public agencies must inspire a liminal public culture open to all but governed by the private sector. Private management of public space does create some savings: saving money by hiring nonunion workers, saving time by removing design questions from the public arena. Because they choose an abstract aesthetic with no pretense of populism, private organizations avoid conflicts over representations of ethnic groups that public agencies encounter when they subsidize public art, including murals and statues (*New York Times,* July 17, 1992, p. C22; J. Kramer 1992).

Each area of the city gets a different form of visual consumption catering to a different constituency: culture functions as a mechanism of stratification. The public culture of midtown public space diffuses down through the poorer BIDs. It focuses on clean design, visible security, historic architectural features, and the sociability among strangers achieved by suburban shopping malls. Motifs of local identity are chosen by merchants and commercial property owners. Since most commercial property owners and merchants do not live in the area of their business or even in New York City, the sources of their vision of public culture may be eclectic: the nostalgically remembered city, European piazzas, suburban shopping malls, Disney World. In general, however, their vision of public space derives from commercial culture.

An interesting application of BIDs' taking the opportunity to re-present public culture is the new "community court" in Times Square, which grew out of a proposal put forward in 1991 by officials close to the Times Square BID. The proposal was to dispense immediate justice for local crimes in an unused theater in the area (*New York Times,* November 15, 1991, p. A1). The goal of this unprecedented decentralization – not even envisioned in the city's criminal justice system since the 1960s – was to clean up Times Square. Prominent city and state government officials in the court system praised the proposal. A neighborhood court, they said, would speed the disposition of cases against minor offenders accused of such crimes as prostitution, shoplifting, trespassing, and running a scam of three-card monte in the street, and enhance community control over quality of life. The theater owner who would donate the use of the theater for a courthouse, who was also the chairman of the Schubert Organization, spoke of the "devastating" impact of crime on a long-delayed Times Square redevelopment plan. The deputy mayor for public safety admitted the proposal for a Times Square court could be criticized as "elitist," but that seemed to be less of a problem than how to finance it. The *Times* printed an editorial in strong support. The only voices of dissent were raised by the Manhattan District Attorney's office, which protested the diversion of time and money to a single branch court, and the Legal Aid Society, which joined the DA's office in criticizing the new pressures on attorneys to run up to midtown from the primary site of the courts in lower Manhattan.

The Times Square court promised to create a new public culture consistent with a historic local identity: "With attentive spectators filling red plush seats, judges and attorneys could be expected to maintain high standards of efficiency and dignity long absent from the Criminal Court. The judges would also be encouraged to use more imaginative and productive sentences than fines or jail time: three-card monte players, for example, might be required to help with street-cleaning" (*New York Times,* November 17, 1991). In fact, once the court was set up in 1994, community service sentences of 10 to 12 days were carried out in the Times Square area. A person convicted by the community court was given a broom by the Times Square BID and told to sweep the sidewalks, not unlike the Grand Central Partnership hiring the homeless to sweep 42nd Street. This is a public culture worthy of Dickens.

Security, Ethnicity, and Culture

One of the most tangible threats to public culture comes from the politics of everyday fear. Physical assaults, random violence, hate crimes that target specific groups: the dangers of being in public spaces utterly destroy the principle of open access. Elderly men and women who live in cities commonly experience fear as a steady erosion of spaces and times available to them. An elderly Jewish politician who in the 1950s lived in Brownsville, a working-class Jewish neighborhood in Brooklyn where blacks began to move in greater numbers as whites moved out, told me, "My wife used to be able to come out to meet me at night, after a political meeting, and leave the kids in our apartment with the door unlocked." A Jewish woman remembers about that same era, "I used to go to concerts in Manhattan wearing a fur coat and come home on the subway at 1 a.m." There may be some exaggeration in these memories, but the point is clear. And it is not altogether different from the message behind crimes against black men who venture into mainly white areas of the city at night or attacks on authority figures such as police officers and firefighters who try to exercise that authority against street gangs, drug dealers, and gun-toting kids. Cities are not safe enough for people to participate in a public culture.

"Getting tough" on crime by building more prisons and imposing the death penalty are all too common answers to the politics of fear. "Lock up the whole population," I heard a man say on the bus, at a stroke reducing the solution to its ridiculous extreme. Another answer is to privatize and militarize public space – making streets, parks, and even shops more secure but less free, or creating spaces, such as shopping malls and Disney World, that only *appear* to be public spaces because so many people use them for common purposes. It is not so easy, given a language of social equality, a tradition of civil rights, and a market economy, to enforce social distinctions in public space. The flight from "reality" (Huxtable 1993) that led to the privatization of public space in Disney World is an attempt to create a different, ultimately more menacing kind of public culture.

In *City of Quartz* (1990), Mike Davis describes the reshaping of public spaces in Los Angeles by surveillance and security procedures. Helicopters buzz the skies over ghetto neighborhoods, police hassle teenagers as putative gang members, homeowners buy into the type of armed defense they can afford . . . or have nerve enough to use. While Los Angeles may represent an extreme, high-tech example, I have also seen "Eyes on the Street" surveillance signs on lamp posts in small towns in Vermont and the design of Bryant Park gives evidence of a relatively low-tech but equally suggestive concern for public order. Indeed, Bryant Park may be a more typical public space than downtown Los Angeles because it has been "secured" within a democratic discourse of aestheticizing both cities and fear.

Gentrification, historic preservation, and other cultural strategies to enhance the visual appeal of urban spaces developed as major trends during the late 1960s and early 1970s. Yet these years were also a watershed in the institutionalization of urban fear. Voters and elites – a broadly conceived middle class in the United States – could have faced the choice of approving government policies to eliminate poverty, manage ethnic competition, and integrate everyone into common public institutions. Instead, they chose to buy protection, fueling the growth of the private security industry. This reaction was closely related to a perceived decline in public morality, an "elimination of almost all stabilizing authority" (Siegel 1992, 37) in urban public space. As public authority eroded, employment in the private security industry tripled, growing from over half a million to 1.5 million jobs, from 1970 to 1992 (Cunningham, Strauchs, and Van Meter 1990). Between 1972 and 1990, 300,000 new jobs for security guards were created, making detective and protective work the 20th fastest growing employment sector in the United States.

Private armies, those of the security companies, have grown faster and stronger than public security forces. In the late 1960s or early 1970s – estimates of the date vary – employment in private security firms of all kinds began to exceed that in public law enforcement agencies. From the mid 1970s, when municipal budgets began to tighten, public agencies have grown to a much smaller extent than private firms. In California today, there are 3.9 private security employees for every public security employee. In the less urbanized Indiana, the ratio is more equal, with 1.7 private security employee to 1 in the public sector. By 2000, researchers have predicted, 73 percent of the country's "protective employees" will work in the private sector, while only 27 percent will work in public law enforcement.

Although many security employees work in private corporations, public-private partnerships are a significant, and growing, part of the industry. In New York, public agencies and private firms share information and emergency duties (*New York Times,* July 13, 1993, p. B2). A private force of 112 armed guards and 20 security supervisors work in the three richest mid Manhattan BIDs, including Bryant Park. In Phoenix, Arizona, private security forces have been used for crowd control (Cunningham, Strauchs, and Van Meter 1990, p. 275). In Los Angeles, Chicago, New York, and New Haven, they patrol streets around private universities; in suburbs, they drive around the perimeter of the campus. The urban public university where I teach hires its own private security guards. In Lexington, Kentucky, which is often said to be a typical American city, private security guards are on duty in public housing projects.

From the viewpoint of political economy, the withdrawal from public to private security employees is part of a general shift to privatization. Fiscal austerity limits government spending increases, even on the police. Yet private security cannot be free. The security costs borne by the private sector are passed on to the public by excluding potential criminal acts from segregated spaces, leaving the rest of the city to watch out for itself and be watched by the police. Crime, the criminal justice system, and private security forces absorb a high percentage of the unemployed, a "reserve army" in a more literal sense than Marx intended in his famous phrase about "the reserve army of the unemployed." While factory jobs disappear, urban workers, especially minority-group members, seek security jobs, and their mainly white colleagues in small, rural towns go to work in prisons.

The geographers John Jakle and David Wilson (1992), and the ecological historian John Wilkinson (1973), have written about Americans' tendency to abandon their farmlands, workplaces, and towns when they stop being economically productive, leaving the country littered with "derelict landscapes" (Jakle and Wilson 1992). From a similar point of view, American attitudes toward cities smell strongly of fear of the old and disdain for those who inherit it. As urban public spaces have included more strangers, those who look and talk so differently they are considered "Others," the Americans who used them before have abandoned them, leaving them to a generalized ethnic Other, a victim of the politics of fear. An anthropologist concluded her study of "urban danger" in Philadelphia (Merry 1981) by saying that people tend to think Others are criminals; eventually, crime becomes a device, an idiom, for thinking about the Other.

In the past, those people who lived so close together they had to work out some etiquette for sharing, or dividing, public space were usually the poor. An exception that affected everyone was the system of racial segregation that worked by law in the south and by convention in many northern states until the 1960s, when – not surprisingly – perceptions of danger among whites increased. Like segregation, a traditional etiquette of public order of the urban poor involves dividing up territory by ethnic groups. This includes the system of "ordered segmentation" that the Chicago urban sociologist Gerald Suttles (1968) described a generation ago, at the very moment it was being outmoded by increased racial and ethnic mixing, ideologies of community empowerment, and the legitimization of ethnicity as a formal norm of political representation. Among city dwellers today, innumerable informal etiquettes for survival in public spaces flourish. The "streetwise" scrutiny of passersby described by the sociologist Elijah Anderson (1990) is one means for unarmed individuals to secure the streets. I think ethnicity – a cultural strategy for producing difference – is another, and it survives on the politics of fear by requiring people to keep their distance from certain aesthetic markers. These markers vary over time. Pants may be baggy or pegged, heads may be shaggy or shaved. Like fear itself, ethnicity becomes an aesthetic category.

Ethnicity and private security services have shaped an urban public culture that simulates inclusion. The old civic virtues for mingling with strangers – civility, security, tact, and trust – have lost their meaning in the fear for physical safety and the dramatization of ethnic diversity. Every tabloid carries the news: public spaces are too dangerous for public culture. Elementary school pupils carry homemade arms, teenagers attack each other in crimes of sexual abuse. Even ethnically homogeneous subcultures lack solidarity. In most states, both crime victims and convicted criminals are disproportionately black and Latino and come from the same inner city ghettos (Ellis 1994). In the city around them, whatever its name, the symbolic geography of neighborhoods has been remade by selective abandonment and redevelopment. People who were perceived as part of "far away" worlds are present in the "here and now" (see Shields 1992a). Spaces inherited from the modern city – department stores, schools and welfare offices, subways and buses – frame encounters that are both intimate and intrusive.

In everyday experience in the city, the "Other" might be the salesperson or waiter who speaks to you in a familiar tone, the supermarket cashier or bank teller who taps on computer keys with inch-long fingernails, the subway driver who roars into the station wearing a turban. At the same time, despite debates stretching from the Chicago School of the 1920s to the "underclass" school of the 1980s, many social practices that were once considered limited to "subcultures" now cross class and ethnic lines. Illegal drug use, out-of-wedlock births, and female-headed families are more common in all parts of the population. Whites watch and copy African-American rap artists ("gangstas," with a nod to previous generations of immigrants who made their mark on society). Lessons are taken from the struggle for existence, both social and sexual, of the older generation. Mass entertainment provides common icons and rituals. *Cocaculturalism,* as Henry Louis Gates, Jr., (1993, 117) calls the whole complex of commercial culture, is the most powerful form of public culture. If this is the only source of public culture, there is less distance between subcultures and between "ghetto" and "mainstream" identities. Then social distance is reestablished by developing new cultural differences, confirming the cultural power of fear.

In such a landscape, there are no safe places. The Los Angeles uprising of 1992 showed that, unlike in earlier riots, the powerless respect fewer geographical boundaries, except perhaps the neighborhoods where rich people live. Carjack-ings – the ultimate American violence – occur on the highway and in the parking lots of fast food restaurants. "If you can't feel safe at McDonald's," a driver in Connecticut says, "is there any place you can feel safe?" (*New York Times,* February 27, 1993). Patrons of 24-hour automatic teller machines are robbed so often that the NYCE Network, with 10,000 machines in New York City, distributes a pamphlet of safety tips worthy of a military base: "As you approach an ATM, be aware of your surroundings. . . . When using an ATM at night, be sure it is located in a well lit area. And consider having someone accompany you." Someone, that is, other than the homeless man who stood by the door with an empty paper cup in his hand, until the New York City Council passed a law that forbade panhandlers to stand within 15 feet of an ATM. Or, as a Spanish-language subway advertisement cautions, "Man-tengase alerta. Sus ojos, oidos y instinto son sus recursos naturales de seguridad en la ATM." In Chicago and Los Angeles, ATMs have been installed in police stations, so resi-dents with bank accounts in the poorest neighborhoods will have a safe place to get cash.

For a brief moment in the late 1940s and early 1950s, working-class urban neighborhoods held the possibility of integrating white Americans and African-Americans in roughly the same social classes. This dream was laid to rest by movement to the suburbs, continued ethnic bias in employ-ment, the decline of public services in expanding racial ghet-tos, criticism of integration movements for being associated with the Communist party, and fear of crime. Over the next 15 years, enough for a generation to grow up separate, the inner city developed its stereotyped image of "Otherness." The reality of minority groups' working-class life was demonized by a cultural view of the inner city "made up of four ideological domains: a physical environment of dilapidated houses, dis-used factories, and general dereliction; a romanticized notion of white working-class life with particular emphasis on the centrality of family life; a pathological image of black culture; and a stereotypical view of street culture" (Burgess 1985).

By the 1980s, the development of a large black middle class with incomes more or less equal to white households' and the increase in immigrant groups raised a new possibility of developing ethnically and racially integrated cities. This time, however, there is a more explicit struggle over who will occupy the image of the city. Despite the real impoverishment of most urban populations, the larger issue is whether cities can again create an inclusive public culture. The forces of order have retreated into "small urban spaces," like privately managed public parks that can be refashioned to project an image of civility. Guardians of public institutions – teachers, cops – lack the time or inclination to *understand* the generalized ethnic Other. "We don't know how to reach Salvadoran refugees, Vietnamese boat people, African-Americans whose neighborhoods are full of crack," says a public school reformer in Los Angeles. "There is a widening gulf between those of us in charge and the successor generation. We can't relate to their reality" (*New York Times,* February 16, 1993, p. A13).

Yet the groups that have inherited the city have a claim on its central symbolic spaces. Not only to the streets that serve as major parade routes, not only to the central parks, but also to the monumental spaces that confirm identity by offering visual testimony to a group's presence in history.

Many places that we think of as great public spaces have become so only over time. Some, like city halls, Grand Central Terminal, or the Metropolitan Museum of Art, were built as representations of centralized power. Others, like Times Square, are places of commercial rather than political culture (Taylor 1992). Public spaces like the Mall in Washington, D.C., may eventually become civic spaces, evoking a sense of citizenship and the memory of sacrifice or heroism that citizenship often requires. Or a public space can be rebuilt or reconfigured to repress the memory of citizenship. The Basilica of Sacré Coeur was built on Montmartre, site of the slaughter of Communards in 1871 (Harvey 1985b); traffic was rerouted around Columbus Circle, in New York, to end the left-wing rallies that gathered there in the 1920s and 1930s.

Until 1914, we are told, "Times Square was the scene of many outdoor forums. When the square became too crowded these activities shifted northward; now in the open space below the [Columbus] monument impromptu discussions are held and groups listen to oratory on every conceivable subject from Thomas Paine and the *Age of Reason* to the advantages of a vegetable diet" (Federal Writers' Project 1939b, 180). Now the discussion at Columbus Circle focuses on which developer is going to build a multistory speculative tower there and how little he will pay the city treasury for the right to build it.

Many social critics have begun to write about new public spaces formed by the "transactional space" of telecommunications and computer technology, but my interest in this book is in public spaces as places that are physically *there,* as geographical and symbolic centers, as points of assembly where strangers mingle. Many Americans, born and raised in the suburbs, accept shopping centers as the preeminent public spaces of our time. Yet while shopping centers are undoubtedly gathering places, their private ownership has always raised questions about whether all the public has access to them and under what conditions. In the 1980s and 1990s, shopping centers became sites for hotels, post offices, and even schools, suggesting that public institutions can indeed function on private property. A recent decision by the New Jersey Supreme Court (*New York Times,* December 21, 1994), moreover, recognized that the great public spaces of modernity – "the parks, the squares, and the streets . . . have now been substantially displaced by [shopping] centers," and consequently, that the private owners of these shopping centers could no longer prevent people from exercising their Constitutional right of free speech. But it will take many years, and many changes in the culture of privatization, for shopping centers to develop into symbolic landscapes of public power. If suburbanization, computerization, and electronic media are to transform the social spaces of shopping malls and internets into public spaces, they require greater subjective legitimacy.

When Disneyland recruited teenagers in South Central Los Angeles for summer jobs following the riots of 1992, it thrust into prominence a new confluence between the sources of contemporary public culture: a confluence between commercial culture and ethnic identity. Defining public culture in these terms recasts the way we view and describe the cultures of cities. Real cities are both material constructions, with human strengths and weaknesses, and symbolic projects developed by social representations, including affluence and technology, ethnicity and civility, local shopping streets and television news. Real cities are also macro-level struggles between major sources of change – global and local cultures, public stewardship and privatization, social diversity and homogeneity – and micro-level negotiations of power. Real cultures, for their part, are not torn by conflict between commercialism and ethnicity; they are made up of one-part corporate image selling and two-parts claims of group identity, and get their power from joining autobiography to hegemony – a powerful aesthetic fit with a collective lifestyle. This is the landscape of a symbolic economy that I try to describe in the following chapters, on sites as geographically and socially diverse as Disney World, the Massachusetts Museum of Contemporary Art, New York art worlds, Times Square, New York City restaurants, and ghetto shopping streets like 125th Street in Harlem. These are my sources; this is my "city."

How do we connect what we experience in public space with ideologies and rhetorics of public culture?

On the streets, the vernacular culture of the powerless provides a currency of economic exchange and a language of social revival. In other public spaces – grand plazas, waterfronts, and shopping streets reorganized by business improvement districts – another landscape incorporates vernacular culture or opposes it with its own image of identity and desire. Fear of reducing the distance between "us" and "them," between security guards and criminals, between elites and ethnic groups, makes culture a crucial weapon in reasserting order. Militant rhetoric belongs to the forces of order. "We will fight for every house in the city," said the New York City Police Commissioner in his inaugural address in 1993. "We will fight for every street. We will fight for every borough. And we will win." This Churchillian call echoes the appeal of right-wing journalist Patrick Buchanan, who explicitly identified cities and culture when he addressed the 1992 Republican National Convention in Houston: "And as those boys [in the

National Guard] took back the streets of Los Angeles, block by block, my friends, we must take back our cities, and take back our culture, and take back our country."

But whose city? I ask. And whose culture?

■ Visual order, physical beauty, and social control: The landscape of Metro Orlando, "one of the 'top 10' U.S. cities in which to work and live."

Photo courtesy Economic Development Commission of Mid-Florida, Inc.

2

LEARNING FROM DISNEY WORLD

Disneyland and Disney World are two of the most significant public spaces of the late 20th century.[2] They transcend ethnic, class, and regional identities to offer a national public culture based on aestheticizing differences and controlling fear. The Disney Company is an innovator of global dimensions in the symbolic economy of technology and entertainment; it also exerts enormous influence on the symbolic economy of place in Anaheim and Orlando. The world of Disney is inescapable. It is the alter ego and the collective fantasy of American society, the source of many of our myths and our self-esteem.

---

2. After I wrote about Disneyland and Disney World as archetypal landscapes of power (Zukin 1991), I thought I had finished with them. I *wanted* to be finished with them. But then I realized they were on *everyone's* mind. At every anthropologists' conference, at least five scholars offered critiques of the Disney Company's theme parks. The business media were filled with prognoses of Euro Disney's success. I was asked to write jacket blurbs for two new books: one filled with enormous detail about every feature of Disney World and the other using "theme park" as a trope for the cultural subtext of urban design. To top it off, the faculty labor union at my university organized a package tour to Disney World. So I could not leave the subject alone. This chapter began as a paper for a conference on Encountering Space: Identity and Place in the Human Sciences, organized by Marc Blanchard in the Critical Theory Program at the University of California, Davis, in 1992. I have expanded and updated it, with special emphasis on the growth of Orlando and the continued growth of the Disney Company.

One reason for its success in creating an inclusive public culture is that Disney is truly a multimedia corporation. It produces large numbers of films and videos, runs a cable television channel, and owns professional sports teams. Its film library contains images that have "peopled" imaginations around the world since the Great Depression, with Mickey Mouse and his friends more effective agents of American culture than the CIA. Disneyland and Disney World are the most important tourist sites of the late 20th century. Not only do they represent an image of America that foreigners want to visit, they also represent a way of life that others want to join. Since the mid 1980s, moreover, when the company was reorganized and new managers took it over, Disney's name has been synonymous with business initiative, global expansion, high profits, and good stock market performance – all very impressive qualities in these years of business cutbacks and economic recession.

The apparent failure of Euro Disney during its first year in operation only dramatized the nearly universal Disney mania. When the European theme park opened in 1992, every newspaper, every architectural magazine, every culture critic had to "review" it – quite different coverage from news articles about the opening of the original Disneyland in Anaheim, California, in 1955.[3] Lower than expected attendance figures in Paris were rumored and then reported in the business press. Within a year, business losses resulted in the company's stock price falling by 60 percent. Yet losses at Euro Disney, only 49 percent owned by the Disney Company, were more than offset by record profits from other corporate activities. And no one rejected the idea of building more theme parks. The city of Anaheim granted the company zoning and environmental approvals and promises of infrastructure improvements for a $3 billion expansion. This promised to modernize Disneyland and bring it into the age of virtual reality. Toward the end of 1993, the company also proposed building a histori-

---

3. Articles about the opening of Disneyland in 1955 emphasized technological innovation and speed in both construction and landscaping (an important factor in the dry, desertlike climate) and assumed a child-centered point of view in delight with the amusements. By contrast, the expansion of Disney World assumed an adult-centered viewpoint, based on an aesthetic appreciation of design, especially the big-name, postmodern architecture.

cal theme park called Disney's America on a 3,000-acre site in northern Virginia. Although the Disney Company got the appropriate endorsements from state and local governments, the project drew the wrath of a specially organized historians' group and got a rather critical hearing – despite lack of jurisdiction – in the U.S. Congress. Around the same time, a corrosive new biography of Walt Disney, the founder of the company and "father" of Mickey Mouse, claimed Disney had been anti-Semitic, alcoholic, and an informer for the FBI.

Could the Disney Company's judgment be less than infallible? One challenge appeared to come from "location-based" virtual reality, the newest synthesis of automation and entertainment, a form of mass amusement much cheaper to install than theme parks. But it turned out that a grandnephew of Walt Disney and two Disney executives already controlled a virtual reality entertainment firm. Another challenge came from critics of the new theme park, Disney's America, but the project was defended by local officials as an economic development strategy before the company itself retreated. Film critics did not like some of the new Disney movies. But two films on a list of box office smashes in the summer of 1993 were released by a Disney subsidiary.

The Disney Company also explored new avenues to the collective imagination. It opened a Broadway show based on the movie *Beauty and the Beast* and received subsidies from the New York City government for its own theater on 42nd Street. It negotiated to buy Progeny, a division of Whittle Communications, that planned to establish low-cost private schools to compete with public schooling. Demonstrating that it had the trust of private investors, the Disney Company issued 100-year corporate bonds, the first such long-term bonds to be sold by any U.S. company in nearly a century. It certainly enjoyed the confidence of middle-class consumers. A local newspaper reported (*Orlando Sentinel,* January 16, 1994, pp. J1–2) that prospective home buyers deluged the Disney Company with requests to be put on a waiting list for Celebration, a long-planned residential community near Disney World in Orlando – before the specific details of the project were even announced. In its cover story on "the entertainment economy" (March 14, 1994), *Business Week* declared that "America's growth engines [were] theme parks, casinos, sports, [and] interactive TV."

But it is not only the Disney Company's business judgment that has so captured the imagination. Its greatest contribution has been to show the apparently boundless resilience of culture industries in a world of increasingly severe material limitations. Disney's success indicates a way to build economic development from an entirely cultural – that is, a "nonproductive" – base. Could this be real?

Learning from Disney World is a humbling experience, for it upsets many of the assumptions and values on which a critical understanding of modern society is based. Not least is the assumption that production, rather than culture, is the motor driving the economy. Yet the entertainment provided at Disney World relies on an extensive work force and an expansive network of material resources. These in turn feed the urban development of the surrounding towns and counties, establishing an image of regional growth that attracts more jobs, more migrants, and more houses. Disney World itself has become a base for attempting synergy with other areas of a service economy. Given the planning capacity of Disney managers and employees, would a Disney Medical Center be out of line? There is, already, a Walt Disney Cancer Institute at Florida Hospital in Orlando, but building a hospital on the grounds of Disney World itself would not be inconceivable.

People have also learned they can derive social benefits from visual coherence. The landscape of Disney World creates a public culture of civility and security that recalls a world long left behind. There are no guns here, no homeless people, no illegal drink or drugs. Without installing a visibly repressive political authority, Disney World imposes order on unruly, heterogeneous populations – tourist hordes and the work force that caters to them – and makes them grateful to be there, waiting for a ride. Learning from Disney World promises to make social diversity less threatening and public space more secure.

For many years, critics have dissected the public culture that Disneyland and Disney World embody. In the early 1960s, before civility became an issue, the architect Charles Moore (1965, 65) wrote that Disneyland offers "the kind of participation without embarassment" that Americans want in a public space. People want to watch and be watched, to stroll through a highly choreographed sequence of collective experiences, to respond emotionally with no risk that something will go wrong. Although Moore praised Disneyland for creating a coherent public space in "the featureless private floating world of southern California," he anticipated the harsher criticisms of European intellectuals, who have tended to write about Disney World since it opened, in 1971, as a simulation of history for people who prefer fakes because they *appear* more sincere (Eco 1986 [1975]; Baudrillard 1986). Disney World works because it abstracts both the technical and architectural elements of a place and the emotions that places evoke. "The more openly fake the buildings are, the more comfortable we are with them" (Goldberger 1992b).

By contrast, North American intellectuals criticize Disney World because it is not "hyperreal," but too real. Between 1982, when EPCOT (the Experimental Prototype Community of Tomorrow) opened, and 1985, when the new corporate management of the Disney Company revitalized the theme park by commissioning new rides and planning new hotels, Disney World began to be understood as a powerful visual and spatial reorganization of public culture. Its exhibits make social memory visible, and its means of establishing collective identity are based strictly on the market. Moreover, its size and functional interdependence make Disney World a viable representation of a real city, built for people from the middle classes that have escaped from cities to the suburbs and exurbs. It is an aestheticization of an urban landscape built without the city's fear or sex – and with its own, Disney money. Moreover, the insular theme park complex suggests very strongly that a separate, smaller city can be walled off within a larger city. While Disney World is an autonomous place with its own price of admission, a walled-off real city – like a gated residential community – promises to control the menace of strangers.

Nevertheless, the vision has its critics. Mike Wallace (1985) accuses the narrative behind the attractions of bleaching the conflicts out of American history. Steven Fjellman (1992) describes the paid amusements as a bazaar of commodity fetishism. While Alex Wilson (1992) calls the architecture and physical layout a supersuburb that eliminates the city,

Michael Sorkin (1992, 208) thinks Disney World is an elaborate modernist utopia that reshapes the city into "an entirely new, antigeographical space." Like television, which provided the original Disneyland with a national audience of wannabe Mouseketeers, visual communication at Disney World "erode[s] traditional strategies of coherence."

The fascinating point is that Disney World idealizes urban public space. For city managers seeking economic development strategies and public philosophers despairing of the decline of civility, Disney World provides a consensual, competitive strategy. Take a common thread of belief, a passion that people share – without coming to violence over it – and develop it into a visual image. Market this image as the city's symbol. Pick an area of the city that reflects the image: a shimmering waterfront commercial complex to symbolize the new, a stately, Beaux Arts train station to symbolize renewal, a street of small-scale, red-brick shops to symbolize historical memory. Then put the area under private management, whose desire to clean up public space has helped to make private security guards one of the fastest-growing occupations.

Visual culture, spatial control, and private management make Disney World an ideal type of new public space. From the 1950s to the 1970s, this space was usually found in suburban shopping malls. From the 1970s, however, as conservative national governments reduced urban renewal funds and competition for private-sector investment discouraged local governments from urban planning, this new public space has increasingly occupied the centers of cities. It has been shaped by both the expansionary strategies of real estate developers and the withdrawal from planning on the part of local governments. In this sense it is an emblem of the reshaping of the Welfare State.

But cities have never been able to control space so effectively as does corporate culture. Disney World admits the public on a paying basis. After getting local governments to pay for the infrastructure, the administration of the theme park secures the right to govern its territory autonomously. Disney World has its own rules, its own vocabulary, and even its own scrip or currency. Not only do these norms emphasize a surrender of consumers' identity to the corporate giant, they also establish a public culture of consumership. This is the model of urban space driving the public-private business improvement districts. Since Disney World provides its own security force and sanitation workers, the area they control is safer and cleaner than real city streets. Disney World has a mass transportation system, outdoor lighting, and street furniture; again, not surprisingly, all this works better than public facilities. Has Disney World been, all along, a not-so-subtle argument for privatizing public space?

"The Disney Company is America's urban laboratory," a journalist writes in the *Village Voice* (Ball 1991). So parts of Disney World have been used in many different places. There are visual and spatial elements of Disney World in urban festival marketplaces and shopping malls, museum displays, ski resorts, and planned residential communities. Moreover, Disney World's control over its labor force and their interaction with consumers have been taken as models for other service firms. The synergies between Disney's various corporate investments are a model for the symbolic economy based on media, real estate, and artistic display. And Disney World is a way of making the whole symbolic economy real, no matter what levels of unreality are explored. When you see Disney World, you have to believe in the viability of the symbolic economy. So learning from Disney World relates to a number of separate agendas: in theme parks, urban planning, service industries, and the symbolic economy as a whole.

▮ Real Theme Parks

While it is relished as a collective fantasy of escape and entertainment, the theme park is a tightly structured discourse about society. It represents a fictive narrative of social identity – not real history, but a collective image of what modern people are and should be – and it exercises the spatial controls that reinforce this identity.

The story of Walt Disney's inspiration for Disneyland is well known (see, e.g., Zukin 1991, 221–32). He had a sentimental attachment to a vision of Americana that he may have experienced during his boyhood in the Middle West. He needed, as well, to anchor his desire for security in an ideal landscape that he could control. His father, an unsuccessful inventor and failed small businessman, drifted from job to job and place to place during Disney's childhood. Walt Disney was also motivated to build an amusement park – an entertainment center, we might say, if the term *theme park* had never been invented – that would be bigger, better, and more wholesome than the tawdry fairs, carnivals, and amusement parks that Americans were used to.

Disney's plans departed from most of the accepted models. From the beginning of the 20th century, the widespread use of electric lighting in commercial architecture had enabled imaginative or obsessive entrepreneurs to build fantasy spaces as public amusements. Usually these were built in urban areas, like Luna Park at Coney Island (1903) or the New York Hippodrome (1905) (see Register 1991). Disney's great idea was to build an amusement park on a large tract of undeveloped land away from public transportation. Moreover, amusement parks featured scary rides and a large number of paying "attractions" in a small amount of space. Disneyland offered a small number of rides in a large amount of open space that would not generate revenue. Indeed, Disney was criticized on these grounds when he showed his plans to a convention of amusement park owners in 1953. The closest parallel to Disney's ambitions was the world's fairs that were held periodically to showcase industrial products and vignettes of exotic culture from other countries, along with a utopian or monumental construction representing a coherent, socially harmonious vision of the future. The 1893 World's Columbian Exposition in Chicago and the 1939 World's Fair in Flushing Meadows, New York, shaped Walt Disney's desire to provide "a place for people to find happiness and knowledge."

Though Disney claimed this was a simple idea, it was really a self-conscious visual presentation different from its predecessors. Disneyland's utopianism projected backward toward the past, with its strangely miniaturized reconstruction of the vernacular landscape of Main Street U.S.A. It also utilized the stage-set qualities of Hollywood studios, which for many years had offered tourists guided visits to the stage sets where films were made. Disneyland incorporated five different stage-set amusement parks: Adventureland, Lilliputian Land, Fantasyland, Frontier Land, and Holiday Land, borrowing motifs from carnivals, children's literature, and

U.S. history. The addition of themed artifacts and costumes – to make the fantasy more complete – was either pure Hollywood or pure Hollywood technique. On the one hand, it is a panorama like that of the earlier Williamsburg, Virginia, with people paid to exemplify and interpret a matching set of cultural products. On the other hand, it is a montage (Sorkin 1992, 226–27), fabricating and aggregating visual images with no concern for logical structure.

Disney World opened in south Florida, near the city of Orlando, in 1971. EPCOT, the utopian village that Disney wanted to build as a planned and highly managed residential community, did not open until 1982 because the technology required for some of the exhibits was too expensive. And until the 1990s, it lacked the homes that were originally envisaged. While the theme park controls 28,000 acres and has built more hotel rooms than any other hotel and convention center developer in the southeastern United States, the company did not want to assume the legal responsibilities for establishing a real town.

Even before EPCOT's corporate pavilions and Disney's Hall of Presidents and other automated exhibits were opened, Disney World continued to combine elements from Disneyland and the world's fairs. There was a wholesome carnival atmosphere that people could enjoy with their families. Architecture and costumes reduced international cultures to a few touristic signs. High-tech machinery was used to keep people moving through the park site. Corporations were identified with an optimistic control of the future. Spaces were designed to foster civilized social interaction. Famously, the social space at Disney World encouraged customers to be polite while waiting in long lines to enter attractions. Consumers (*guests,* in Disney language) were bombarded with demands to buy every element of the leisure experience, from tickets to food and souvenirs. As every critical visitor points out, moreover, Disney World teaches that site is sight. Space is experienced in postcards, photographs, and videos. Just as public highway signs in many countries indicate places with scenic views, so photo opportunities at Disney World are marked by Kodak signs. Guests pay extra for a photo op with Mickey.

At Euro Disney, which opened in France in 1992, space was designed as though never seen by the human eye, only by a camera – either a director's movie camera or a tourist's VCR. This strategy caters to younger visitors, who tend to come to Euro Disneyland through other Disney products, primarily movies and images of earlier theme parks. "It's wonderful," a 14-year-old French girl was quoted as saying at the opening of Euro Disneyland. "I love watching the Disney cartoons" (*New York Times,* April 13, 1992, p. 1). Indeed, Disney cartoons are broadcast on TF 1 every Sunday morning to an audience of 6 million French children, and the long-lived *Journal de Mickey* has a circulation of 10 million (Zuber 1992, 15).

As for architectural fantasy, Euro Disney looks like the movies. Reversing the world's fairs, it offers exotic Americana for foreign tourists, with visions of cities, the old West, and California in the 1950s or early 1960s – the last and best of modern times in America. Thus the theme park reproduces what Europeans who visit the United States want most to see: New York City, the West, and Disneyland. So Euro Disney "[built] a skyline that rivals London, Paris, New York or whatever, in terms of a recognizable set of landmarks," a Disney official says. The hotels are stage sets for Western action movies: the Hotel Cheyenne, Sequoia Lodge, Hotel Santa Fe, and Camp Davy Crockett. A reporter describes the Hotel Santa Fe as

> *most startling. . . . a cross between a Southwestern Indian pueblo and a 1950s motel. The lobby echoes a Pueblo Indian kiva, or ceremonial chamber. The cafeteria uses an on-the-road theme, serving salads out of an aging pickup truck and dispensing water from old oil drums. Hallways showcase kachina dolls, Indian pottery and convincing Mexican-made copies of Navajo rugs (C. Watson 1992).*

Like all the world's fairs that preceded it, this is a visual narrative for a compact tourism of exotic places. And it is a world's fair brought to you by a world-class corporation, whose references to its own cultural products are so entangled with references to those of real places that Disney World is indistinguishable from the real world.

▓ A Shared Public Culture

The production of space at Disneyland and Disney World creates a fictive narrative of social identity. The asymmetries of power so evident in real landscapes are hidden behind a facade that reproduces a unidimensional nature and history. This is corporate, not alternative, global culture, created in California and replicated in turnkey "plants" in Florida, Japan, and France. We participate in this narrative as consumers. The products we consume are imported from other places. Because they are sold in a coherent visual scheme, they appear to perpetuate or reconstruct a place with its own identity. Main Street and EPCOT make obvious fictions for yesterday and tomorrow. But the experience of going to Disney World, and waiting to consume the various attractions, locates us in an endless present, when we are concerned only with getting somewhere and waiting to get back.

The big question is how we have come to use these public spaces to satisfy private needs. The need to be together, to be entertained, has created a mass market for high-quality consumer goods in high-status consumption spaces. The need to "connect," to form social communities, creates a market for many kinds of associations and convention centers for them to meet. Private corporations' desire to project a benevolent public spirit – helped along by zoning laws – creates large plazas, atria, or lobbies devoted to "public use," either through art exhibits or facilities for eating and shopping. People "experience" these spaces by seeing each other experiencing them. Disney World has become such a monumental phenomenon because it visualizes a public that comes together only in transitory, market situations.

At the same time, Disney products have become the logos of a public culture. Naturally, there have been some changes over the years. Mickey Mouse started out in 1928 as a cartoon character. The Great Depression was Mickey's formative childhood experience. In a Christmas tale published in 1934 (*Mickey Mouse Movie Stories* repr. 1988), Mickey and his dog Pluto walk hungrily through the snow on Christmas Eve. They pass a rich household, where the spoiled child amuses himself by teasing the butler, a dog dressed in a morning coat. The butler asks Mickey if he will sell his dog, which Mickey refuses to do. Mickey and Pluto then pass another house,

where a poor family of kittens is asleep. Mickey rushes back
to the first house, sells Pluto to the butler, and buys gifts for
the kittens, which he leaves in their home. Warmed by his
good deed, Mickey sits in the snow – where Pluto finds him,
for he has run away from the rich child, dragging the rich
family's Christmas turkey with him. How does this lean and
hungry Disney symbol relate to the sleek, self-satisfied mouse
who is the mascot of a major transnational corporation?

During the 1980s, Mickey Mouse's ears were unasham-
edly stolen from popular culture by high-status arts, beginning
with architecture. The architect Arata Isozaki designed part
of the Team Disney Building at Lake Buena Vista, Florida
(1987–90) in the shape of a giant pair of mouse ears – pop art
fed back to a corporate sponsor. This design has been defended
aesthetically as a pure geometric abstraction, in contrast to
the anthropomorphic dolphins, swans, and mice used by the
architect Michael Graves on other Disney corporate buildings
(Asada 1991, p. 91). Once they are abstracted from the mass
culture of Disney cartoons, however, mouse ears become symbols of a shared public culture. They even appear in a political
cartoon on the Op-Ed page of the *New York Times* (June 5,
1992), worn by both a Republican elephant and Democratic
donkey.

As Disney symbols are introduced into high culture, artists shake off the ironic detachment with which they might
once have regarded them. When a modern dance company,
Feld Ballets/New York, set two recent ballets to Mozart sym-
phonies, they dressed the soloist in mouse ears and had the
dancers sing "M-I-C-K-E-Y M-O-U-S-E" along with the 31st
symphony (*New York Times,* February 29, 1992). While they
do not offend in cultural performances, Disney symbols may
be too suggestive for political affairs. A British painter, John
Keane, caused an uproar in London in 1992 by exhibiting
Mickey Mouse at the Front, a painting critical of the United
States for mounting the Persian Gulf War (Porter 1992). The
artist Bill Shiffer showed an assemblage, *New World Order,*
in New York in 1993 that featured Mickey Mouse on top of a
hammer and sickle, stars and stripes, cross, and Jewish star.
Professional culture critics may even see Disney forms where
none are intended. When the Sugar Cubes, a far-out rock
group from Iceland performed recently in New York, the *New*

York Times (April 20, 1992) described the lead singer's hair as pinned up in Mickey Mouse ears on each side of her head – or maybe they were just Viking braids.

Mickey Mouse infiltrated standard American English a long time ago. Yet the meaning is ambiguous because it joins irony and simulation. The adjective *Mickey Mouse* means both outlandish and false, "a caricature of normal practice . . . [and, as in the military, a] mindless obedience to regulations" (Rosenthal 1992). Despite this ambiguity, and his changing form, Mickey Mouse has become a criterion of authenticity in cultural production. He is both icon and exemplar, a talismanic Ralph Lauren that enables mass market reproductions to be discussed as high culture. Which is more authentic, the cultural critic of the *New York Times* has asked: an idealized version of the past or the real past with all its warts? "The Disney version, like Mr. Lauren's environments, corrects all the mistakes, and paradoxically gives you a much better sense of what the experience of being in a lavish Victorian seaside hotel ought to have been" (Goldberger 1992a, 34).

◼ The Spatial Reality of Virtual Reality

The virtual reality of Disney World most resembles the metropolitan region of Orlando. Orlando's rapid growth since Disney World opened relates at least as much to the theme park and the tourist economy it spawned as to the proximity of high-tech industry at Cape Canaveral, low-wage labor, and open land. The theme park brought Orlando subjective legitimacy as a place where businesses and people wanted to be. "Spend less Orlandough," says a United Airlines poster in a travel agency window on Madison Avenue in New York. People are attracted to the city because it has the image of public space that Disney World projects. "People come here because they know it's going to be safe," says the head of Universal Studios, Florida. People need never worry about bad weather or crime. The author of a best-selling book of investment advice who lives in Orlando says, "The best place to live is where everybody wants to vacation" (quotes in "Fantasy's Reality," cover story, *Time* May 27, 1991, 52–59, on 54).

Orlando in some ways reiterates the mythology of Los Angeles. The city has youth, a population of migrants, jobs in manufacturing as well as services, and an image of leisure. Orlando is a boomtown of the 1970s and 1980s, one of five "hot spots" of regional economic development, on the same level as greater Boston, metropolitan New York, Los Angeles, and San Francisco (Thurow 1989, 192–93). The population in metropolitan Orlando more than doubled between 1970 and 1990, rising from half a million to over a million people. Employment in the same period more than tripled, from 193,000 to 662,000. A fifth of the population moved to Orlando between the late 1980s and early 1990s. At that time, the city had the youngest median age in Florida. About 80 percent of the 1990 population was white. "Non-whites" make up 13 percent of the population, and "Hispanics," 7 percent but growing fast. Still, 85 percent of the 1990 work force was white. Corporate CEOs named Orlando "one of the three most attractive emerging, major U.S. markets in which to relocate a business during the next five years" (Economic Development Commission of Mid-Florida 1991, 89–90; *New York Times,* January 31, 1994).

Race must have something to do with Orlando's extraordinary growth. Companies that have set up offices in Orlando recruit the kinds of middle-middle-class white workers that used to live in the Northeast and Middle West. The defense contractors that spurred the region's employment growth in the 1980s have not located in areas with large racial minorities for years. Metro Orlando is the site of corporate headquarters for Tupperware Home Parties, the American Automobile Association, and five large national insurance companies. AT&T, Alfa Romeo, the restaurant operator General Mills Restaurants, and Southern Bell Telephone Company have large offices there. The California-based Campus Crusade for Christ relocated its corporate headquarters to the area. The Naval Training Center, a government agency, employs nearly 17,000 people. In all, service jobs increased nearly tenfold, from 27,000 in 1970 (23.5 percent of total employment) to 200,000 in 1990 (35.5 percent of total employment).

Manufacturing has grown in Orlando even though it has grown smaller throughout the United States. Defense and aerospace industries account for much of this growth, with Martin Marietta employing more than 11,000 workers, along with Litton Laser Systems, Westinghouse Electric Corporation, and other producers of micro-electronics equipment, simulation training systems, and electronic assemblies. All of these are bound to survive military cutbacks because they are used in the mobile armed forces and aerial bombing strategies with which "regional" wars are fought. Nevertheless, as the presence of Disney World, Universal Studios, and Sea World suggests, one of every four jobs is tourist related. More than 50,000 men and women work in hotels, resorts, restaurants, and tourist attractions, over 30,000 at Disney World alone.

Despite the comfortable lifestyle that Orlando represents, most of these jobs are neither secure nor highly paid. Temporary placement agencies were responsible for the hiring of 38,340 people in 1990, mainly in clerical, secretarial, word processing, and light industrial jobs. During the same year, permanent placement agencies were responsible for the hiring of only 3,000 people (*Orlando Business Journal,* 1992). Aside from the defense complex, Orlando is typical of any medium-size city dependent on a service economy, with an added advantage for employers in its new labor force. People in Orlando are young, fairly well educated, unencumbered by a history of labor union militance.

Orlando's other advantages include a lot of undeveloped land, very clean streets, homeless people who live in mobile homes rather than on the sidewalks, and no ethnic conflicts (*Time,* May 27, 1991, 54–55). The city also has low property taxes. Local government shows no inclination to raise taxes in order to clean up polluted lakes, build new highways and schools, or maintain an existing symphony orchestra – after all, the tourists do not come to hear Mozart. Yet the four-county complex that surrounds Disney World and supports a single public agency for economic development has been able to convince people that private development, aided by the state, creates significant public benefits. Convention business increased so much during the 1980s that a 4 percent tax on hotel rooms paid for the construction of an Orange County Convention/Civic Center, half of the Orlando Arena, and a portion of the renovation of the Citrus Bowl (DePalma 1991).

Besides helping to shape the growth of Orlando, Disney World influences the shape of other places. The commercial and critical success of planned residential communities with strict building and design rules, like Seaside, Florida, planned by the architects Andres Duany and Elizabeth Plater-Zyberk, show that people like benevolent authoritarianism, as long as it rules by imposing visual criteria. In smaller development projects, re-creating the 19th-century town green has been highly marketable. But the old town and town green represent more than aesthetic images; they embody broader strategies of social control. The organization of space is accompanied by a carefully planned distribution of population by age and income level. This goes hand in hand with acceptance of an internalized political authority. Ironically, the town government legislates a certain amount of diversity. No white picket fence in Seaside may look like any other white picket fence. Other regulations control the density, size, and style of construction, as well as the use of space. Controlling diversity determines the aesthetic power of the place. In social class terms, this is a middle-class space, the equivalent of Disney World's Main Street. It reproduces the white middle-class exclusivity – the safe, socially homogeneous space – of the 1950s, within acceptable limits of aesthetic diversity.

Since four-fifths of the visitors to Disney World are grown-ups, the look of the place must appeal to what adults want. Disney World exemplifies visual strategies of *coherence,* partly based on uniforms and behavioral norms of conformity, and partly based on the production of set *tableaux,* in which everything is clearly a sign of what it represents in a shared narrative, fictive or real (see Boyer 1992). Disney World also uses a visual strategy that makes unpleasant things – like garbage removal, building maintenance, and pushing and shoving – *invisible.* Disney World uses *compression* and *condensation,* flattening out experience to an easily digestible narrative and limiting visualization to a selective sample of symbols. Despite all the rides and thrills, Disney World relies on *facades.* You cannot go into The Magic Kingdom, but it is a central place at Disney World.

These visual strategies have influenced the building of shopping complexes with historical themes like South Street Seaport in New York and shopping malls with amusements like the West Edmonton Mall in Canada. They also shape consumption space as a total experience, as at the Mall of America in Minnesota. But defining a consumption space by its look is especially suited to transnational companies in the symbolic economy, which try to synergize the sale of consumer products, services, and land. Disney World is, of course, the prime example. It is followed by the Ashley resort, or "recreational village," built by the Laura Ashley Company in Japan, where the home furnishings, fabrics, and fashion company designs and sells hotel rooms, restaurants, gardens, stables, helipads, apartments, and houses (Gandee 1991). The look is the experience of the place. Controlling the vision brings market power.

Disney World's strategies for organizing space also influence New York City's business improvement districts (BIDs). Their first goal is to *clean up* an area, to keep it free of litter that the city's sanitation services cannot control. They also secure space by erecting barriers or otherwise limiting public access and making rules about appropriate behavior. Private security guards help enforce that strategy. They control the public's mobility by keeping people moving through public space and organizing where and how they sit – and also determining who may sit. Another strategy of establishing social control is to influence norms of body presentation. The dress and grooming codes for employees at Euro Disney got a lot of attention in the press because they seemed to violate French culture. How could French men not be permitted to wear a beard? Or French women not to wear black stockings? Yet in every culture, dress rules are a means of managing socially engendered diversity. As an American visitor to Euro Disney, a long-time resident of Paris, observes, conforming to Disney's work rules made French workers seem to be "professionals"; it gave them an air of civility. "Perhaps one can conclude that class boundaries are erased at Euro Disney, if only for a few hours" (Zuber 1992, 15).

These social strategies have the political effect of creating an impression of trust among strangers. This differs from the fatalistic trust found among passengers aloft in an airplane – or below ground in a New York City subway car. It is comparable to the sociable but reserved behavior you find in small country "inns," where everyone trusts that the other guests are the same social type. Politically, it is important that these are all spaces to which you buy entry. The ticket price alone – at Disney World, a hefty, though not extraordinary, $35 a day – ensures some gatekeeping, some exclusivity, some sense of confidence that equal access is not threatening.

Establishing confidence by means of spatial controls creates a precedent for public-private partnerships and private developers in cities. Unable to wall off their sections of the city, they have to make them accessible to the public but do not want to encourage the disorder of loiterers, muggers, the homeless, and the unruly. Like Disney World, these agencies set up private jurisdictions over which they have nearly absolute control. They have fiscal and financial power to create "public" services. These differ from previous arrangements because the services do not supplement public goods: they *replace* public goods.

BIDs, as we have seen in Chapter 1, create a privatization of public goods that many city dwellers find attractive. The BIDs' political autonomy derives from their financial autonomy: in addition to paying legally required city and state taxes, the property owners assess themselves an additional local tax based on square footage, and these taxes are collected for them by the city government. The BIDs then use the money to fund public improvements that local governments cannot or will not pay for. Activist BIDs develop because of the city government's inability to generalize improvement strategies – which is, of course, the problem with the BIDs themselves (see Wolfson 1992).

These BIDs create their own sense of place not only by re-creating the attentive municipal services of another era (such as sanitation and security), but also by following Disney's lead in identifying theme and style with social order. The extreme example is the BIDs' use of uniform design to reinforce their public identity. In 1992, the Times Square BID commissioned an award-winning theatrical costume designer to create uniforms for its private sanitation force (*The New Yorker*, July 6, 1992, 12). Jumpsuits and caps are bright red to match the trash cans; T-shirts and logos are purple to match the plastic liner bags. "Until now," says a member of the sanitation crew, "we wore the same dull-blue work pants and shirts that ten thousand other people wear in New York. But now when people spy you on the street, they'll know you're part of the Times Square team. These are sharp – I mean, this is Broadway, right?"

Property values lie at the heart of the BIDs' drive for public improvements. But property values do not merely reflect use, as David Harvey (1973) has written. Instead, they reflect Disney World values of cleanliness, security, and visual coherence. The 34th Street BID, on a heavily used shopping street between the Empire State Building and Macy's, hired retail consultants to write guidelines on proper storefront design because the stores' presentation of a public face was too messy (Griffith 1992). For years, 34th Street has been a "populist" shopping street, a magnet for working-class families of every ethnic group. But, since Macy's filed for a bankruptcy reorganization in 1991 and the Empire State Building was bought by a private investor in 1992, the bazaar look has not projected a desirable image. Signs were oversize, up to six stories high, and merchandise spilled out onto the street from stalls at newsstands and through open windows. Images of brand names, store names, logos, and murals were overwhelming. So the BID decided to push the enforcement of municipal regulations. BID employees reported such violations as awnings that were too big, illegal sidewalk stalls, and newsstands that "have turned into bazaars," as an assistant commissioner of the city's Department of Consumer Affairs says. If found guilty by an administrative law or Criminal Court judge, violators face fines, jail terms, and suspension of licenses. Ironically, the murals and signs and "carnival atmosphere" on 34th Street deplored by a retail consultant are the lively aesthetic element so desired – after years of public criticism – in the redevelopment of Times Square.

The BIDs' strategies for managing public space suggest what an important role vision plays in defining spatial identities. To some extent the importance of visualization reflects the cumulative influence of photography, film, and television from the end of the nineteenth century, but it also reflects the influence of Disney World on public culture. In New York, advocates of both historic preservation and new construction accuse each other of "Disneyitis" (see Gill 1991), as they try to regulate, or free from regulation, aesthetically or narratively incoherent segments of the city. Occasionally these efforts are too strenuous. In a village on the eastern end of Long Island, where many affluent New Yorkers have vacation homes, some old-time residents criticized the village improvement associa-

▨ The impact of Disney World on 34th Street: The 34th Street Partnership rides shotgun on visual display, before (above) and after (below).

Photos courtesy of 34th Street Partnership.

tion for "trying to turn Water Mill into Disneyland," by cutting down two trees on the village green to preserve a windmill that is a national historic landmark (*New York Times,* December 30, 1991).

The general question behind "Disneyitis" is which visual strategy – historic preservation, imitation, or imaginative recreation – is morally legitimate. While strategies based on theme may be transparent, techniques of simulation decontextualize the production of space and so may be difficult to decode in a critical way. Moreover, simulation is economically productive, for it provides opportunities to develop new products and a market edge, as well as to export work to new markets, especially in Japan and Southeast Asia. By the same token, simulation gives art and architecture critics something to discuss, rhetorical grist for the critics' mill. The architecture critic of the *Boston Globe* defends a new, pseudo-neo-Georgian office tower in Boston by the architect Robert A. M. Stern because it "is architecture for an age of simulation" (Campbell 1992). He also praises the way the social diversity and unruliness of the work force contradict the apparent aesthetic harmony and political coherence that real neo-Georgian architects aimed for in the early 20th century. Between postmodern architecture and the new informality, public space enshrines spontaneity and chaos – but to what purpose and at what cost? "A long-haired messenger boy in bicycle tights . . . transforms the building at once, by his mere presence, into a stage set. . . . An attorney in running shoes and earmuffs simply by being here alchemizes [the building] into a museum representation of a dead culture, becoming, herself, a tourist in that museum."

▓ Disney World as a Service Industry

Just as Disney World shapes representations of space, so it consciously sets a model for service industries. In 1990, a survey of "hundreds of business experts" conducted by *U.S. News & World Report* (July 9, 1990, 74) found the Walt Disney Company to be the best service provider in the United States, followed by the retailers Nordstrom and L. L. Bean. Disney was praised for a high level of staffing, cleanliness, and "chipper" employees. Translated into the rhetoric of the *Harvard Business Review* and other formulators of management ideology, this means that competitiveness in the services is based on the quality of the service product – that is, on the bodily and emotional presentation of the work force. Indeed, during the 1980s, the *Harvard Business Review* laid equal emphasis on cost cutting and contact with the customer. The usually abstract product in service transactions appears to be a socially constructed interaction – a "moment of truth" in service industry ideology – when the employee is responsible for managing impressions more than for doing anything "real." Certainly Disney World does create a real product in all the ways I have already outlined: cleanliness, visual coherence, social order. The dependability of this product accounts for much of the success in exporting Disney theme parks from the United States (as it also does, in part, for the transnational success of fast-food chains). But the employees of Disney World also work like crazy to make sure all the customers have fun.

The burdens placed on employees are similar to those on flight attendants, historically women (see Hochschild 1983), and waiters in upscale, but not pretentious, restaurants. While women's service work of this type has been called *emotional labor,* Disney World employees produce *emotive* labor. Those in the front regions, in direct contact with customers, are often entertainers – actors or musicians who are glad of the chance to put on a costume and perform. Together with waiters and some retail sales clerks, these employees interpret and exemplify the consumption experience. They "act out" rather than merely sell a product. They are hired because they bring to the job some cultural capital that they have developed outside the work relation. Their ability to simulate empathy with customers is similar to that of successful salespersons in clothing stores: the saleswoman who exemplifies "the look," the salesman – often gay – who develops "the perspective" on a wardrobe (Peretz 1992).

This interpretation of an ideal type of service work contrasts with the "post-Fordism" that some critics find in contemporary industrial strategies. In contrast to that depiction of the labor process as flexible, self-propelling, and intellectually demanding, many service industries rely on extreme standardization of labor, multiple levels of managerial authority, and rote performance. Because contact with the customer is so important – and managers cannot directly and continually monitor that performance – delivering a quality product depends on employees' internalization of their service role. In the Disney World model, this requires selective recruitment, training, and a distinctive corporate culture that aims at both employees' identification with the firm and self-discipline. "You can't force people to smile," says the director of Walt Disney Company's three-day training seminars for business executives from other firms. "Each guest to Disney World sees an average 73 employees per visit, and we would have to supervise them continually. Of course, we can't do that, so instead we try to get employees to buy into the corporate culture" (McGill 1989).

This lesson appeals to companies whose business depends on field representatives. A manufacturer of household alarms, who attended Disney's management training seminars, says, "There's no way we can control those moments of truth in the field, unless we have a culture that insures they know what's right and wrong. If we're going to compete with the Japanese, we've got to develop that service orientation." A hospital administrator from New York applied Disney World's strategies for dealing with problems to the hospital: "They have long lines and lots of waits, which is not dissimilar to what we have here when a machine breaks and people have to wait longer than they should" (McGill 1989).

Disney's training programs for employees make up Disney University. New employees' first class, Traditions, is a mandatory, one-day orientation with a slide show and tours of the facilities. It teaches the history of the company through its key products and images. New employees also learn the Disney language, in which employees are called *cast members* and are said to be *on stage*. Job performance norms are taught in the form of such slogans as "What does Disney make? It makes people happy" and "Don't take yourself seriously, take your job seriously" (McGill 1989). Employees in supervisory "front" positions, called *leads*, must attend a lead development class and a class to learn performance appraisal of subordinates. All leads also attend a one-time-only class called You Create Happiness, which teaches techniques of conflict resolution and how to handle guest complaints. Employees must attend classes periodically to revitalize their commitment to service norms or "recharge your pixie dust," as a former employee of Disneyland told me.

Like other service jobs in Orlando, these jobs pay wages that are higher than minimum wage, between $5.50 and $7.75 an hour in 1989–92 (*Monthly Labor Review,* February 1989, 53–54). In fact, these hourly rates represent the settlement of a long contract dispute with 11,400 of 36,000 employees at Disney World. Yet the theme park faces a chronic labor shortage. At Disneyland, where almost all employees come from the Los Angeles area, the work force is encouraged through a Share the Spirit program to recruit friends to apply for jobs there. Yet Disneyland did not recruit from the inner city of Los Angeles until after the riots of 1992.

The mainly suburban work force is represented by an array of labor unions, including the Food and Commercial Workers, the Hotel Employees and Restaurant Employees, the Teamsters, the Service Employees, the Transportation-Communications Union, and the International Association of Theatrical Stage Employees. In contrast to the Disney image of harmony, competence, and grace under pressure, the division of labor among these unionized trades often makes it very difficult to get tasks done on time. Not surprisingly, employee benefits are highly dependent on seniority. Since getting a "good" shift depends on seniority, employees tend to stay in their jobs a long time. They can retire on a maximum monthly pension of $530 after 25 years, which many reach in their middle age.

New employees are hired at the lowest level, as casual temporary workers. They can then rise through casual regular jobs, working all year round on weekends, at night, and during the summer, to regular part-time and finally regular full-time jobs. From their first day as Disney World employees, they are subject to a dress and grooming code and constant performance appraisals.

Disney World also provides a significant number of student jobs through the Walt Disney World College Program and special internships. An ad in the *Black Collegian* (January–February 1990, 94–99) describes a 10-to-14 week internship as a momentous experience in career dedication at a crucial point when college students are committing themselves to their future work. In reality, however, the internship offers a minimum of 30 hours a week working in an hourly nonsupervisory position in food and beverage, merchandise, attractions, and resort operations – selling soft drinks and Mickey Mouse dolls and greeting customers. These sound like low-wage jobs in the hotel and travel industry, but they pay more than most college internships. The internship also includes class sessions in management training, housing – for which rent, including utilities and transportation, is deducted from the paycheck – and the opportunity to use the parks and attractions. "Come and learn how to make magic."

A special internship in aquaculture is offered by The Land Agricultural Student Program, part of the Kraft General Foods' exhibit on agriculture in Future World at EPCOT Center. The juxtaposition of scientific student internships, Disney World, and corporate management is significant. It deepens both the corporate nexus on which EPCOT depends and the model of a new service economy that Disney World represents. Although the aquaculture program is part of the Kraft facilities, all employees, including marine biologists and student interns, are hired by the Walt Disney Company. Two student interns are accepted every six months. They are paid $300 a week and given air transport to Orlando and a small relocation allowance. They must own a car.

Working with scientists with advanced degrees in a variety of agricultural specializations and 16 additional professional agricultural support staff, the students grow the 30 crops in the show on The Land. They plant, prune, harvest, install irrigation systems, and sterilize the growing areas by steam. They take part in a research project "which benefits both The Land and the student" (Walt Disney World Company, announcement of internship, 1992). More concretely, 20 working hours out of 40 are spent in maintaining the facilities of the Kraft exhibit, including cleaning tanks. Ten hours are devoted to "husbandry – health monitoring, handling, harvesting, nutrition and food preparation." Six hours are spent taking group tours through the greenhouse and four hours are spent in training, field trips, and meetings. These jobs sound like low-wage labor on an ecologically astute farm. But they probably look good on a job resume.

Although the catfish, tilapia, and bass grown in The Land are sometimes served in The Land Grille Room Restaurant, the ultimate goal of the Kraft exhibit appears to enter the rapidly growing industry to breed artificial food. With world demand for fish increasing and natural supplies dwindling because of demographic factors and water pollution, the companies that control fish production are bound to profit. This is what interests Kraft, Ralston-Purina, Johnson and Johnson, and other big corporations involved in research on mariculture. Although they are not resistant to disease and cannot reproduce, farm-raised fish are a consumer's dream, a clean industry staffed by workers with advanced degrees. The brochure published by the Florida Department of Agriculture and Consumer Services about Farm-Raised Florida Hybrid Striped Bass could have been written by Disney imagineers:

> *A sleek, silvery fish with bold black lines, these beautiful fish are the product of a fish biologist's whimsy. The female striped bass are mated with the males of the white bass. The offspring, a hybrid, are hardy fish that grow well in tanks or ponds and readily adapt to consuming pelletized foods.*
>
> *The hybrid striped bass is a predator. On the farm, the fish are graded numerous times and fed frequently so that smaller, slower growing fish do not become dinner for their tank mates. A high protein, grain-based feed is used to satisfy their voracious appetites.*

▓ Disney's Symbolic Economy

The sponsorship of marine culture at Disney World represents an integration of primary products and visual symbols. Like Disney World itself, this symbolic economy accepts incongruities that violate historic material forms, both economic and ecological. Buy "fresh salmon steak, farm raised and grain fed," as a supermarket poster in New York proclaims. In the symbolic economy, employers hire a work force with cultural capital or higher education to do productive labor and provide a labor-intensive service called fun. Because of language requirements, business establishments use "European" employees in front regions in direct contact with customers and "minority" employees in the back. The Disney World model suggests that a local or regional economy can be created on a primary base of services, which spin off real estate development, attract other "clean" businesses, and generate creative business services like advertising and entertainment (Zukin 1990).

This model of the symbolic economy creates its own internal stratification, with low-wage workers, temporary workers, and unionized workers performing low-status tasks of maintenance, security, and food preparation. One of the crucial social issues is how this model handles status disparities. Much of the burden is borne by corporate culture and job security, but the cost may be employee burnout, achievement limited to the benefits provided by the firm, and vulnerability to corporate mind control. Will producing fun create a different kind of personal identity than producing widgets?

The corporate managers that took over the Disney family business in 1985 have bet on the development and diversification of new mass culture products: Hollywood films, syndicated television programs, and videocassette releases of old Disney movies. They have also taken on the role of hotel developer at Disney World and expanded the theme park by building new rides, linking them with such high-price talent as Michael Jackson, Steven Spielberg, and George Lucas, and multiplying "participation agreements" with large corporate sponsors. Corporate synergies are not new to Disneyland. Back in the 1950s, Walt Disney received a $500,000 investment and a loan guarantee of $4.5 million from the televison network ABC to build Disneyland.

In return, the network owned one-third of the park and got to show Disney's first weekly television program. Walt Disney also sold Coca-Cola an exclusive soda concession for Disneyland; Kodak bought exclusive rights to sell film at the park. Under a Disney license, Hollywood-Maxwell sold underwear from a corset shop on Main Street, and a building company sold real estate from another store. At EPCOT, the large corporations that sponsor pavilions invested $75 million apiece in construction funds and guaranteed operating expenses for ten years.

Under CEO Michael Eisner and CFO Frank Wells, the new Disney management negotiated a new contract with

Kodak so that Kodak paid for part of the construction costs of the Michael Jackson ride as well as for theater renovations at Disneyland and Disney World. General Motors, which had its own pavilion, The World of Motion, and also supplied Disney World's "official car," paid a share of the costs of joint advertising campaigns. A new corporate sponsor, Metropolitan Life Insurance Company, agreed to spend almost $90 million for a health-theme pavilion at EPCOT.

By late 1988, the Disney Channel was also achieving Eisner's goal of cross-promotion for other company ventures. Kids watching Winnie the Pooh or Mickey Mouse cartoons became a target market for Disney toys. Showing episodes of The Mickey Mouse Club, *which had been filmed at the Disney-MGM Studios Theme Park, enticed 14-year-olds into pressuring their parents to take them to Orlando* (Grover 1991, 150).

In any event, the Disney World theme park is almost infinitely expandable even within the southern tier of the United States. While Disney World has helped to create a new transatlantic and Latino tourist zone in south Florida, a completely new Disneyland in Anaheim, Westcot Center, will focus on "our humanity, our history, our planet, our universe." The new Disneyland resort will include Westcot, the original Disneyland, a resort hotel district, a centralized Disneyland Plaza linking the old and new theme parks, and Disney Center, a commercial area for shopping and strolling around a lake.

The virtual reality of Disney World is expandable not only in economic and geographical terms. Visually, too, Disney World is a model of how to think about the past and how to reproduce it. While technology aids this process, Disney World's real attraction is that it is a new social space, an alternative to cities. The conceptual challenge Disney World raises to public culture reflects the fact that a completely artificial space, a space that has never been a real place to live, can so resonate with social desires.

Disneyland and its marketing world developed together with broadcast television. Like Niagara Falls and Yellowstone National Park (Sears 1989), Disney World emerged at a crucial point – after the Vietnam War, before the fall of the Berlin Wall, during the Decade of Greed – when American identity was contentious, divided, unfocused on a patriotic vision. Because there is no longer a public identity that cities embody, the artificial world of Disney has become our safe place, our cities' virtual reality.

Cities impose visual coherence in many ways: by using zoning to impose design criteria for office buildings, by making memory visible in historic districts, by interpreting the assimilation of ethnic groups in street festivals, by building walls to contain fear. Disney World is not only important because it confirms and consolidates the significance of cultural power – the power to impose a vision – for social control. It is important because it offers a model of privatization and globalization; it manages social diversity; it imposes a frame of meaning on the city, a frame that earlier in history came from other forms of public culture. That frame is now based on touring, a voyeurism that thrives on the video camera and the local television news.

It is unreasonable to propose that people sit at home and cultivate their gardens, but Disney World raises serious questions about the social and political consequences of marketing culture, from cultural tourism to cultural strategies of urban development.

■ Can cultural tourism save North Adams from economic decline? Raw space in old factory to become Massachusetts Museum of Contemporary Art.

Photo by John M. Kuykendall, courtesy of Massachusetts Museum of Contemporary Art.

3

A MUSEUM IN THE BERKSHIRES

(with Philip Kasinitz)

The tortuous story of the Massachusetts Museum of Contemporary Art (MASS MoCA) demonstrates the appeal of cultural strategies of development to even the smallest cities.[4] The old factory town of North Adams, Massachusetts, is an unlikely spot to build a modern art museum. It is quite a wager that this museum will create a tourist industry and that tourism will save the town from economic decline. But when the last factories have closed their gates and neither business nor government offers a different scenario, ordinary men and women can be persuaded that their city is ready to enter the symbolic economy.

---

4. When I first heard about plans for the Massachusetts Museum of Contemporary Art (MASS MoCA), I told Phil Kasinitz, who was then teaching at Williams College, in Williamstown, Massachusetts, that this was a topic for us. Phil had been my research assistant on *Loft Living* (1989 [1982]), and MASS MoCA seemed to bear out our most extreme speculation about the material impact of art and culture on urban space. Phil handled the field work in the Berkshires while I thought about the politics of the art world. In discussions, we reversed these roles. An early version of the chapter was written by both of us and presented at the 1993 annual meeting of the American Sociological Association, and I presented other versions in lectures at Syracuse and Columbia Universities and a conference on The Humanities and the City at the City University Graduate Center in 1994.

There have been, in fact, in only a few short years, two successive plans to build a modern art museum in North Adams. Each in its own way broke with traditional notions of what a museum ought to be. The first was to have been a megaproject spearheaded by the Guggenheim Museum in New York City, which would have created in this remote corner of the Berkshires an outpost of a global cultural empire. This project died when it ran out of political support and its sponsors could not raise funds from private sources. The second plan, which replaced the first in 1994, opted for a more modest regional center, a teaching museum, that would put visiting artists in close contact with local residents. Despite their differences, both plans exuded confidence in the symbolic economy as a form of development that creates jobs without demanding too much government support. MASS MoCA was born and died and was reborn as a cultural strategy to revive a declining community.

North Adams differs from the surrounding hills and valleys of northwestern Massachusetts (see map of cultural tourism in the Berkshires), which have long been a center of bucolic cultural tourism. The valleys of the Berkshire Mountains are dotted with summer festivals of symphony music, dance, and theatrical performances. In winter, the rolling green hills become ski slopes, with the ever increasing A-frames of American chalets. Nearby are the restored and reused summer "cottages" of 19th-century rich folk and literati. Edith Wharton's summer home, The Mount, is the headquarters of a Shakespearean acting troupe. North Adams is the anomaly in this happy scene, with its empty urban complex of 19th-century, red-brick factory buildings, untouched by modernization. In towns like North Adams, there are few alternatives to cultural tourism, even when there is little to see or do.

Cultural strategies of redevelopment find much support in areas that have been "disorganized" by economic decline or natural disaster. Old industrial dynasties have disappeared and no new power barons take their place. Wages are low, jobs are scarce, talk is cheap. Because they have grown up with the symbolic economy of the post-1970s world, cultural strategies work on the basis of valorizing vision. They rehabilitate vernacular architecture and make it the base of guided tours, hotels, and restaurants; they create selective land-

▓ Cultural tourism in the Berkshires: Art museums, performance festivals, and historic restorations.

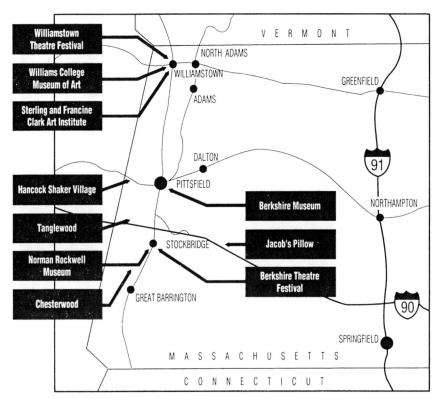

Source: Massachusetts Museum of Contemporary Art 1989a.

scapes of consumption. But cultural strategies only work within certain limits. Art museums, historic districts, and ethnic heritage zones are favored when the land they sit on is not more valuable to investors for other purposes. They have to target a middle class with literacy, mobility, and disposable income. Government usually offers subsidies for development, prodded and helped by an organized local constituency of patrons of the arts. Painful memories of place must be buried deep in the past – or presented as an aesthetic sight.

During the 1970s, cultural tourism was identified with the gentrification of inner cities. Both promised urban renewal without demolition and despair, a revival of community identity and civic pride. In contrast to the slash-and-burn strategies of earlier urban renewal, cultural strategies of historic

■ Bucolic cultural tourism in the Berkshires: Visitors relax on the lawn at Tanglewood.

Photo by Walter H. Scott, courtesy of Tanglewood.

preservation satisfied both elite protests against mass demolition of landmark buildings and populist demands for slowing change. A new mode of development seemed inspired by both an incremental view of economic growth and a reverential view of older landscapes (Zukin 1989 [1982], 1991; Wright 1985; Smith and Williams 1986; Hewison 1987; Logan and Molotch 1987).

During the 1980s, the artists' loft district of SoHo in New York, the shops and aquarium at Baltimore's Inner Harbor, and the themed marketplace at Faneuil Hall and Quincy Market in Boston became great tourist attractions. In Cheltenham, in Britain, Georgian and Victorian townhouses were converted to insurance company offices (Cowen 1990). In Lowell, Massachusetts, and Lancaster, in northern England (Urry 1990a), 19th-century cotton mills were featured in tourist promotions because they evoked a vanished industrial past. Lowell is an interesting case, because in 1978 local business leaders and politicians, coordinated by former U.S. senator Paul Tsongas, managed to convince the Congress to transform an assortment of old textile mills into a large eco-museum and place it under the stewardship of the National Park Service (*Wall Street Journal*, February 1, 1985, p. 1). In a less successful example, the dying automobile city of Flint, Michigan, drew state, private, and foundation funds to create Autoworld, a theme park "extolling the virtues of the automobile" (Lord and Price 1992, 159). The state of New Jersey tried to lure cultural tourists to devastated inner cities by building a performing arts center in Newark and an aquarium in Camden; the aquarium could not compete with other aquariums on the East Coast, including Baltimore's, because the fish were not exotic enough and tourists felt unsafe driving into the city (*New York Times,* October 17, 1994).

Cultural strategies of redevelopment are complicated representations of change and desire. Their common element is to create a "cultural" space connecting tourism, consumption, and style of life. They appreciate archaic living and working sites, but push them deeper into the past. They incorporate these sites into an image of local identity by defusing their contentiousness. Regardless of their bloody past or current social tensions, the sites become "a happy face." Cultural strategies, moreover, are often consensual strategies of change. They preserve rather than tear down; they rely on alliances between unlikely groups.

But I am uneasy about some basic questions. Are cultural strategies clutching at straws or improving the quality of life? Which cultural strategy will work in a particular time and place? Whether the cultural space is docks in London and Liverpool converted into art galleries, farmers' markets set up in public spaces in New York City, bistros carved out of pensioners' Art Deco hotel residences in Miami Beach, or a riverfront walk in San Antonio, cultural strategies give rise to a Machiavellian manipulation of local identity. When they succeed, they seem to confirm the private sector's command of "market logic." When they fail, they seem to confirm the ineptitude of public sector planning.

The examples of Flint and Camden suggest there are some places where a lot of money can be spent on buildings but tourists will not come and cultural strategies just will not work (see Urry 1990b, 132). Camden has an almost entirely black and Latino population; Flint also has a significant population of ethnic minorities. Aside from its mainly white population, what makes North Adams different?

■ Trouble in the Berkshires

In 1986, Thomas R. Krens, then the ambitious young director
of the Williams College Museum of Art, in Williamstown,
Massachusetts, announced to almost unanimous acclaim a
plan to build the world's largest museum of contemporary art
– a museum devoted primarily to large-scale art of the 1960s
and 1970s – in a complex of 28 derelict, 19th- and early-
20th-century industrial buildings in nearby North Adams.
The Massachusetts Museum of Contemporary Art was
intended to help North Adams in several ways. It would take
abandoned, non-tax-producing property out of the hands of
local government and redevelop it. It would bring the tourist
industry to a small, deindustrialized corner of the Berkshires
that had been untouched by previous waves of tourist growth.
In addition to an estimated 644 jobs in the museum complex,
itself, MASS MoCA would theoretically create employment in
hotels, restaurants, and shops connected to tourism (Massachusetts Museum of Contemporary Art 1989a, sec. 2, p. 9).

Even after Krens moved to New York in 1988 to become
director of the Guggenheim Museum, he continued to work on
plans for MASS MoCA, and the Guggenheim was eventually
named (though it later withdrew as) its operating partner.
With these close relations, large works of art belonging to the
Guggenheim could be stored and displayed in North Adams,
which would act as the larger museum's northern annex (see
map). This would be consistent with the overall strategy of
the Guggenheim, which under Krens's leadership has created
affiliated "branch" museums in Italy, Spain, Austria, and
downtown Manhattan, as well as proposing to do so in North
Adams.

A potential gain of employment means a lot to North
Adams. Mountainous and relatively isolated, western New
England has never been heavily populated compared to southern New England and New York. Several of the rural hill
towns had more inhabitants 200 years ago than they do today.
North Adams reached its peak population of 24,200 in 1900,
declining to 19,195 in 1970 and 16,797 in 1990. In 1980, 15
percent of town residents were living below the poverty level
(Berkshire County Regional Planning Commission 1985). In
1985, when Krens first conceived the MASS MoCA plan, the
unemployment rate was a dramatic 14 percent – in contrast

▓ MASS MoCA site in relation to New York and Boston.

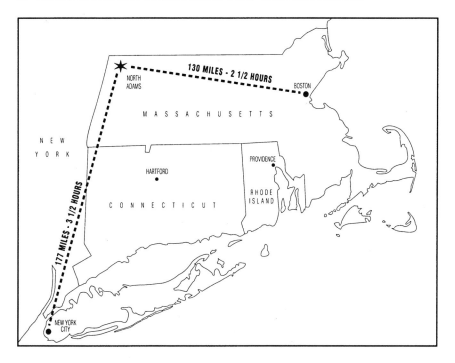

Source: Massachusetts Museum of Contemporary Art 1989a.

to the "Massachusetts miracle" of high tech-led prosperity, which reduced unemployment to record low levels across the state ("Thinking Big" 1987). And the town suffered from the social problems that accompany economic decline. At various times during the 1980s, North Adams led Massachusetts in teenage pregnancy rates and per capita reported cases of child abuse. In 1991, its high school dropout rate was five times the statewide average (Gaines 1992).

North Adams has lived through two periods of industrial growth. From 1860 to 1880, the town's textile mills, print works, shoe factories, and tanneries prospered (Spear 1885; Cougan 1988). Steam power from the Hoosac River and the completion of the Hoosac Tunnel in 1875 enabled industry to locate there and expand after the Civil War. North Adams was also an important rail link between Boston and Albany, New York. The work force, moreover, was quiescent. Early efforts at union organizing by the Knights of St. Crispin were crushed when employers temporarily replaced striking native-born workers with Chinese laborers; and after the depression of 1873, the labor union was tamed (Spear 1885, 105; Rudolf 1947; McCunn 1988, 33–35). Many streets still bear the names of 19th-century factory owners.

The decline of textiles and shoemaking in the 1920s emptied industrial plants all over New England. But unlike the larger mill towns of eastern Massachusetts, such as Lowell, North Adams experienced a second period of industrial growth in the 1930s, when the electronics industry began. Small electronics companies found that the mills of North Adams and nearby Pittsfield provided cheap startup space near a supply of experienced industrial workers. Throughout World War II, North Adams gained employment, especially when the Sprague Electric Company (later, Sprague Technologies Inc.) took over the former Arnold Print Works on the river and several smaller manufacturing buildings to form the Marshall Street Complex. This is now the MASS MoCA site.

Among its wartime activities, the complex produced firing capacitors for atomic bombs. In the boom years of the 1950s, the plant manufactured a variety of products, the most important of which were television components. From a high point of employing 4,000 workers, Sprague Technologies began to decline until, in 1979, it had only 1,800 employees. The firm was sold to the companies that formed General Electric Company and, in 1981, was sold again, to the Penn Central Corporation, which closed the Marshall Street plant in 1985. Around 1,500 employees were laid off. From 1980 to 1985, four other manufacturing plants in North Adams, with 849 employees, were also shut down (Seider 1985).

Without its manufacturing backbone, North Adams provides mainly service employment. Williams College, less than five miles away in Williamstown, is the largest employer of town residents, followed by North Adams Regional Hospital, Sprague's remaining plant and pension operation (with fewer than 600 employees), and North Adams State College. Several small manufacturing plants remain open. This is a typical scenario of industrial decline in upstate New York and western New England (on Pittsfield, Massachusetts, see J. Nash 1989).

The surrounding region of the Berkshires tells a different story. From the 1860s, when textiles and shoemaking spurred

North Adams's industrial growth, the Berkshires became a summer residence for affluent New Yorkers. Even earlier, such writers as Herman Melville and Nathaniel Hawthorne had established second homes there. With the construction of a railroad line between Stockbridge, Massachusetts, and New York City, travel became much easier to contemplate (Federal Writers' Project 1939a, 108). From 1890 to 1920, the small, rustic houses of artists were gradually replaced by grander country houses, modestly called *cottages.*

In 1902, Edith Wharton built The Mount, following principles she had set out five years earlier, with Ogden Codburn, in *The Decoration of Houses.* Frederick Law Olmsted designed gardens in the area, and McKim, Mead and White built churches in the center of Stockbridge (Owens 1984). Despite this reconstruction of a "rural" landscape for urban elites, city dwellers who came to the Berkshires claimed to enjoy the tranquility and the play of nature. An 1894 profile of Lenox, Massachusetts, then at the height of fashion, maintains that the same people came to Lenox as to Bar Harbor, Maine, and Newport, Rhode Island, resorts for social elites from New York and Boston. In Lenox they preferred to take long walks and watch the colors change on fall foliage rather than engage in more taxing social rituals. At the same time, land prices rose dramatically as prime-quality lots were bought up for summer homes and estates (Hibbard 1894).

With the Great Depression, most of the cottages fell into disuse. Many were converted into schools, hotels, or country clubs; some were simply abandoned. (The Mount was a virtual ruin when restoration began in the 1970s.) From the 1930s, however, a new wave of tourists came to the Berkshires looking for organized cultural experiences, similar to those of the recently established European music festivals at Glyndebourne and Bayreuth. These cultural tourists were primarily New Yorkers and Bostonians; many were political and cultural radicals. They transplanted an urban culture to the deliberately rustic setting of the Berkshires. In contrast to the quaint New England villages and bucolic landscapes of the region, and the folk and primitive art those places inspire, they came to the provinces to see performances of quintessentially modern music and dance. Unlike the Gilded Age cottage builders, these were middle-class cultural tourists.

Tanglewood, in Stockbridge, became the summer home of the Boston Symphony Orchestra, led by Serge Koussevitzky, in 1937. Programs frequently included contemporary works by Bartok and Copeland, as well as heavy doses of classical and romantic composers, notably Beethoven, Wagner, and Mahler. Listeners initially attended these concerts either in the open air or under a circus-style tent. When the tent was replaced by a permanent structure, it was called the *Music Shed*. After Koussevitzky's retirement in 1948, Tanglewood continued to attract star performers and guest conductors, most notably Leonard Bernstein, who was long affiliated with its famous summer music school. Tanglewood now draws approximately 300,000 visitors a year (Lenardson 1987; Pincus 1989).

In an even more rustic setting nearby, the Jacob's Pillow Dance Festival, founded in 1931, brought Ted Shawn, Paul Taylor, and other mid-20th century avant garde choreographers to spend their summers in the region (Tracy 1982). In the 1950s, the Williamstown Theater Festival was established on the campus of Williams College. Directed by Nikos Psacharapoulos, the festival presented serious, contemporary American drama and the classics instead of light, "straw hat" summer theater. Williamstown also became home to the Clark Art Institute, a small but well-respected Impressionist museum established by private collectors who had long spent summers in the area. From the 1970s, the culture-based, summer tourist economy was strengthened by the building of winter ski condominiums, retirement homes, and more summer houses. Autumn also offers a brief opportunity for bucolic cultural tourism when "fall foliage season" is joined with "antiquing."

But North Adams has not participated in any of the tourist booms. In contrast to the hill towns whose economic decline took place in the eighteenth century, and left no ungainly buildings to detract from a view of nature, North Adams still has a visible industrial base. The river was dammed for industry, the Marshall Street MASS MoCA site alone is as big as ten football fields, and housing is still used by working-class families. These descendants of Irish, Italian, and French-Canadian millworkers differ from the populations of the more picturesque hill towns. They are Catholic rather than Protestant, classic "Reagan Democrats" who vote for right-of-center populist candidates regardless of party affiliation. The long-time mayor of North Adams is a Democrat. By contrast, wealthy residents of the nearby college town of Williamstown are liberal Democrats, but are often perceived in North Adams as elitist.

North Adams's belated attempt to adopt a cultural strategy of redevelopment was grafted onto more traditional, slash-and-burn strategies of urban renewal (Pearl 1989). In the first of three phases of urban renewal, the town demolished 251 substandard dwellings near the center in the early 1960s, replacing them with a small shopping center and the first section of a highway through town. In the second phase, in the late 1960s, North Adams tore down more dilapidated housing, but also razed the historic center, including the old city hall, two banks, and an old hotel. Much of the cleared land remained vacant. In the third phase, 1979–80, some of the vacant land was used to build a Kmart and a 400-car parking lot in the center of town. A Heritage State Park, consisting of a small shopping center with a local arts and crafts theme, was also built with state funding. By the early 1990s, most of the stores there had gone bankrupt and their space was vacant. A hotel built in the third phase of urban renewal has been vacant since 1986.

In the mid 1980s, the work force of North Adams was dispirited and dispossessed. The labor unions had lost hope of attracting other industrial employers. Unlike in some other economically depressed regions, no small-scale industrial or commercial entrepreneurs tried to open up shop. There was some talk about making a museum of the industrial past, but no Museum of Industry, as in Youngstown, Ohio, or eco-museum, as in Lowell, was planned. Ideas were few and far between.

▓ Global Art Worlds

Williams College is an interesting beachhead from which to launch a cultural strategy for the economic redevelopment of North Adams. Aside from being a home for professors and the summer theater festival, the college is the training ground of a generation of influential art museum directors. Known as the *Williams Mafia,* this is a cohesive group of men in their 40s, institutionally and personally ambitious, maintaining strong ties to faculty at the college (Nathan 1989). They include the director of the Brooklyn Museum, the deputy director of the National Gallery of Art, the director of the Art Institute of Chicago, the director of the San Francisco Museum of Modern Art, the director of the Los Angeles County Museum of Art, the director of painting and sculpture at the Museum of Modern Art, and Thomas Krens, the director of the Guggenheim.

A Williams College graduate, Krens has an MBA from Yale and an MA in studio art. Appointed director of the small Williams College Museum of Art when in his early 30s, Krens turned the museum from a dowdy, teaching-oriented institution into a regional center for avant garde art. Prior to his arrival, the museum featured an eclectic collection. Krens tightened and professionalized the museum's organization. He acquired at least one major collection (the Prendergast collection), supervised remodeling, and oversaw a 35,000 square foot addition ("Thinking Big" 1987, 36). He brought in controversial shows of avant garde work, particularly German Expressionism. For all this he aroused national attention, as well as both admiration and resentment from his original mentors on the college faculty.

Krens was first described as a visionary when he was appointed director of the Guggenheim in 1988. Not least of his innovations was his attempt to solve space problems at the Guggenheim by integrating it with MASS MoCA, using the idea he had originally dreamed up in 1986 (Weisgall 1989). Like a number of similar museums, the Guggenheim faced several challenges. First, it had too many pieces to exhibit in its museum on Fifth Avenue. Not until a long-awaited expansion to a second building (envisioned in an early version of the Frank Lloyd Wright design but not actually built) was completed in 1992 was the museum able to show more than 1.5 percent of its permanent collection. Second, it had a large operating deficit – in 1988, nearly $2 million on an operating budget of $11 million. Third, many felt that the museum had to revitalize its mission of showing modern art for the 21st century. Works by early 20th-century artists that had made the museum's reputation had to be joined by contemporary works.

Krens's solution was to establish the Guggenheim's identity as a global cultural institution. His strategies included forming close ties with overseas museums, courting potential foreign donors, and setting up branches of the Guggenheim in other countries. In this way the museum would be able to circulate new art works from all over the world, tap into overseas capital, and participate with a new voice in global discussions of culture. The museum, incidentally, would also be better able to compete in New York with the larger and better known Museum of Modern Art (MOMA) and the Metropolitan Museum. Both had undergone significant recent expansions (see Chapter 4), and the Metropolitan was increasing its collections of modern art. The Guggenheim already operated a small museum in Peggy Guggenheim's palazzo in Venice. With Krens's arrival, the museum began expanding its presence there. Although the curator of the Peggy Guggenheim collection claimed that Krens's administration neglected that facility, rumors flew thick and fast that the Guggenheim was negotiating with city officials to open another museum in the Dogana di Mare, perhaps with a Disney-type art park or grand hotel (Richardson 1992, 21–22). Simultaneously, the museum negotiated an agreement to establish a branch museum near Milan and explored the creation of a satellite museum in Salzburg.

Museum expansion always stirs envy, but this degree of globalization was severely criticized in the art world. Under Krens, moreover, the museum engaged in controversial policies of deaccessioning works, selling well-known pieces by Kandinsky, Chagall, and Modigliani. At the same time, the Guggenheim accepted a collection of large contemporary pieces under questionable conditions. Count Giuseppe Panza di Biumo gave 211 Minimalist pieces by American artists of the 1960s and 1970s to the museum, but only half of these pieces were given outright. The other half were to be paid for over the next six years, with the count pledging to donate 105 other works over five years.

The Guggenheim faced the problem of how to pay $30 million for the Panza collection – and where to house it (McHugh 1990). When the expanded, renovated Guggenheim

Museum opened in July 1992, the immediate critical reaction fell into two camps. Some critics limited themselves to discussing the architectural changes and generally praised them (e.g., Goldberger 1992c; Kimmelman 1992; Gill 1992). Others linked the architecture and installation to the whole range of controversial policies – expansion, branch museums, deaccessioning, and the acquisition of Minimalist art – and damned them all (H. Kramer 1992; Richardson 1992). In particular, the art critic Hilton Kramer suggested that expansion to a tall, new building was unnecessary if Krens was going to distribute the permanent collection among branch museums.

▇ The Conceptual Museum

From its inception, MASS MoCA was presented differently to different audiences. Emblematic of its multiple images was the model of the proposed museum displayed at the exhibit on the project site in 1989, entitled "From Mill to Museum." The model showed the word *ART* coming out of the old mill's central smokestack.

The project, as originally proposed, relied primarily on state funding in the form of a $35 million dollar bond issue, as well as a limited amount of direct state grants for the planning process. Thus political support was essential. In the context of Massachusetts politics, MASS MoCA was initially portrayed as a *local* enterprise (albeit one managed by a major international institution) whose purpose was primarily to revive North Adams by expanding the arts-based tourism already characteristic of the Berkshire region. In the art world, however, MASS MoCA was presented as a project of *international* significance connected with institutions around the world and largely independent of its local context. After Krens's move to the Guggenheim in 1988, the proposed museum was increasingly seen as a single component in the Guggenheim's multi-site expansion plans. In 1989, Krens described MASS MoCA as a branch of the world's first "multinational" museum (Weisgall 1989, 35).

In the museum's new strategy, expanding to North Adams simultaneously solved the problems of where to exhibit Count Panza's collection and how to establish the identity of a global, avant garde cultural institution. First, however, Krens had to market a conceptual reordering of both the museum and the industrial complex in North Adams. "MASS MoCA is indeed a museum without a collection, but a museum of space," he said (Nathan 1988). It is also a museum of selective, rather than encyclopedic, presentation. Krens thought of museums since the 1970s as *interpreters* of cultural epochs" rather than "treasure houses and repositories." Thus MASS MoCA could well be "definitive: a Sixties, Seventies and Eighties art museum." To understand this period in art, people would have to travel to North Adams ("Met Grill" 1988). This conceptual reordering to fit a specific visual image also fit the art work Krens wanted to install in North Adams: the Panza collection, huge sculptures, Minimalist pieces by Donald Judd that were boxes or sheds, and light strips by Dan Flavin.

Both the museum concept and the museum's Conceptual art were controversial in the art world. First, the press discovered that many of the "pieces" in Count Panza's collection had never been fabricated. They existed only as artists' notations

▨ Art for a conceptual museum: Donald Judd's plywood construction, *Untitled* (1981).

Photo by Glenn Steigelman, © Donald Judd Estate.

on paper. In addition, artists complained that Count Panza planned to shortchange them by paying others less money to do some of the constructions. Critics raised the question of exactly what the museum was buying from Count Panza for $30 million (Glueck 1990b; Kramer 1990).

Ironically, much art of the 1960s and 1970s was initially conceived as a rebellion against the idea of art as decoration or as a collectible commodity. Artists created sculptures so huge they could not be shown in most rooms, site-specific installations that could not be moved, plans that existed only on paper. Yet, in the booming art markets of the 1980s, people did indeed collect these works. Not only were such pieces collectible, they were expensive. It was precisely such art that MASS MoCA's eccentric, cavernous, industrial spaces were uniquely configured to display and store. The role of museums in establishing the value of such art is absolutely crucial, for despite the escalating prices fetched by Minimalist and Conceptual works in the heady 1980s market, the noninstitutional market for this art is ultimately quite limited: few individuals are able to display it in their living rooms. Finally, the MASS MoCA plan was announced at a time when much Minimalist and Conceptual art of the preceding decades was in danger of losing critical acclaim. The establishment of a major museum devoted to such art was thus greeted with considerable enthusiasm on the part of many major collectors. But when doubts were cast on Count Panza's generosity, many in the art world ridiculed the conceptual museum.

▓ Cultural Politics

Throughout its history, the project has been threatened by political and financial conditions in Massachusetts. Initially, Krens had been hailed as a visionary in the national press ("Art Comes to the Rescue," trumpeted *Newsweek* in 1987), and local newspapers saw MASS MoCA as the salvation of North Adams. The administration of Governor Michael Dukakis, eager to spread the "Massachusetts Miracle" to an isolated corner of the state that had been bypassed by the high tech-driven "boom" was extremely supportive of the proposal. Yet criticism billowed in the wake of the severe economic recession that began in New England in 1988 and Dukakis' failed presidential campaign that same year. When a fiscal crisis erupted in Massachusetts shortly thereafter, the press, following the lead of some state officials, found flaws in the museum proposal.

As early as June 1988, four months before the presidential election, an art consultant hired by the *Berkshire Eagle* questioned the realism of the museum plan, and the idea of building a convention center at the museum was dropped. Extremely optimistic attendance projections, overlooked in the initial blush of publicity, came to public attention. In August 1989, a marketing study commissioned by the museum found that the concept of contemporary art on which MASS MoCA was based was too narrow. "Most potential visitors would rather see scenery, theater or dance, hear music, shop at outlet stores or bookstores or visit a wildlife sanctuary than see contemporary art" (Densmore 1989). No one knew whether enough out-of-towners would drive from New York or Boston on relatively narrow roads to justify the state's, and private bondholders', investment (Glueck 1990a; Gamerman 1990).

The state's worsening fiscal crisis jeopardized the $35 million bond issue approved for MASS MoCA by the State Legislature earlier that year, pending a $1.8 million, state-financed feasibility study to be written by a planning team headed by Krens. In fact, the MASS MoCA funds had little direct relation to state budget cuts, as the museum was to be funded by a bond issue rather than by the state's operating budget. This distinction, however, made little impression on the general public. Many people simply saw the state spending money on an extravagant museum at a time when essential services were being curtailed. When the legislators decreased the state's arts budget from $27 million in 1988 to $17.3 million in January 1990, they became more vigilant in checking the operating subsidies granted the interim MASS MoCA staff. As early as 1989, MASS MoCA had to borrow $100,000 from the Massachusetts Industrial Finance Corporation to pay a $175,000 gas bill – a point not missed by the now-critical local press (*Berkshire Eagle,* July 29, 1989). Meanwhile, because of inflation, projected costs for converting the Marshall Street complex rose from $77.5 to $85.7 million.

Yet local support for MASS MoCA remained strong (Kernek 1990). In October 1988, town residents stood in line to enter an open house held by the museum's planning staff and said they were proud the museum was coming (Bruun 1988). Four months later, a fund-raising ball for the museum was oversubscribed (Tichenor 1989). "This is a sweet moment for me," said Mayor John Barrett III. "A lot of people said, 'Who's going to come to the northwestern part of Massachusetts?' But they came [to the ball], from Germany, England, and New York. South County has Tanglewood and Jacob's Pillow, but we said take us as we are, and they took us, right here in an old mill building" (*Boston Globe,* February 13, 1989). Such officials may have been less impressed by the art than by the few hundred jobs in the services the museum staff promised. " 'I'm a blue-collar mayor from a blue-collar community,' Mayor Barrett told the state legislature. 'I really don't understand contemporary art nor do I pretend to, but I do recognize it as a vehicle that could create a couple of hundred jobs for us' " (Gamerman 1990).

To a great extent, this attitude reflected a lack of alternatives. It was too expensive for the town to clear and redevelop the Sprague site. With a state-imposed cap on property tax levels and no possibility of help from any tax-paying private institutions, the town council had to find other sources of revenue. Pressure came from unemployment in the local work force, increased by more layoffs in 1990 and closings at several plants. In 1992, as support for the museum eroded in other parts of the state, a local merchant told the *Boston Globe,* "MoCA is a good idea. At this point, anything is a good idea" (Gaines 1992).

Nevertheless, the cultural and geographical distance between Museum Mile on Fifth Avenue in New York City, where the Guggenheim Museum is located, and the town hall in North Adams, has continually created opportunities for doubts and misunderstandings about respective commitment to the project (Bruun 1990). These doubts were magnified by questions about the relative advantages each side would draw from their collaboration. Once the Guggenheim was named MASS MoCA's operator (*New York Times,* December 19, 1990), suspicions increased that the Marshall Street complex would be used primarily as a warehouse for the Guggenheim's overflow collection.

The state's fiscal crisis and ethical questions about the Guggenheim's role in the project may have simply masked the project's weak institutional support. Within the state of Massachusetts, MASS MoCA represented a way for state legislators to attack Governor Dukakis. "It's a question . . . of priorities: to protect people and save lives, or to provide capital projects for the rich," said a Democratic state representative from Uxbridge (Phillips 1990a), a middle-class town in the southeastern part of the state where voters resisted raising taxes.

While North Adams's politicians continued to promote the project as an economic development tool, MASS MoCA lacked the support of a significant community of local arts patrons. Residents who support the arts seemed satisfied by the modest aspirations of the Berkshire Museum in nearby Pittsfield, the county seat, and the Williams Museum and the Clark Art Institute, both in Williamstown. Indeed, around this time, the directors of the Berkshire Museum dismissed an energetic curator who "imported" shows of contemporary art by New York artists. Neither did the small number of local artists, most of whom work in a folk art or arts and crafts tradition, stand to gain much from MASS MoCA or the studio space it promised. It was debatable whether local artists would enhance their market if MASS MoCA were built as planned.

Building MASS MoCA as Thomas Krens envisaged went beyond the adaptive reuse of old buildings for cultural consumption. It did not respond to a local perception of needs. Input from local communities, both political and cultural, was minimal. The formation of an all-star museum design team, including the internationally known architects Frank Gehry and Robert Venturi and the architectural firms Skidmore, Owings and Merrill and Bruner/Cott & Associates (of Cambridge, Massachusetts), dramatized the gap in resources between the museum and the town. The entire strategy of combining historic preservation of industrial buildings and Conceptual art reversed the redevelopment strategy North Adams tried to develop over the preceding 20 years. Although that strategy obliterated the historic center, rebuilding the center around MASS MoCA suggested a drastically new symbolic geography.

Yet the preservation of the industrial buildings on the Marshall Street site remained a key local selling point for the museum project. From the beginning, MASS MoCA's planners willingly and consciously embraced the contradiction between types of art emblematic of high culture at its most international and decontextualized – bearing no relation to the specific historical context of North Adams and its residents – and historic preservation strategies utterly dependent on that local context. "Respect these noble buildings," the original MASS MoCA proposal commanded. In 1989, during negotiations over the eventual funding of the project, the planning staff mounted a small exhibit on the site itself. The exhibit, "From Mill to Museum," was primarily devoted to the industrial history of the site and to placing the MASS MoCA project within that context (Massachusetts Museum of Contemporary Art 1989b). Guided tours of the site were begun. While these attracted some tourists and art aficionados, they also drew local residents eager to take another look at the now silent structures in which they had spent much of their working lives ("MASS MoCA Starts Tours of Project" 1990). The cavernous industrial buildings, with their central red-brick clocktower, were the most powerful visual image museum proponents could muster. They became the dominant focus of publicity

MASS MoCA site, main courtyard with clocktower.

Photo by John M. Kuykendall, courtesy of Massachusetts Museum of Contemporary Art.

packets and of a local television commercial made for the proposed museum.

In June 1990, the state inspector general tried to cut off additional state funding of MASS MoCA on the grounds that its financial backing was illegal (Phillips 1990b). In contradiction to its authorizing legislation, which mandated $10.7 million in startup funds from the town of North Adams, the museum listed a contribution of only $500,000. The planning staff counted on including the value of donated art works and the value of the Sprague Electric Company buildings in the Marshall Street complex. Despite disagreement by the economic development director in Governor Dukakis' administration, Massachusetts began to withdraw support from MASS MoCA. By the time the Republican governor William Weld was elected in November 1990, a simmering tax revolt made it unlikely the state would commit more funds.

In September 1991, the Weld administration pushed for a scaled-down version of the museum. "It's time to get real," state economic affairs secretary Daniel Gregory told reporters, referring to the original plan for $35 million in state-backed bond funds approved by the legislature two years earlier. "Somebody must have thought they'd hit the Easter bunny." North Adams politicians responded that only a project on the scale originally envisioned would generate the economic spinoffs necessary for a viable economic development strategy (Phillips 1991).

On October 18, 1991, after considerable debate, the Weld administration approved the release of $688,000 to fund MASS MoCA for one year, during which time the museum had to raise $12 million (of the projected $35 million) in private funds. In the meantime, MASS MoCA obtained the necessary building permits. The staff also solicited bids from several museums to act as operators for the North Adams site. Krens had previously removed himself from the chairmanship of the MASS MoCA Cultural Development Commission, to avoid the appearance of a conflict of interest. To no one's surprise, but to the relief of the project's backers, the Guggenheim's proposal was approved in the spring of 1992 (Densmore 1992). At the end of that year, Governor Weld granted MASS MoCA a seven-month extension to raise private funds.

Despite surviving a series of cliffhanger deadlines imposed by the state, the museum planners were unable to raise development funds from private patrons of the arts. Neither were expressions of interest by commercial developers matched by financial commitments. In 1993, the museum staff cut its salaries by half. Later that year, the mayor of North Adams said he doubted the necessary private funding would ever be raised, and he refused to seek another extension from the state. Meanwhile, in New York, the Guggenheim Museum was running out of operating funds. Despite a successful fund-raising campaign, staff members were fired, hours were reduced at both the main museum and the SoHo branch, and the library was temporarily closed (*New York Times,* February 3, 1994). MASS MoCA appeared to be dead.

In 1994, however, a new vision of MASS MoCA arose from a new consortium of arts institutions. More modest in scope and to be built in phases, the revised project includes a museum with exhibition and performance spaces and a technology production laboratory. The operating consortium is made up of the Jacob's Pillow Dance Festival, in the Berkshires, and two outsiders, the Japanese-American Community Center of Los Angeles and the American History Workshop of Brooklyn, in New York City. A new artist-founded museum, to be called the *North Adams Collection,* will be a fourth operating partner. Mentioned in the local press as possible limited partners are the Guggenheim Museum, the Disney Development Company, North Adams State College, the Walker Center for the Arts in Minneapolis, the Henson Foundation, the Brooklyn Academy of Music, and the Flynn Theater in Burlington, Vermont (Sliwa 1994a; Borak 1994). The governor, "initially lukewarm to the project, gradually has grown supportive . . . to the point of enthusiasm" (Sliwa 1994a). Perhaps the governor changed his mind because MASS MoCA's new director is Samuel Miller, an arts administrator who built an impressive track record for fiscal and artistic responsibility at Jacob's Pillow (Borak 1994).

According to the president of the American History Workshop, the point of the new MASS MoCA plan is to make an art center that is relevant to year-round residents of the Berkshires and "build on the existing summer cultural economy of Berkshire County" (Sliwa 1994b). With this goal in mind, resident artists will be asked to live and work in North Adams while developing new projects and techniques. They will hold teaching workshops and master classes; they will collaborate with local musicians, artists, crafts people, and performers. In the viewing museum – a museum in the traditional sense – the artists whose work will be shown are not the Conceptual and Minimalist artists of the 1960s and 1970s, but a more established avant garde of abstract painters and iconoclasts, including Robert Rauschenberg, Agnes Martin, Richard Tuttle, Ellsworth Kelly, and Louise Bourgeois (Sliwa 1994b).

Yet the new plan has just as much hype as the old one. Instead of Krens's "museum of space," the new project describes a "seamless continuum" of "the creation, production, and experience of works of art" (Massachusetts Museum of Contemporary Art 1993). While the first plan would have displayed works of art originally conceived as antiheroic in a way that only dramatized their creators as artistic heroes, the new plan emphasizes the process of creation "by turning the making of work inside out, by revealing to visitors what goes on behind the stage curtain or studio wall, by involving them in the process of creation itself." The artist is not a hero, but a gentle craftsman, a teacher, a fellow performer and explorer. There are even some elements of Disney World in the promise of visual imaging to glorify local history. In a scenario entitled "Imagining MASS MoCA," the new sponsors foresee

> the public arriving at the Massachusetts Museum of Contemporary Art . . . [and entering] the Visitors Center. There, they learn about both the history and evolution of the mill complex as well as the range of exhibitions and activities occurring within. In one orientation gallery, visitors crowd around a wall of computer touch screens to conjure up the people and places of New England's nineteenth and twentieth centuries. Children and young adults line up to try the virtual reality helmets and joysticks that recreate the old mill buildings, first as a textile mill, then as the Sprague Electric Plant. Recordings of stories and memories documenting New England's long history as a center for crafts and industry fill the room. . . . Video interviews with resident artists are on

*view. Opportunities for adults and children to participate
abound; so, too, are there places for quiet contemplation
and reflection.*

The new project also offers a "seamless continuum" of
different art activities by utilizing the various buildings of
the mill complex in different ways. One building will be a
music center; "for many artists, the state-of-the-art sound
stage at MASS MoCA presents an alternative to the commercial studios of New York." Another building will house dance
companies, both resident and on tour. A third building will
offer facilities for silkscreeners and other artists to show the
public how they work. Space for rehearsal, performance, "for
quiet contemplation": the museum that is now projected offers
something for everyone – a bit of history, of the region, of
exotic visitors, and of a resting place from the dizzying art
world of the Guggenheim and New York cultural markets.

Yet again, the new plan is careful to establish the museum's value as a tool of economic development. "Artists will
live in housing available in the city while they work at the
center; many products and services needed by the MASS
MoCA partners and tenants will be purchased in the community." Moreover, in contrast to the first plan, which saw local
residents as hotel and food service workers, catering to a
tourist market, the new plan suggests more meaningful jobs,
jobs with a future: "Activities at the center – from day-care
to food service to set design to production to new applications
of multi-media technologies – will provide training and
employment for area residents." The museum complex, in its
own way, will guide North Adams into the symbolic economy.

Following the twists and turns of the MASS MoCA story
over several years, we were never sure what the outcome
would be. Would the state of Massachusetts cast off the
museum without a cent? Would the Guggenheim manage to
raise enough money to run the project as originally conceived?
If the conceptual museum was built, would anyone come? But
we were always sure a museum project of some sort would be
retained. We were sure it would be impossible to eliminate a
cultural strategy of redevelopment.

Nevertheless, the experience of *almost* building a conceptual museum in North Adams, Massachusetts, and its replace-

ment by an alternative vision, raises serious questions about art, regional identity, and global culture.

▧ Museums and Metropolitan Culture

As MASS MoCA evolved into an element of the Guggenheim Museum's expanding international network, it raised the issue of the cultural preservation or homogenization of local identities. Would a conceptual museum of avant garde art overshadow the humble folk art traditions of North Adams? Would the preservation of the old factory buildings also preserve a local working-class identity? Under any circumstances, making a museum the arbiter of local identity risks undermining the cultural understandings that support any social community. In a fragile economy, making that community financially and emotionally dependent on a transnational museum adds irony to tragedy.

Avant garde art is usually associated with metropolitan centers. It diffuses slowly to other areas. Tourism may accelerate this process, as it did with modern music and dance in the Berkshires, but it does so within limits. Local museums outside a metropolitan setting rarely present avant garde works. They perform educational and curatorial functions. They commemorate local histories. They preserve fossils found on native soil, paintings and sculptures by regional artists, and encyclopedic – rather than topical – displays.

We do not know whether Conceptual and Minimalist art, and its descendants in feminist and other installations, can command a loyal audience in rustic or humble surroundings. Until now, the summer visitors who patronize arts festivals in the Berkshires come for mainstream modernist and Impressionist works. They fill evenings in their vacation schedules.

The MASS MoCA proposal essentially argued that space does not matter: art can be appreciated anywhere. The North Adams site was a "museum of space," in one meaningless expression, which meant that it was to be considered an outpost of global culture rather than a local social institution. Thomas Krens theorized that visitors would go to North Adams to see a definitive display of a highly specific art that was created elsewhere. While this strategy works for the Guggenheim's core museum in New York and the Clark Art Institute in Williamstown, few people thought it would work for North Adams. But who creates the social and spatial context in which a specific cultural strategy "works"? Could avant garde art "work" without a critical mass of avant garde artists to produce and view it, without a public already trained to "see" it?

Local audience was the least thought-about issue in the first MASS MoCA project. Aside from projections of out-of-town visitors and promises of educational projects (an afterthought to appeal to political officials), interviews with MASS MoCA planners, especially Thomas Krens, focused on getting artworks and negotiating their market value. Making deals with collectors, with other museums, and with the state was the dominant theme of the museum proposal. From a strictly economic point of view, the absence of either a proven local audience for contemporary art or a strong base of cultural institutions made the state-backed bond look like a risky investment. In New York, by contrast, despite fiscal problems at least as severe as in Massachusetts, a $60 million city-backed bond to finance the Guggenheim's recent renovation and expansion did not arouse controversy. New York City has an established audience for avant garde art among residents and tourists, a strong network of elite cultural institutions, and a significant constituency for state support of the arts. The financial impact on the Guggenheim and the ethical questions raised by using the museum's collections as collateral on borrowed funds are another matter.

But even if the idea of building a conceptual museum in North Adams is crazy, serious people, business people, shared this craziness. A letter included in the executive summary of MASS MoCA's 1989 feasibility study expresses the interest of Akira Tobishima, president and CEO of the Japanese real estate investment firm that bears his name, in participating in the development of a luxury hotel on the MASS MoCA site. Thanking Thomas Krens for his recent tour of North Adams, Tobishima writes, "As you know, we own the Stanhope Hotel in New York [across the street from the Metropolitan Museum] and the luxury hotel in the midst of the planned museum complex fits the image we are pursuing, that is to own and manage luxury hotels in highly cultural environs."

Despite their boosterism, neither the MASS MoCA planners nor local elected officials showed a desire to confront, or
nurture, the art itself. Elected officials and local residents
still see the museum primarily as an economic development
tool. The Guggenheim conveyed a sense of going after this art
because it interests critics, or it has value on the global art
market, or it is relatively underrepresented in the world's art
museums, and thus provides a convenient way to renew the
Guggenheim's mission. "To differentiate itself programmati-
cally from urban museums, MASS MoCA will specialize in
areas where others cannot compete. . . . For art-interested
patrons, MASS MoCA's scale, style, and concentration on key
moments in contemporary art will make it a must-see on the
international art circuit" (Massachusetts Museum of Contemporary Art 1989a, 3-7). The museum's feasibility study did
emphasize "the imperative of space," the spatial requirements
of "time-intensive" and site-specific works (Massachusetts
Museum of Contemporary Art 1989a, 3-1–3-4). But there was
little sense of the rebellion the art implied at its creation or
its connection to later work. Indeed, installing it in a major
museum of its own decontextualizes the art to the same extent
as the old industrial buildings on the site.

Serious art in a rural setting has long been a cornerstone
of Berkshire County tourism. Yet while the works presented
at Tanglewood, Jacob's Pillow, and the Williamstown Theater
Festival were once regarded as avant garde, they are now
more or less a mix of the classics and mid-20th century modernism. In the summer of 1993, the resident troupe of Shakespearean actors at The Mount performed both Shakespeare
and plays adapted from Edith Wharton's short stories. The
Boston Symphony Orchestra closed its season at Tanglewood
with a Beethoven concert, and the much smaller Contemporary Music Festival featured three student orchestras performing early Stockhausen. Jacob's Pillow presented modern
dance companies from the United States and Spain. To a great
extent, the audiences for these institutions have aged with
them. They might well be more interested in works by Louise
Bourgeois and Robert Rauschenberg than in Conceptualist
and Minimalist art.

Even so, creating a museum as large as MASS MoCA
involves major problems of scale. An enthusiastic Krens told

an interviewer early in the project, "I don't think anybody really understands the tangible excitement that can generate from something that takes place on this scale. . . . We see MASS MoCA as a small city. . . . What about the possibility of connecting the complex to downtown North Adams, to main streets, to making it part of the town, part of the city" (Johnson 1988, 98). The 1989 feasibility study cites the Italian city of Florence as a relevant example of how museums can be integrated into the urban fabric (Massachusetts Museum of Contemporary Art 1989a, 4-14). Allowing for a certain amount of enthusiastic exaggeration, this raises the question whether a museum, like a textile mill, can overshadow a town.

A proposal to build a major museum raises concrete issues about satisfying the cultural needs of local audiences, establishing visual links to the rest of the city, and understanding the implications of redeveloping an industrial town around a symbolic economy. Local residents may not really debate these issues. A North Adams State College professor who studies mill workers says informally, "A lot of people will go to a city council meeting and argue for hours about raising the sticker fee for the town dump from $6 to $7, but never say a peep about MoCA and its impact on the town."

By the same token, the more museums depend on government support, the greater is the possibility that the museum's mission will be transformed into an economic development strategy. Culture, in this case, is used mainly for its potential to create service-sector jobs, its tie-ins with hotels and restaurants, and its "gate" or ability to attract a paying audience.

There are also problems in connecting economic redevelopment to the economic value of individual art collections. Krens said in an interview, "The smart collector, if he sees it evolving the right way, will then try to get in on the ground floor." Marketing a collection is, then, a small step away from marketing a museum and marketing culture: "You've seen a revolution in the Olympics since Los Angeles [1984]. They called it the marketing of the Olympics. . . . If we've got MASS MoCA under our belts and we approach it the right way – I'm absolutely certain we could get corporate support to [fund it like the Olympics]" (Johnson 1988, 98). The post-1990 downturn in both the art and real estate markets cautions against the public's getting a free ride on this synergy. Moreover, the public may be tired of the incessant commercial drive behind the expansion of major museums in the 1980s. The marketing strategies of museums may well have reached their limits. When the art concerned is conceptual art, many of whose examples are limited to concepts jotted down on paper, the public may show a healthy distrust of art's economic benefits.

A successful museum and tourism complex in North Adams would surely create tension between the economies of scale required for a successful tourist industry and the quality of small town life. At best, residents would have to endure environmental and social irritations such as traffic congestion. At worst, property values would rise so high residents would no longer be able to afford to live there.

It may be too cynical to indict a lack of fit between the "modernism" of North Adams's economic needs and the "post-modernism" of the symbolic economy. The success of the new MASS MoCA plan indicates a middle position, based on the importance of institutional support and a contextual program. The ability of the new MASS MoCA plan to gain official approval indicates the limits of cultural strategies of redevelopment. Such simple factors as numbers of people, political support, and local identity pose serious obstacles. The value of culture cannot be conceived outside a specific social and institutional context. This was easily forgotten in the dizzying art and financial booms of the 1980s. In such a market, concepts can indeed become commodities: from junk bonds to unfabricated works of art, from the "art of the deal" to the art being dealt.

The substance of a symbolic economy – what art is to be featured, how it will be seen, and who will produce it – must engage the strategic considerations of cultural officials and city planners. The contrast between successful museums in Lowell and Old Sturbridge Village, Massachusetts, and MASS MoCA's problems suggests that the choice of visual strategies is crucial. Which visual strategy is most appropriate to the region and the audience: the *panorama* of historical re-creation or the *context* of adaptive reuse? Whose culture and whose vision shapes the expression of local identity? MASS MoCA's problems dramatize two central issues in developing and maintaining a symbolic economy: the autonomy of vision, on the one hand, and the diversity of cultural production, on the other.

■ High art in public space: The Metropolitan Museum of Art has periodically built extensions into Central Park.

Original buildings, 1880–94. Photograph © The Metropolitan Museum of Art. All Rights Reserved.

Part of early building (at left), flanked by expansions. Photo by Richard Rosen.

4

HIGH CULTURE AND WILD COMMERCE IN NEW YORK CITY

Unlike North Adams, New York City has long had the kind of metropolitan base that supports a wide variety of cultural institutions. It also has a vastly more complex and diversified economy. But even before that isolated corner of the Berkshires turned to a cultural strategy of economic development, New York's mayors, business leaders, and real estate developers were talking up culture in a big way.[5] As early as 1954, the *New York Times* claimed many corporate executives wanted to be in New York because of the city's cultural attractions, including "the theatre, the opera, nightclubs." At the end of the 1950s and beginning of the 1960s, "articles [in *Fortune* and *Business Week*] evoked a lifestyle for urban executives consisting of corporate suites, posh apartments, exclusive social clubs, fine restaurants, fashionable stores, and cultural

5. When I was asked to give a paper at a conference on postindustrial New York City at the University of Bremen, it occurred to me to discuss art, money, and real estate, topics ignored by the other conference participants. Although I did not attend the conference, my paper was published as "Hochkultur und 'wilder' Kommerz: Wie New York wieder zu einem kulturellen Zentrum werden soll," in *New York: Strukturen einer Metropole,* ed. Hartmut Haussermann and Walter Siebel (Frankfurt: Suhrkamp, 1993), pp. 264–85, and even found its way onto German radio. The present chapter is a greatly revised and expanded version of that publication. Thanks to Jenn Parker for research assistance and to Hartmut Haussermann for his encouragement.

pursuits" (Wallock 1988a, 46). In the New York City Plan of 1969, discussion of culture became even more instrumental. Culture was now seen less as a perquisite of old money or new organizations and more as an engine of economic growth. The movers and shakers wanted New York to be the "national," and eventually the "global," center of a symbolic economy based on finance, business services, and property development. Cultural institutions and culture industries could be a significant factor in consolidating that role.

Since the 1970s, the belief that New York is the world capital of culture has been used as if it were a fortune-teller's benediction to ward off all evidence of economic decline. Rhetoric acknowledging the economic importance of culture transcends political differences. Speaking at a conference in 1993 on the culture of racial tolerance organized by the New York City Department of Cultural Affairs, the deputy mayor for planning and development in a liberal Democratic administration gave a perfunctory nod to culture as a unifying force: "The role that the arts play in humanizing the city and in binding our social fabric takes many forms." Then she emphasized,

> *The signature role that the arts community has played in the revitalization of our neighborhoods is evident throughout the city. The proliferation of restaurants, shops and other small businesses that appear in areas where artists live and work have brought substantial gains to the fabric of our neighborhoods. We should remember also, particularly in this period when the statistics on unemployment are rather staggering, that culture in New York City is a six billion dollar industry. ("Tolerance as an Art Form" 1993, 3; italics in original).*

Around the same time, Martin Segal, a businessman and chairman emeritus of Lincoln Center, protested proposed cuts in the budget of the New York State Council on the Arts by proclaiming art and culture a "megaindustry" in New York City, with an annual economy "conservatively estimated" at $8 billion. "Art and tourism combined constitute one of the largest generators of tax revenues, some $2.5 billion in direct city, state, and Federal tax receipts" (letter to editor, *New York Times*, March 12, 1993).

One year later, after rumors circulated that he was thinking about cutting city government funding for small, nonprofit cultural institutions and was bitterly criticized for this by other public officials, newly elected Republican mayor Rudolph W. Giuliani echoed these themes. "It really is the core of a great city to maintain and preserve the arts, certainly as part of the spiritual identity of the city but also because this is an important industry. . . . This is vital to our economic renewal" (*New York Times,* January 25, 1994). Together with the growing numbers of cultural producers who work both formally and informally in service industries and the nonprofit sector, the consensus on the significance of the arts in New York City suggests that we have finally arrived at an "artistic mode of production" (Zukin 1989 [1982]).

Yet the commitment to culture has to be qualified. Public officials and developers are more at ease discussing the image of the city as a culture capital than attending to demands for support by artists, musicians, theater owners, and museum workers. The consensus surrounding the value of the arts often breaks down over specific issues of land, labor, and capital – especially when demands for low-cost artists' housing compete with pressures for gentrification, demands for theaters and rehearsal space compete with pressures for midtown office development, and demands for a guaranteed number of jobs in the orchestra pit compete with pressures to cut labor costs in concert halls and Broadway musicals. When push comes to shove, culture has been an interim development strategy, useful in periods of uncertainty and risky development projects. Artists have been welcomed as "bridge" gentrifiers – but not as statutory tenants deserving protection when property values rise. Cultural zones and art installations have been encouraged – when plans to build skyscrapers have fallen through or when sponsored by real estate developers. In general, the synergy between art, finance, and politics benefits high culture institutions and the tourist industry while creating only sporadic gains for independent cultural producers.

But public officials need cultural strategies of development. The dramatic decrease in manufacturing jobs since 1960 and the prominence of business services demand a new, more abstract representation of growth. In New York, as well as such large cities as Boston and San Francisco, the nonprofit sector, including cultural organizations, plays an important role in the service economy, with more jobs than in manufacturing. The number and diversity of cultural attractions are believed to work to the city's advantage. Representing the allure of a culture capital, they supposedly compensate for the disadvantages of living and working in New York. Moreover, since the early 1980s, researchers connected with government agencies have argued that cultural activities – including television production, Broadway performances, museum exhibits, and auction sales – have important multiplier effects on the urban economy (Port Authority 1983, 1993; also "Arts and New York" 1978).

If art is the city's business, it is hardly a new one. New York has been the center of "information" in the United States almost since the country's creation (Pred 1973). Its position at the center of numerous transportation systems, and as a point of transit between the United States and Europe, helped it to become the leading site of cultural diffusion from the end of the 19th century. Cultural products were inspired, then cross-fertilized, by social elites, business leaders, and constant streams of immigrants. The restless pace of new money joining old opened opportunities for the production of new cultural symbols.

The growing concentration of cultural producers in New York, and the economic advantages in each cultural sector of "importing" products made in New York over creating new regional magazines, theatrical productions, and fashions supported New York's base in culture industries for nearly a century. In economic terms, concentrations of cultural producers, their intermediaries, and suppliers formed agglomeration economies. Especially in Manhattan's central spaces, New York City spawned specialized social enclaves of artists, writers, musicians, and performers (Wallock 1988b). Most of all, from the 1940s through the 1960s, Cold War politics that fought Soviet Communism with "cultural freedom" brought popular attention to the New York School of abstract painting, making the city the art capital of the country, the century, and some say, the world (Guilbaut 1983).

What has changed since 1970 is our understanding of culture and its relation with the city. Earlier, men and women thought of "culture" as an amenity, a beautifying factor, a

gloss on public life. The arts were a symbol of collective identity, showing some cities and their elites to be more honorable,
more innovative, and ultimately more productive than others
(see Horowitz 1976). If monuments of culture – great public
spaces, statues, buildings – were supposed to inspire, they
were shaped, in turn, by the material civilization that conceived and constructed them. Culture was a fait accompli. But
"culture" today – a secular, generalized, visual culture – is
more malleable and more ambiguous. It responds to the
demands of many collective patrons who compete over both
the definition of symbols and the space to put them. In their
hands, culture is an agent of change. It is less a reflection
than a tool of material civilization, using images not only as
salable commodities but also as the basis of tourist and real
estate markets and visions of collective identity. The ambiguity of material culture nurtures speculation. Culture is both
a commodity and a public good, a base – though a troubling
one – of economic growth, and a means of framing the city.

▓ Measuring the Arts Economy

New York incontestably has the largest base in high culture
of any city in North America. In 1977, arts employment in
the New York metropolitan region represented 30 percent of
all arts employment in the United States. Revenues of the
region's museums represented 25 percent of the nation's.
Operating receipts of legitimate theaters in the city were 34
percent of the operating receipts of all U.S. theaters. For symphony and dance companies, operating receipts represented
29 percent of the national total. And the region's nonprofit arts
operating receipts represented 26 percent of all such operating
receipts in the nation ("Nonprofit Sector" 1982, 3). Fifteen
years later, in 1992, New York continued to outshine its nearest competitors, Los Angeles and Chicago, in the number, size,
and diversity of its major cultural institutions. The New York
metropolitan region has almost 500 commercial galleries, 49
museums, 34 for-profit theaters with annual budgets over
$300,000, 31 dance companies, and 26 symphony orchestras.
Most important, these days, nearly half the out-of-region visitors to these cultural sites say they come to New York especially for the cultural attractions (Port Authority 1993).

If estimates can be believed, in 1992 the loosely linked symbolic economy of art galleries and auction houses, commercial theater, nonprofit cultural institutions, movie and television production, and tourist spending by visitors to arts events was worth $9.8 billion a year (Port Authority 1993).[6] This amount is considerably higher than the earlier estimate of $5.6 billion that so impressed the deputy mayor. It also challenges several indicators of economic decline that could be expected to affect the arts: a recession involving huge job losses that began in 1989, two years earlier than the national recession; falling profit rates in financial firms that reduced both their sponsorship of the arts and the free-wheeling spending of high-income earners; and fiscal cutbacks in New York City and New York state in the early 1990s due to tax shortfalls and reduced spending by the Reagan and Bush administrations. The contrast between a vital and growing arts economy and the overall impoverishment of New York City is reflected in a "livability index" comparing more than 300 metropolitan areas in North America. While New York is in, or near, last place for jobs, crime, and cost of living, it is in first place for art (Savageau and Boyer 1993).

Within the arts, three fields – film, television, and video production; nonprofit cultural organizations; and tourist spending – have a multibillion dollar effect on the city's economy. Movie and TV production has the greatest effect in direct expenditures ($1.4 billion) and the greatest overall economic impact ($3 billion) (Port Authority 1993). The nonprofits have $1.3 billion in direct expenditures, for an overall economic impact of $2.7 billion. Visitors who come to the city primarily to attend arts events spend $1.3 billion, for an overall economic impact of $2.3 billion. Although profits and production in the

---

6. The data collected by regional economists at the Port Authority of New York and New Jersey was analyzed by their own input–output model. Direct expenditures include both primary payments by cultural institutions (the largest category of which is wages) and secondary payments to materials and services suppliers. The model subtracts expenditures that leak out of the metropolitan region. I cite multiplier effects despite my grave reservations about both their statistical reliability and the validity of using them to measure the value of cultural activities. Nevertheless, they have been cited so often by public officials and the media that they exert an important influence on representations of the city. Also, flawed though they may be, they at least suggest that cultural activities do have quantitative significance.

commercial theater have both declined, for-profit theaters generate $451 million in direct expenditures and have an economic impact of $905 million. Art galleries and auction houses spend $398 million on operating costs and have an overall economic impact of $840 million excluding sales. Because of the economic recession, growth in each of these sectors stopped in the middle to late 1980s and only slowly began again around 1992. While the economic impact of movie and TV production rose from $2 to $3 billion, the effect of nonprofit cultural institutions and visitor spending stayed the same.

Wages are the biggest category, accounting for almost half of all operating costs. This portion varies from 37 percent in art galleries and auction houses and 48-54 percent in small and large nonprofit institutions to almost 60 percent in the theater and movie and TV production. Not surprisingly, the nonprofits have tried to cut costs by turning to outside contractors and part-time workers, especially in the smaller institutions. All in all, the arts directly and indirectly support a work force of about 107,000 men and women. Although this is 8.5 percent less than in 1982, the arts may be losing fewer workers than other sectors of the economy. A note of caution concerns the relation between "direct" and "indirect" jobs. Although the 1993 report on the arts does not distinguish between them, the 1982 report did. At that time, only 35,323 jobs properly belonged to the arts labor force; an additional 80,000 jobs were counted indirectly in other fields – in support services and tourism.

Tourist spending and wage bills are not the only economic benefits of a symbolic economy. Developing the city as a culture capital also creates qualitative benefits for the service economy as a whole. Cultural centers for display and performance effectively reserve public space for upscale stores and services. Because they are often located in downtown areas, they appropriate space from populist, manufacturing, or tawdry uses and transform it into the "clean" entertainment, commercial, and residential zones preferred by professionals, managers, and white-collar workers. Cultural spaces in their many guises also enhance the economic value of commercial and residential property. If, in the 18th and early 19th centuries, the cultural tone of New York City neighborhoods reflected the social class of their inhabitants, by the 20th century cultural spaces could make or break class boundaries.

Cultural institutions have a long history of raising property values. When they were built in the late 19th century, the Metropolitan Museum of Art and the American Museum of Natural History reserved key access points to Central Park and the neighborhoods surrounding the park for the upper classes. The next generation of urban planners and architects, the City Beautiful movement, influenced by the Chicago World's Fair, developed more comprehensive schemes for unifying public buildings in civic centers that would attract high-class real estate investment (Boyer 1983, 51–55). Around the same time, but with less orchestration by business and political elites, Times Square established a new kind of public space in whose vaudeville halls, legitimate theaters, and winter gardens different social classes mingled with near abandon (Taylor 1991). Powerful New Yorkers learned how important even low-status cultural institutions could be in framing new real estate development.

The Rockefeller family wanted the Metropolitan Opera House to anchor Rockefeller Center when it was built at the end of the 1920s. They were unsuccessful; instead, they built Radio City Music Hall and got the Rockettes. Thirty years later, with the help of the power broker Robert Moses and federal urban renewal funds, the Metropolitan Opera joined the New York Philharmonic, Fordham University, and ballet and theater companies to form Lincoln Center for the Performing Arts, a major recipient of funding from the Rockefeller Foundation.

In the 1970s, pressures to use culture to stabilize neighborhoods came from the educated middle classes. Loft living testifies to the effectiveness of a coalition of artists, middle-class homeowners, and political and social elites that defeated plans by major real estate interests, banking leaders (including the Rockefellers), and labor unions to tear down old manufacturing buildings and replace them with such signs of urban renewal as an expressway, a sports stadium, and high-rise commercial and residential development (Zukin 1989 [1982]). The architectural salvation of the loft districts of SoHo and Tribeca led to their use as the base of an arts economy and to broader commercial success. These neighborhoods showed that historic district ("landmark") designations and concentrations of arts facilities did not only represent aesthetic amenities, they also raised property values and attracted commercial development.

It could be argued that "saving" SoHo and Tribeca pitted the art collecting and philanthropic roles of social and business elites against their real estate interests. Since their founding in the 19th century, however, "public" museums have consistently helped elites across the board in their social, business, and real estate dealings. Even now, high culture institutions offer excellent networking opportunities. Their boards of directors are meeting places and clearinghouses of ideas, especially for linkages between the public and private sectors (on Louisville, Kentucky, see Whitt 1987 and Whitt and Lammers 1991). The democratization of these august institutions since the 1960s may not have redistributed to a great extent the benefits they offer to elites.

Certainly the marketing strategies of major museums, their blockbuster exhibits, and their use of new display techniques have somewhat expanded their audience. Cultural institutions have also included minority representatives in both governing boards and programming decisions. The power of old elites has, moreover, been diffused by the entry of new money – first, that of national corporations and the federal government, then that of Wall Street – and new political scrutiny of cultural institutions. But museums, overall, still bring most benefits to the elites who serve on their boards and the arts professionals and affluent middle-class cultural consumers who visit them.

While museum attendance in the New York region doubled during the 1960s, arts professionals constituted about 25 percent, the largest share, of weekday museum-goers in Manhattan (Johnson 1969). By the 1990s, a survey of visitors to four exhibits at the Metropolitan Museum, Museum of Modern Art (MOMA), and Guggenheim Museum showed most (24–43 percent) were in the affluent middle classes – professionals, managers, and executives – followed by arts professionals (12–17 percent), teachers, students, and retired persons (Arts Research Center 1993). The highest proportion of affluent professionals among museum visitors was achieved at the historic Henri Matisse retrospective at MOMA. Of the

four exhibits, including Magritte, Jusepe Ribera, and the early
20th century Russian and Soviet avant garde, the Matisse
exhibit had both the greatest name recognition and greatest
snob appeal.

■ High Culture as Space and Symbol

During the 1980s, the expansion of major museums depended
on their ability to organize big-ticket exhibitions. Their visibility in turn confirmed the museums' importance to the mergers
of new and old elites. New York's cultural institutions worked
out an explicit synergy between museums, department stores,
and self-promoting philanthropists who shared commercial
promotions and charity events (Silverman 1986). Collaboration between the men and women in these different spheres
helped unify finance, politics, entertainment, and high society.
Because they are the two largest cultural complexes with
the closest elite connections, the Metropolitan Museum and
Lincoln Center played a prominent role in these arrangements.

   Such speculative activities as real estate and finance
became a major source of funding for New York City's central
cultural institutions. This was especially important in the
belt-tightening aftermath of the fiscal crisis of 1975, which
reduced both city and state expenditures for art and culture.
During the 1980s, private investment in culture developed an
extremely high profile. Museums basked in the celebrity of
Wall Street's new multimillionaires. Patrons added luster to
their image by sponsoring big art exhibits and capital projects
– special facilities or new wings – in museums, especially
the Metropolitan, which kept expanding into Central Park or
rebuilding its already extensive galleries. Art in general, and
specifically collecting, became the focus of the media because
of the astronomical prices paid at auction sales. The auction
houses Sotheby's and Christie's capitalized on an interest in
the work of living artists, which brought prices of these works
to near-parity with those of Old Masters. A new nexus of
auction houses, art galleries, art museums, art producers,
and cultural and social elites – many of them international –
contributed to New York's renewed reputation as a culture
capital (P. Watson 1992). As in the Gilded Age of the late 19th
century, capital invested in the visual arts from the 1960s

through the 1980s helped to create a new, coherent landscape of power out of the turbulence of financial speculation.

The dependence of art institutions on private-sector financing, including both donations and stock market–based endowments, produces a creative tension between high culture and speculative, partly unregulated, "wild" commerce. This peculiarly American system of funding the arts has become more market driven as government budgets have been pared and cultural institutions have become more dependent on admissions fees, gift shop sales, and image differentiation. High art has become more like for-profit culture industries in many ways. Artists who prided themselves on their aloofness from the marketplace are lionized by new collectors and begin to socialize with them. Younger artists take the earning power of some living artists as their model, setting up studios where "assistants" produce their signature works, endlessly reproduce the same style, or switch to new styles to stay in the critics' eye. Museums organize ever more spectacular exhibitions. Auction houses, like investment banks, shed their fustian traditions and promote themselves as a global business. But there is a problem here. Museums, as quasi-democratic institutions, connect art, money, and public space. In the 1980s, they joined the authority of art to both the cultural hegemony of a new financial elite and the politics of public goods.

On this point, the symbolic economy is consistent: the production of symbols (more art) demands the production of space (more space). The more space there is for art, the larger is the public for cultural institutions. Yet as this public has been enlarged, new interests and demands have been brought to bear on the symbolic economy. On the one hand, social groups have urged cultural institutions to attend to their desire to be represented in canonic displays of art, music, and theatrical performance. These groups have joined "ethnic" demands for the representation of their cultural identity to the "aesthetic" agenda of professional arts administrators and the old elites that have supported them. This has both democratized cultural institutions and challenged their sense of mission. On the other hand, the expansion of the public for cultural institutions has encouraged those institutions to seek still more space for their activities. Art museums complain they need more galleries to display a larger portion of their collections and need more room for gift shops to finance their operations. As museums and other cultural institutions physically expand, they occupy space that might be intended for other uses in the symbolic economy, especially high-rent real estate development. In New York, in particular, museums no longer seem like adjuncts to property development projects: they are development projects in their own right. This increases competition for the land where such museums are found, usually central spaces of the city.

A complete history of how high culture has been used to re-present central spaces would begin with the Metropolitan Museum of Art and Lincoln Center. Those institutions created precedents for today's public-private partnerships, showing how the city's elites use the powers of government to appropriate space in the public domain (see Rosenzweig and Blackmar 1992; Caro 1974). Each institution took public space for a public purpose but remained under the control of a private board and private management. Each required a large, presti-

Cultural power joins market power: Gift shop of the Metropolitan Museum of Art, Prince Street, SoHo, one of 16 Metropolitan Museum of Art Shops from coast to coast.

Photo by Richard Rosen.

gious building project that simultaneously enhanced the reputation of political, business, and social elites and provided patronage in the form of construction contracts to politicians' friends (including, in the 20th century, labor unions). And each claimed, or reclaimed, an area of the city that was becoming central to urban development. The ability to project a cultural mission for this space served several functions. Above all, with strong elite support, a cultural project overrode competing claims for the site. It permitted the project's supporters to speak in lofty terms about national, even international, prestige and the city's honor. In crass economic terms, however, cultural projects took up a large swath of urban land and anchored markets in upscale real estate development.

Higher property values in turn suggested different uses, taller buildings, denser forms: upper-middle-class rather than working-class housing, apartment houses for the rich, a new physical and social topography for the Upper East and West sides. While the Metropolitan Museum was built on a squatters' settlement in the newly designated Central Park, Lincoln Center was built on the site of a residential neighborhood after it was condemned to be torn down because of "urban blight." For the first time, in the early 1950s, the allure of culture legitimized the use of urban renewal funds by the city's growth machine. But the hands that shaped Lincoln Center were those of Robert Moses, the Baron Haussmann of mid-20th century New York, and the Rockefeller Foundation. While building Lincoln Center gained New York City international prestige, on a local level it confirmed the cultural hegemony of the city's postwar elite.

New York City has not built a big cultural center since the 1950s. Since that time, however, the process of using culture to re-present central spaces has been defined by incremental changes: the enactment of historic preservation laws, the expansion of museums, and the planned rehabilitation of Times Square. All three projects share an intellectual and political history that spans the decades from the 1960s to the 1990s. This history grows from elite mobilization to challenge the large-scale, modern mode of urban renewal through a diffusion of art and culture in state-financed programs of community and economic redevelopment. At various points, different meanings of culture, even within an emerging common framework, pit group against group, groups against institutions, and one part of the symbolic economy against another. Landmarks, museums, and Times Square show some of the conflicts that arise from combining high culture, wild commerce, and community participation. These are all, in a way, unfinished stories of the symbolic economy.

▓ Landmarks

The opportunity to designate historic landmarks that are protected from real estate development marks a sea change in the re-viewing of a city's central spaces. In the early 1960s, a rather elitist historic preservation movement arose to protest "the worlds we have lost." Led by architects and critics of urban planning, historic preservation focused on landmarks, core buildings in a city's material civilization, as signs of a spirituality obliterated by Modernism. Many of the buildings that inspired their devotion were public buildings, designed by famous architects, used by business and government. Over time, the belief that old buildings represented the culture of cities spread to residential areas and less significant examples of architectural styles. The diffusion of a preservationist ethos offered legitimacy to the shifts of middle-class residents from one neighborhood to another and increases in property values associated with gentrification. But it also coincided with the rise of new urban politics, whose keywords were decentralization and community control. So historic preservation became both a goal of grassroots mobilization and a means of establishing community identity.

In 1965, consistent with its new role as a culture capital of the world, New York was the first city in the United States to establish an official public agency for historic preservation. Through arduous procedures of nomination and certification – reminiscent, in the power to decide not to hear certain cases, of the U.S. Supreme Court – the New York City Landmarks Preservation Commission decides which buildings and districts of the city will remain frozen in time. While existing improvements are "grandfathered" and permitted to stay, a historic district designation exerts serious moral pressure on building owners to remain in, or restore, an area's "character." Owners can plead for an exemption because of economic hardship, but the legal pressure for visual conformity is usually overwhelming. Demolition is ordinarily verboten.

Plans for exterior and sometimes even interior improvements have to be approved by the commission. Consequently, the agency is constantly criticized by building owners of every size and kind, whose ability to sell, renovate, and otherwise change their property is affected by the commission's decisions. Sometimes, for the sake of visual purity, the commission's decisions displease the very homeowners and residents they are intended to protect. In 1993, the commission ruled against tree planting in Tribeca – one of the city's most economically successful cases of historic preservation – because trees were not part of the urban landscape in the early 1800s, the period chosen as the aesthetic baseline for preservation. After that decision was publicly ridiculed, the commission relented and allowed trees to be planted on certain streets.

Needless to say, the very idea of excluding property from redevelopment is a compromise. While property development is still held sacred, the laws on historic preservation make it possible to limit development for "historic" or "aesthetic" reasons. Yet since the commission was established, aesthetic judgment has had the force of law. It is not only an important criterion; it is often the sole *legitimate* criterion for opposing development in central spaces. Design and scale have joined the zoning system's "non-conforming use" as means of blocking development.[7]

However, without a blanket classification of the central city as a historic zone, engaging in historic preservation is a piecemeal process. Each landmark designation of a district or building is proposed, justified, and selected individually. Thus each proposed designation incites both a strategic and a tactical battle, with people arguing over the validity of a mode of development that privileges *sight* as well as the merits of preserving individual *sites*. Even so, in its first 25 years, the Landmarks Preservation Commission designated 856 build-

---

7. At the beginning, in the 1960's, the historic preservation movement included both aesthetic motivations and community stabilization. The 1965 New York City law on historic preservation aimed to save buildings important to the city's "cultural, social, economic, political or architectural history." Over time, the aesthetic issues became dominant.

ings, 79 interiors of buildings, and 9 parks or other outdoor places (Goldberger 1990). It also designated 52 historic districts, containing nearly 15,000 buildings. The contrast between the demolition of Pennsylvania Station in the early 1960s and the proposal in the mid 1990s to re-create the former terminal's public space in the current Post Office Building, also designed in the Beaux Arts style by McKim, Mead, and White, shows just how important an effect historic preservation has had on New York City and its *mentalités*.

The conflict between producing symbols through historic preservation and producing space through speculative development makes strange bedfellows. Because churches are prohibited from either tearing down, or selling the air rights over, their landmark properties, the elite Episcopal St. Bartholomew's Church became embroiled in a major lawsuit in the mid 1980s to set aside this restriction. Alternately pleading economic hardship – to continue funding their charity programs – and exemption as a charitable institution, St. Bart's lost an appeal before the U.S. Supreme Court. Afterward, churches worked together with developers in lobbying City Council members to restrict the Landmarks Preservation Commission's power. Just how political landmark designations are was underlined in 1991, when the City Council shifted the appeals process, for those protesting a landmark designation, from the Landmarks Commission to the council itself. Nevertheless, the designation process gives fairly wide latitude to the individual judgment of Landmarks Commission members, who are responsible to the mayor.

Although landmark designations reflect cultural judgments, the effects of historic preservation are mediated by real estate markets. Sociologists' research on gentrification suggests that a landmark designation may raise rents and taxes so high that lower income residents are forced to move away. The time-consuming procedure and costs of officially approved renovation of landmark properties also influence some property owners to reduce maintenance. This worsens living conditions for rental tenants. Still, some local residents, usually homeowners, pursue a landmark designation that privileges the *look* of a place over such other sources of community identity as social class, ethnicity, and residential stability. In the Upper West Side Historic District, many residents involved in the preservation movement in the middle to late 1980s explicitly wanted to preserve the look of the area, although they realized that limiting new residential development would reduce the potential housing supply. In SoHo, the designation of 19th-century cast-iron loft buildings in 1973 opened the door to intense residential settlement by artists and others who followed their path. While landmarking the buildings effectively barred demolition and large-scale redevelopment, it also discouraged already weakened manufacturers from staying in the area. So historic preservation is never just a cultural category: the mediation of aesthetic qualities by real estate markets has a strong impact on social communities.

In terms of race, if not class, historic preservation has made the city more aware of how symbols can be used in the production of space. The first African-American chairman of the Landmarks Preservation Commission held office from 1983 to 1989. Since the election of New York's first mayor of African descent, David N. Dinkins, in 1989, mayoral appointments to the Landmarks Preservation Commission have shown greater ethnic diversity. Geographically, this means that more members are appointed from areas outside downtown Manhattan and the Upper East Side. Even earlier, the commission broadened the grounds for landmark designation by including important historic sites of African-American settlement and plebeian as well as patrician buildings. Yet the results have not been startling. From 1983 to 1989, 12 new historic districts and many individual sites in Harlem were proposed for landmarking; but only four of the 220 individual buildings designated during these years were in Harlem and no historic districts (Wolfe 1993, 66). An interesting argument that arose during this period, however, was whether landmarking could effect neighborhood revitalization. Non-European ethnic and racial groups, in particular, could use the cultural power of landmark designation to change the social class base of their communities. If this is so, it indicates a shift in the meaning of landmark from aesthetic category to public good.

The Landmarks Preservation Commission has always been responsive to advocacy groups, from the Friends of Cast Iron Architecture and the New York Scenic and Historic Preservation Society to neighborhood organizations. But those groups have all argued in terms of aesthetic categories, well within the parameters of the original movement for historic preservation in the 1960s and 1970s. Beginning in the late 1980s, however, community groups from historically black neighborhoods, especially Harlem, have publicly pressed for designation of more historic sites, such as the Audubon Ballroom, where Malcolm X was assassinated in 1965. The history embedded in these sites is not the history of architecture, it is a political history. It responds not only to a community's need to construct its own political identity, but also – in this case – to a rejection of Columbia University's plan to use the Audubon site to build biotechnology laboratories. Because the plan was seen as a political bombshell and an economic development strategy, the Audubon's landmark designation was not even handled by the commission. Instead, an agreement was brokered by the Manhattan borough president's office and signed by the New York City Economic Development Commission and the university.

■ The democraticization or politicization of historic preservation? Audubon Ballroom, site of Malcolm X's assassination, with new biotechnology buildings behind it.

Photo by Alex Vitale.

At the beginning of the 1990s, the co-chairperson of the
landmarks committee of the local community board in central
Harlem proposed a radical revision of the Landmarks Preservation Commission's mandate, a change from looking at space
aesthetically to looking at social consequences. Arguing in
favor of designating a building that has only modest architectural significance, she said, "It's time for a new kind of Landmarks Commission. We've designated all the major
landmarks. Landmark designation could be such an encouragement, such recognition for what the tenants in this building and other buildings are trying to do" (*New York Times,*
January 26, 1992). The use of this argument is not limited
to minority communities. It also appears in the successful
lobbying effort to designate a historic district in Jackson
Heights, a multi-ethnic area of Queens. " 'This will bring pride
and stability and everything else that this community
deserves,' said Adrienne M. Sumowicz, the president of the
Jackson Heights Beautification Group, which led a three-year
effort to win the designation. 'This community is a real gem' "
(*New York Times,* January 27, 1994, emphasis added).

The Jackson Heights designation was accepted unanimously by the City Council, partly in response to serious
protests by the outer boroughs that they were being neglected
by the powers that be in Manhattan, seconded by the passage
of a referendum by Staten Islanders in favor of secession from
New York City. But it may be too great an extension of its
mandate to shift the Landmarks Preservation Commission
from aesthetic considerations to social intervention. The commission refused to hold hearings on the St. Agnes apartment
house, one of 25 sites proposed in Harlem in 1990 and 1991.

At the same time, the commission did not handle the
compromise on the Audubon Ballroom. Parts of the facade
and auditorium were preserved and restored while Columbia
University built biotechnology laboratories around them and
promised to hire neighborhood residents. Even so, the grounds
of the compromise were contested. The president of the Upper
Manhattan Society for Progress Through Preservation, a
group that lobbied in support of landmarking the Audubon,
said, "This is just further proof that the history of black people
is trivialized. Malcolm X is one of our country's most important

political figures. Yet we can only save half of the auditorium? Would people have been content if only part of the Ford Theater, where Lincoln was shot, were saved?" (quoted in Wolfe 1993, 56). With landmarking laws in effect, the issue of defining the "cultural significance" of a building is crucial to constructing narratives of political history. *Whose* house is landmarked is important for public culture, though not necessarily the aesthetic or political reasons behind it.

In the 1960s, preservationists complained that physical demolition and urban renewal caused the loss of a cultural heritage. Today, with a preservationist ethos widely accepted, the question is which cultural heritage will be preserved and whose culture will control the designation. With many old buildings saved from demolition, the battle has shifted to devising more inclusive criteria for re-presenting central spaces. Instead of complaining about the loss of monuments of the past, preservationists now complain about the banality of contemporary design. Their shibboleths are themed developments and derivative architectural styles, all evidence of the city's "Disneyization" (Gill 1991). Tall, dense, bulky buildings, the kind that make up most of midtown Manhattan, are considered incompatible with the "historic city." Such buildings can, of course, be constructed on the borders of historic districts, where they reap the profits of their unique location. So preservationists have proposed a broader vision of preservation using a sight-based "context" rather than a narrow site (Oser 1990).

Expanding the use of aesthetic and historic criteria for re-viewing central spaces also expands the possibility of viewing a much greater portion of New York City as a culture capital. But the production of these symbols often conflicts with the speculative production of space.

▓ Museums

Great museums also contribute to the development of the city as a culture capital. From the 1970s, New York museums have led the way in developing blockbuster exhibitions of spectacular cultural products that attract highly visible paying admissions, with special marketing strategies, commercial tie-ins, and crowds. They have also aggressively pursued large donations. When they entered this growth period of the symbolic economy, the major New York museums tried to ensure their survival by developing expansion plans that echoed those of financial corporations. The Guggenheim and MOMA planned to build skyscrapers, and the Metropolitan continued to build outward into the public space of Central Park. These projects were identified with the self-promotion of new money as well as with the self-interest of city officials and museum administrators. During the 1970s, the arts – mainly, the big museums – were the fastest growing area of philanthropic donation ("Nonprofit Sector" 1982).

A public hunger to see cultural products encouraged museum directors to try new strategies. At the Metropolitan Museum, the administration changed its policy and bought work by living artists. Museum administrations made museums more accessible to the public by borrowing exhibition techniques from television. They found subjects that resonated with the public's imagination. MOMA turned its entire building into Cézanne and Picasso retrospectives. The Whitney Museum of American Art established branches in the lobbies of several midtown and downtown office buildings by leasing space from the Philip Morris Company, the Equitable Life Assurance Company, and the U.S. government. This was the first time a major museum had tried setting up branches since museum professionals rejected the idea in the 1920s. In the 1980s, the Guggenheim began planning its global expansion. Despite the disappearance of neighborhood movie theaters and the rise of suburban malls, New York City museums emerged as even stronger centers of cultural power.

The Metropolitan Museum is in an enviable position because it has been granted approval over the years to expand behind its main building into Central Park. The addition of the Temple of Dendur, various sculpture and furniture collections, and galleries of 19th century art endowed by generous patrons have virtually created museums within the museum. The Metropolitan's major errors in financing these expansions have been tactical – suffering cost overruns and removing donors' names from previous bequests when larger donors came on the scene (Golway 1991). The museum was also severely criticized in the late 1980s for permitting wealthy individuals to rent museum space for evening parties. Less scrutinized is its policy of renting space for corporate and charity dinners.

The Museum of Modern Art adopted a more audacious strategy: it became a real estate developer. In 1976, MOMA announced a plan to build a 49-floor condominium apartment tower, including six museum floors, on top of its existing buildings on West 53rd Street. Museum Tower would include 250 rental and condominium units, replacing space then occupied by the museum's office and bookstore buildings (see, for example, H. Kramer 1976). But the museum could not act alone. Commercial building owners on 53rd and 54th Streets protested that a high-rise extension of the museum would block their tenants' air and sunlight. Historic preservationists and some architects protested that the museum's main building, designed in the 1930s by Philip Goodwin and Edward Durell Stone, would be overshadowed by a mediocre glass tower. Several of the remaining brownstone townhouses on 53rd Street were to be torn down, and the new tower would destroy the area's low scale (Hoelterhoff 1977). Moreover, the way the museum arranged to sell its air rights was controversial. Although at first the museum announced a selling price of $5 to $7 million, after a few weeks of public debate in the newspapers, the museum raised the price to a more realistic

■ Museum Tower: Real estate venture of the Museum of Modern Art.

Photo by Richard Rosen.

$17 million. Further, the museum picked a shady real estate development firm as its initial partner. The firm's publicly traded stock had fallen in value over the previous five years from $25 to $4 a share.

Yet a collaboration between the museum, the real estate developer, and the New York City government made it possible for the museum to build the high rise on the basis of tax diversions and quasi-zoning variations. The arrangements set a new precedent for linkages between the public and private sectors, linkages set out by Richard Weinstein, an architect and city planner connected to Mayor John Lindsay, who left office in 1974, the City Planning Commission, and the Rockefeller Brothers Fund. Weinstein reasoned that museums could not meet rising prices for art work without corporate support and financing. But they could help themselves in rising real estate markets by building on their unique locations. To do so required a complex web of legal changes. First, the city government endorsed New York state legislation on June 26, 1976, establishing a special cultural trust to administer MOMA's air rights. One of the trust's major functions was to channel the development project's profits back to MOMA and collect tax equivalency payments in lieu of real estate taxes (Anderson and Di Perna 1977). As the architecture critic Ada Louis Huxtable described it, the arrangement "permits the museum – through the trust – to designate a developer and control the design and to receive the tax value of the developed land that would otherwise go to the city, as well as sharing profits with the developer" (Huxtable 1977). The tax equivalency payments would be used by the Trust for Cultural Resources, which was set up solely for the museum, to pay for MOMA's expansion.

The local community board had a chance to oppose MOMA's expansion in a standard ULURP (Uniform Land Use Review Program) procedure. Throughout the review process, a subcommittee of the community board remained suspicious, contending that neither the museum nor the cultural trust had proven the development would resolve the museum's financial problems and lack of space. At last, the subcommittee was convinced that the museum and the developer had arranged to derive the most possible income from the project. However, when the full board met, with 150 people attending, it voted to exempt the museum project from zoning regulations on grounds of economic hardship (Horsely 1977).

Compared to the Metropolitan and MOMA, the Guggenheim Museum's expansion plans on Fifth Avenue were relatively mild. At least, they were limited to the museum's own property. Claiming that space in the landmark building designed by Frank Lloyd Wright was grossly inadequate to show their permanent collection, in 1985 the museum announced an 11-story addition. During the next three years, community groups, historic preservationists, and architects opposed the expansion. They filed at least one lawsuit against the museum, forcing delays and modifications to the original plans. Plaintiffs in the suit represented a variety of cultural and upper-class constituencies, including the Frank Lloyd Wright Foundation and ad hoc groups called Guggenheim Neighbors and Carnegie Neighbors. As at MOMA, neighbors believed the proposed expansion would block air and sunlight from their apartments. Architects felt the expansion would overshadow Wright's original building. While the lawsuit filed in New York State Supreme Court ultimately cost $9 million, it failed to prevent the museum from building the addition. Similarly, a letter writing campaign against the expansion by such Fifth Avenue residents as Woody Allen, Jacqueline Onassis, and Paul Newman had little effect.

After the citywide Board of Standards and Appeals granted the museum a zoning variance in 1987, the Board of Estimate accepted a modified expansion plan for a six-story addition in 1988. Among the witnesses who testified in favor of the museum expansion at the Board of Standards and Appeals hearing in 1986 were the directors of the Metropolitan and Brooklyn museums; Leo Castelli, a senior statesman among gallery owners in New York who specialize in contemporary art; and the dean of the Columbia University School of the Arts. Opponents of the Guggenheim expansion at this hearing included the Friends of the Upper East Side Historic District; the Landmarks Conservancy, a private preservation group; Guggenheim Neighbors; the director of the program in historic preservation at Columbia University; and the chairman of Taliesin, the community dedicated to preserving Frank Lloyd Wright's legacy.

In contrast to MOMA and the Guggenheim Museum, the Metropolitan Museum has had a free ride in Central Park. Yet all three museum expansions pose the issue of whether a privately owned cultural institution can be a real public space. Just as there is a troubled consensus about whose culture the museums represent inside their galleries, in their private space, there is little consensus about whose city they represent outside the galleries, in public space. Museums in fact serve two masters. As universalistic high culture institutions, museums stand completely outside a specific urban context of neighborhood constituencies and local identities. As public spaces, however, they are responsive to the city's political priorities.

The problems of expansion met by New York City's museums point to an issue dramatized, paradoxically, by the redevelopment of Times Square: the use of culture to "clear" space for real estate development.

▇ Times Square

The changing fortunes of Times Square in the 1990s illustrate how important culture has become in economic development strategies in New York City. Once ignored, then derided, the mass, popular, and urban cultural forms associated with this area of the city for many years have been aestheticized and reborn – as logos and spearheads of revitalization. QED: the production of space seems to rely on the production of symbols.

"Times Square" in fact represents a multiblock commercial area on the economically undervalued West Side of midtown Manhattan. The Times Square Business Improvement District (BID) stretches from the northern edge of the Garment District on 40th Street between Seventh and Eighth Avenues to 53rd Street, almost to the Ed Sullivan Theater at 54th Street, where *Late Show with David Letterman* is taped; it extends westward from behind the office buildings of Rockefeller Center on Sixth Avenue to various points midblock between Eighth and Ninth Avenues, including the offices of the *New York Times,* William Zeckendorf's corporate office development Worldwide Plaza, and the corporate headquarters of the Equitable Life Assurance Company. The legitimate theaters and restaurants on the area's most famous thoroughfare, 42nd Street, were converted piecemeal between the Great Depression and the 1950s to pornographic movie houses and peep shows, cheap stores, and diners.

In other American cities, the degeneration of this area would not be surprising. After World War II, the spatial con-catenation of docks supplying international shipping lines, intercity bus stations and their transient populations, and old vaudeville and movie houses and pinball parlors doomed downtowns that could not resist suburban development. In New York, however, too much power was invested in the local real estate industry to give up completely on Times Square. Moreover, the centrality of this space – to both the city's image as a culture capital and its image of itself – posed a constant challenge to the ideology of growth.

But how to redevelop the area? By and large, Times Square has been a carnival area for working people of the city. As long ago as the 1930s, its shoddy buildings, cheap amusements, and reputation for street crime and lawlessness scared off potential real estate investors. Even then, the city government was obsessed with cleaning up its image. From its early 20th century development as a center of commercial culture, reflecting the movement northward of the city's the-ater district, Times Square had been an unplanned, anony-mous, but highly identifiable space. It was, the historian William Taylor (1991) says, "a constant talking point . . . and a challenge to its own civic identity." Neither a traditional agora nor a Beaux Arts civic center, Times Square became a central image of New York despite, not because of, elites' concern with monumentality. During the 1970s, the idea of redevelopment was seriously and repeatedly discussed by the city administration, corporate property owners in the area, and real estate developers. At that point, there was substan-tial agreement on creating a new, more coherent visual image to replace the area's massage parlors and pawn shops. Propos-als aimed to create a standardized American downtown that would get people out of the disorder of the streets. With neither consensus on a program nor a single financial "package," plans ricocheted from a convention center to legalized gambling casinos and shopping malls. Beginning with the construction of a John Portman hotel that turns away from the street to a soaring "sky lobby," projects were approved that reduced the number of Broadway theaters and replaced low-rise buildings with tall office towers and hotels. The new image of Times Square negated its history and raucous public character. It borrowed from mainstream America.

As in any midtown redevelopment, public agencies collaborated with private interests. The Rockefeller family, who until the 1990s were the owners of Rockefeller Center, led a working group of business leaders that mobilized the city and state governments (Fitch 1993). The New York State Urban Development Corporation (UDC), which has the right to execute plans without public approval, set up a subsidiary, the 42nd Street Redevelopment Corporation. In 1976, this subagency took possession of all buildings except one on the south side of 42nd Street between Ninth and Tenth Avenues west of the exit from the Lincoln Tunnel. Two years later, the Ford Foundation, whose headquarters is across town on East 42nd Street, invested half a million dollars in a study and site model for 42nd Street between Seventh and Eighth Avenues. The block was to be converted from low-class and pornographic movie houses to cultural and tourist facilities and legitimate theaters. These would anchor a 550,000 square foot park and visitor center. Yet once again, deals for Times Square were left undone, victims of the city's fiscal crisis of 1975 and a continued lack of private investors.

By the early 1980s, however, New York was experiencing another boom in midtown office construction. In 1984, UDC drafted a 42nd Street Redevelopment Project, focusing on four startlingly tall office towers at 42nd Street and Seventh Avenue, the very heart of Times Square. This time, the commercial theater industry that is still based on Broadway was seen as both a national resource and a powerful drawing card. The 1983 Port Authority study *The Arts as an Industry* had emphasized the amount of money spent by tourists coming to see Broadway shows and the economic effect of employing people in the theater. While experts were aware that regional theaters increasingly produced the innovative plays that Broadway lacked, the UDC plan for Times Square acclaimed a sevenfold increase in yearly box office receipts at Broadway theaters since 1948 (perhaps more indicative of inflation than of a larger theater public). The plan implicitly criticized the fact that the number of theaters on Broadway had been reduced from 39 in 1948 to 33 in the early 1980s. The total number of productions had also continued to decrease. If commercial culture was to renew the economic value of the Times Square area, Broadway theater needed help.

To some degree, the redevelopment of Times Square needed the allure of Broadway theater because no private investors with deep pockets were interested. The city and state governments declared that the image of Times Square was so bad, it threatened property values *in half of midtown.* Without the project, the UDC's draft proposal said, "There will be a continuing problem of 'image' in West Midtown, particularly in the Times Square area, affecting the city's overall reputation" (New York State Urban Development Corporation 1984, vol. 2, 222). Yet the theater industry was not really in shape to anchor redevelopment, even symbolically. Producers had trouble raising capital, theater management could not control price increases, and suburban subscribers were more and more unwilling to come to Times Square. Perhaps the theaters were only window dressing, for the major product of Times Square's renovation, from 42nd Street to 47th Street, was going to be office buildings.

Once the city government and UDC got directly involved in producing space, the property market changed. A Special Midtown Zoning District established by the City Planning Commission permitted taller and bulkier buildings than had previously been allowed on the West Side and a redirection westward of subsidies formerly available on the East Side. As a result, land prices in the immediate 42nd Street project area more than doubled from 1983 to 1984. Since the more generous subsidies for building in Times Square were planned to expire by 1988, real estate developers rushed to file plans with the city's Buildings Department. Owners sat tight and waited until the last minute to sell. To hurry things along, UDC used its right of eminent domain and began to condemn and assemble the privately owned properties along 42nd Street between Seventh and Eighth Avenues, a block that included many old theaters. The agency also offered a writedown of public purchase and assessment of land and a city tax abatement, subsidies said to be worth $100 million for land acquisition alone. By 1987, the financial incentives drew two private development firms, the Prudential Insurance Company of

America and Park Tower Realty, led by a developer personally selected by Mayor Edward I. Koch. They hired the architect Philip Johnson to design signature office towers. The plan to create another midtown office district was, the architecture critic Ada Louise Huxtable (1991) charged, what everyone involved in the redevelopment project had always wanted – despite officials' claims that they wanted to preserve the theaters in Times Square.

But this was the 1980s. In the 15 years it had taken for wishes to percolate into plans, the preservation movement had redefined the terms in which the historic city was viewed. Times Square, no matter how tawdry, was now defended as public art. With debate limited mainly to aesthetics, as in the case of landmark designations, public critics of the Times Square redevelopment project focused on the design and scale of the towers and the desirability of keeping the area's neon signs and giant billboards. Although building 4 million square feet of offices in Times Square was ridiculed, few voices challenged the urgency of remaking this central area of the city.

During the next three to four years, the office towers remained on the drawing board awaiting a commitment on the part of large corporate tenants. But they drew a great deal of criticism. The Municipal Art Society, which as a champion of historic preservation took prominent positions on large-scale development in Manhattan, led a vocal campaign against them. As a result, their height was reduced. Then, changes were made in the design to deal with a perceived neglect of Times Square's sense of place. Questions were raised, however, about whether the 42nd Street Redevelopment Project could legally ignore any restrictions on its choices. A particularly sore point was the change that mandated developers to continue the use of the neon and electric signs that had been used for years for advertising around Times Square. If not the actual buildings, the signage was supposed to maintain the raucous visual character of the area. The former *New York Times* Motogram, which had wound around the Times Tower on 42nd Street since 1928, now became an object of preservation – even though the tower itself was to be replaced. As Huxtable (1991) writes, the veneration of this electric sign showed the movement from "news as advertising to advertising as entertainment." Or, we could say, from electric medium to aesthetic form.

What was built during the 1980s had already repudiated the former visual coherence of the area. The blend of anarchy and the archaic and the small scale of low-rise storefronts were obliterated by the megaliths of hotels that now buffered Broadway as it slashed through Times Square. And the modern design of skyscrapers at the northern end of Times Square inexorably shifted the social character of the area upscale. Yet without investors to build the merchandise mart that had periodically been planned since the 1970s and without corporate tenants to anchor the new office towers, redevelopment stalled. By the recession of the early 1990s, several new office buildings at the northern end of Times Square were vacant and had reverted to bank ownership. In 1992, the city government gave subsidies worth $11 million to the German media conglomerate Bertelsmann, the owner of RCA Records and the U.S. publishers Dell, Bantam, Doubleday, and *Parents* magazine, to buy one of these vacant buildings.

But this was the 1990s. In the time it had taken to sign up several corporate tenants for the office towers proposed on 42nd Street and for those tenants, skittish in the economic recession, to back out of the towers' leases, culture had been recognized as a public good. The big guns of speculative development were replaced by the smaller, though no less noisy, pop shots of cultural renovation. An "interim" plan for Times Square, supposed to last from the mid 1990s to 2004, was rumored in the press as early as 1991 (McHugh 1991) and publicly announced over the next few months. The new plan featured outdoor art exhibits, a children's theater, renewed legitimate theaters, restaurants, and a visitors' center – resurrecting the cultural elements of an entertainment zone from the office development plans of the 1970s and 1980s.

Moreover, the "new" Times Square was inaugurated by a unique summertime outdoor art exhibit that deliberately carried the feel of SoHo's nonconformist art to midtown's public spaces. The UDC subsidiary responsible for redevelopment joined Creative Time, a nonprofit arts organization, and the New 42nd Street Inc., another nonprofit organization established to renovate Times Square's theaters, to commission more than 20 artists and designers to install works on "storefronts, facades, vitrines, marquees, billboards, and even roll-down grates" (Dunlap 1993). The dramatic installations were in some ways a commentary on the street and its commercial culture, but in other ways they blended so closely with the area's visual schlock and sleaze, they were hard to distinguish from the real thing (Vogel 1993). The exception, of course, was that the artists' installations were meant to create an ironic detachment from the skin trades that had dominated the street for so long. Their appropriation of symbols of sexism and pornography framed the street as a cultural object and helped the redevelopment authorities appropriate space. When small stores and convenience shops were evicted, their buildings condemned and taken over by New York state, they were temporarily replaced by video projections of big red lips, a studio for live plaster casting of faces, window displays for an "American She-Male" boutique, mirrored texts, and sculptures. Empty theater marquees presided over the block, bearing brief messages by the conceptual artist Jenny Holzer. The Whitney Museum at Philip Morris, three blocks away on East 42nd Street and Park Avenue, led free tours of the site for adults and children.

The retail consultants hired to design 42nd Street's new image defined the future as a view of the past: "Commercial facilities selected for 42nd Street will generally be popular-priced establishments which together will generate excitement, fun and round-the-clock entertainment. . . . Forty-second Street cannot be pigeonholed like a 'festival marketplace,' a shopping mall, or Main Street, USA. The street will always mirror New York City with all of its vitality and turbulence" (Dunlap 1993). So the production of this most central of New York's spaces faltered on finance and returned to art: an image of the symbolic economy.

But this symbolic economy is not that of Broadway's Great White Way. It is the modern symbolic economy of large culture industries, art, entertainment, and finance. In 1992, the Times Square BID was formed, representing 404 buildings with 30 million square feet of office space. In 1993, the interim plan to rebuild Times Square as a carnival proceeded in tandem with efforts to lure corporate tenants in culture industries. By the end of 1994, city and state agencies had negotiated subsidies – low-interest, long-term loans and rent

■ Times Square: Old (pornographic) district.

Photo by Danny Kessler.

Times Square: New (ironic) cultural district. New Amsterdam
Theatre, proposed site of a Disney theatre.

Photo by Alex Vitale.

payments in lieu of taxes – for the Disney Company to create an entertainment complex in a 92-year-old theater on 42nd Street, the New Amsterdam, where the Ziegfield Follies had once played. The bookstore chain Barnes and Noble and Virgin Records planned to open superstores. Moreover, New York City and New York state gave subsidies worth $80 million to the investment banking firm Morgan Stanley to buy a vacant building on Broadway near Bertelsmann, which had been built and abandoned in the same speculative boom. " 'It's really exciting that Bertelsmann and Morgan have taken these two buildings,' said Gretchen Dykstra, president of the Times Square Business Improvement District. 'It adds to the eclectic mix and harkens new retail activity. We're happy this is all happening without Times Square losing its finger-snapping vitality' " (Bagli 1993; see also *New York Times,* September 15, 1993).

▓ Jobs and Money

Art, real estate, and financial markets led the boom in the symbolic economy in the 1980s. The astounding prices paid at art auctions, especially in New York, enhanced the city's reputation as a culture capital and encouraged people to view art as a money-making industry. In 1965, a Jackson Pollock canvas painted in 1946 sold for only $45,000. By 1973, Andy Warhol paintings were selling for over $100,000; and Jasper Johns's *Double White Map* (1965) was sold for $240,000. Ten years later, Mark Rothko's *Maroon and White* was sold for $1.8 million. In 1986, someone paid $3.6 million for Jasper Johns's *Out the Window*; and in 1988, Jackson Pollock's *Search* was sold for $4.84 million (D. Nash 1989).

Between 1983 and 1987, the proceeds from auction sales increased 427 percent. Understandably, in 1987, the chairman of Sotheby's reported the most successful year in the auction house's history. Sotheby's accounted for more than 60 percent of the international auction market, achieving for the first time more than $1 billion in sales (Sotheby's 1987).

Auctions and the publicity surrounding them set a new career model for aspiring artists. Yet the market value of some art and the artist as celebrity contrast with the living and working conditions of most New York artists. At the end of the 1980s, half of a survey sample of about 500 New York painters, writers, and actors earned an annual income of only $3,000 or less from their art work, and nearly half reported they earned only $10,000 or less from all sources (Research Center for Arts and Culture 1989). Lacking rent controls on production, performance, rehearsal, and residential space, and without the possibility of full-time employment in creative work, artists depend on the government for grants and subsidies.

The city government created an independent Department of Cultural Affairs in the mid 1970s as part of the general consensus on support for the arts. Previously, Cultural Affairs had been a division of the Parks Department. The new department's first annual budget – around the time that auctions of postwar and Pop art began to take off – was just half a million dollars. By 1988, the department's budget reached $124 million. In 1990, when the city reached the low point of job loss from the finance and service sector–led recession, the department's budget peaked at $170 million. This amount was only $3 million less than the budget of the National Endowment for the Arts and more than three times as large as the budget of the New York State Council on the Arts (Munk 1990). By 1995, however, a new fiscal crisis reduced the department's budget to $96 million.

The major portion of the department's budget – over 90 percent until 1988, 80 percent since then – goes to the biggest cultural institutions. Although under Mayor Dinkins the department gave more money than before to small and community groups, they got a larger share of a shrinking pie. In 1991, almost $10 million was given to the Metropolitan Museum of Art, over $8 million to the Bronx Zoo, nearly $7 million to the American Museum of Natural History, $6 million to the Brooklyn Museum, $5 million to the New York Botanical Garden. In 1992, each institution's share of the budget dropped by almost one-third. Smaller institutions, such as the Bronx Museum, the Studio Museum in Harlem, and the Staten Island Children's Museum, received around half a million dollars a year from the department. A much smaller portion of the department's budget, 5 percent, goes to specific cultural programs, including community programs. These are all small grants, between $3,000 and $15,000 each.

Although during the 1980s several Cultural Affairs Commissioners said they wanted to use city programs to support artists' housing, only about $1 million was available to renovate space for cultural groups in city-owned buildings. When a reporter asked the commissioner how the department could aid a small cultural group that wanted to expand, she replied that the only funds for that purpose were in a program development fund whose budget line of $821,000 had been eliminated at the end of the previous year. So it is not surprising that many artists consider the Department of Cultural Affairs unwilling or unable to support them (Munk 1990).

Both major and marginal cultural institutions were hard hit in the 1990s by severe cuts in grants from the city, state, and federal governments. While the city and state reduced funding because of their budget deficits, the federal government in the Bush administration also penalized cultural producers who offended the sensibilities of members of Congress and their organized constituents. These sanctions seem to have especially hurt New York artists, whose material and language are often sexually explicit. Moreover, before his term ended in 1992, President George Bush criticized some grants as "pork barrel politics" – that is, political favoritism – a charge repeated by Republican Mayor Rudolph Giuliani's deputy mayor for finance in 1993. Under these conditions, the City Council, the Manhattan borough president, and various nonprofit arts groups began small programs such as economic development assistance, revolving loans to buy or rent space, giving energy credits to theaters, and awarding grants for emergency repairs. Following the reduction in government funding, some nonprofit theaters closed their doors, while others reduced the number of productions, coproduced shows with other theaters, and laid off employees. Some visual artists formed art galleries not only to show their work, but also to become eligible for group health insurance plans.

Compared to budgets, data on employment in the arts is redundant yet incomplete and altogether unreliable. What is clear is that underemployment and unemployment in cultural production result in a synergy with other areas of the symbolic economy. An arts labor force of actors, musicians, and artists enhances consumer services such as restaurants and catering firms that rely on the cultural personae of their waiters.

Underemployed artists, writers, and performers also offer a depth of qualified personnel for culture industries from television soap operas and film production to art galleries and nonprofit arts organizations. And they do temporary office work in corporate firms.

While it is hard to gauge employment in the visual arts because artists hold so many different jobs, it is tricky to estimate employment in the theater because jobs are not continuous. Employment data are reported by work week. Workers in both production and performance are constantly shifting between film, television, and theater jobs. Moreover, theater workers do not always work in the city. Even when they are employed, they may be on the road. Although theater employment requires membership in a union, union membership does not indicate employment. In the early 1990s, only 40 percent of Actors Equity members were employed in the theater in any week. Many had nonunion acting gigs at conventions, at sales meetings, and in "industrials" (private training films). In the stagehands' union, 50 percent were employed in the theater in any week.

If we combine data from entertainment industry unions, the New York State and City Departments of Labor, and the U.S. census, we find a number of major occupations involved in the theater, including production and maintenance workers, actors, and directors. In the Garment Center, 1,500 factory workers produce theatrical costumes. There are about 1,700 porters and cleaners in legitimate theaters and major art and athletic centers (such as Lincoln Center and Yankee and Shea stadiums). There are 900 stagehands, including studio mechanics, carpenters, and electricians, working on Broadway and for television. Of these, 25 percent work only for Broadway theaters, 25 percent solely for television, and 50 percent shift between the two. The Stage Employees Union, Local 1, New York City, has a membership of 1,800 stagehands. Three hundred wardrobe attendants dress performers, do their makeup, and also (for extra pay in off hours) take care of the costumes by tagging them, cleaning and repairing them, and looking after accessories. Wardrobe attendants also work at other jobs in the entertainment field. And New York theaters employ 380 treasurers and ticket sellers.

Despite the large number of people who work in the arts in New York City, such work is precarious. In an average work week, 2,748 actors and actresses are working in unionized acting jobs in New York City (Actors Equity figures for 1990; all data in this paragraph are from interviews with union representatives). The total number employed nationwide is less than twice this figure. Six hundred twenty stage directors and choreographers work in the New York region, which includes New York State, New Jersey, and Connecticut. Most of them live in New York City. A large percentage of the 2,200 designers, costume and lighting designers, and scenic artists who work nationwide in theater, film, and TV, work in New York City. To qualify for a medical plan, according to the union, members must have an annual income greater than $12,000. Only 980, or fewer than half of them, qualify. Around 11,000 musicians are certified by union membership to work in New York City theaters. Fewer than 10 percent of them are employed at any one time.

As if to spite the dismal job conditions, New York State labor market data for New York City indicate that artists, musicians, and writers and editors are now among the top 45 major growth occupations (New York State Department of Labor 1990) (see table). But the fastest-growing of these categories – writers, artists, and musicians – are often underemployed or work on a free-lance basis. Other cultural occupations that have experienced and will continue to experience decline – journalists, newscasters, correspondents – are connected with mass media organizations that have been dramatically changed by corporate takeovers. In terms of both

▨ Cultural Occupations Among the 45 Fastest Growing
   Occupational Categories in New York City, 1990

Occupation	1988	1992
Writers, editors, including technicians	14,750	15,300
Broadcast technicians	2,010	1,790
Designers	14,320	13,710
Artists and related workers	12,890	13,550
Musicians	11,770	12,450
Dancers and choreographers	550	590
Producers, directors, actors, entertainers	12,280	12,940

Source: New York State Department of Labor 1990.

jobs and money, the symbolic economy has already been hol-
lowed out.

▓ A Culture Capital?

So the force field of culture is pulled in different directions.
If the arts are an industry, they mirror the corporate economy,
with growth in a large pool of free-floating workers who rely
on temporary and low-wage work, as both part-time employees
of nonprofit cultural institutions and independent contractors
(Port Authority 1993, 20-1, 23). New York City's major for-
profit culture industries include advertising, publishing,
music recording, the theater, and television: the very industries that for the past few years have continually engaged in
mergers and acquisitions, with large corporations buying up
smaller independents, jobs becoming more precarious, and
work contracted out (see Storper 1989). The costs of production, whether for Broadway shows, broadcast news, or MTV,
are so high they argue against maintaining a giant production
establishment. As a result, the possibility that a culture capital will offer lots of permanent jobs may be as remote as ever.

Even nonprofit cultural institutions are engaged in struggles over jobs and work rules typical of earlier periods of
industrial organization. In the 1990s, musicians' unions had
serious contract disputes over work rules in symphony orchestras and Broadway theaters. The restaurants in the Museum
of Modern Art replaced a union with a nonunion shop over the
protests of the vendor's unionized employees; several months
later, MOMA employees went on a one-day strike over a proposed 2 percent pay raise. Just when the governor's spokesper-
son declared New York "the cultural capital of the planet"
(*New York Times,* October 26, 1993), the rapid commercial
failure of a play by a well-known dramatist, Brian Friel,
caused Broadway theatrical producers to shake with anxiety
about the entire season.

Moreover, the growth of the symbolic economy since the
1970s has been much less centralized in New York City than
in previous eras. While performance artists, in general, continue to flock to large metropolitan areas where the theaters
are, visual artists have spread out to smaller cities and towns
(Heilbrun 1992). More and more, the threat to New York

City as a culture capital comes from the growth of regional theaters, local concentrations of artists, often connected to design schools and universities, and subcontracting from the city's culture industries to cheaper areas of the country.

New York still leads its closest competitors, Los Angeles and Chicago, in the number of artists employed in all creative occupations except actors and directors, where Los Angeles is way ahead (see table). But the rate of growth in most of the occupations where New York is adding creative artists and performers – actors and directors, photographers, authors, designers – is much slower than in Los Angeles and Chicago (see graph). In some categories – dancers, musicians and composers, and painters, sculptors, and craftspersons – New York has actually lost creative artists while Los Angeles and Chicago have gained. The artistic occupations in which New York excels are connected with jobs in business services rather than culture industries: these are architects, designers, and to some extent, photographers. Moreover, architects, the group that grew the most in New York during the 1980s, produce space in the form of rentable real estate at least as much as they produce visual art. These data paint a much gloomier picture of New York's symbolic economy than "the arts as an industry" suggests.

New York still exerts a considerable magnetic pull on cultural producers. But New York City's mission may now be

■ Employed Artists by Creative Occupations:
New York, Chicago, Los Angeles, 1980–1990

	New York		Los Angeles		Chicago	
	1980	1990	1980	1990	1980	1990
Actors and directors	13,824	16,983	16,081	24,048	1,839	3,503
Dancers	2,439	2,124	1,010	1,251	348	433
Musicians and composers	12,340	11,666	10,961	11,638	3,763	4,001
Painters, sculptors, craftspersons, and printmakers	15,640	15,058	9,032	11,464	5,903	6,970
Photographers	7,342	9,240	3,505	9,166	3,495	4,242
Authors	8,084	11,549	5,569	11,127	1,439	2,994
Designers	31,653	37,411	18,564	32,614	12,945	18,589
Architects	6,109	10,200	5,192	7,613	4,646	5,857
Total	97,431	114,231	69,914	108,921	34,378	46,589

Source: Adapted from Port Authority 1993: A6, Table A-17; based on National Endowment for the Arts, from U.S. Census data, 1980, 1990.

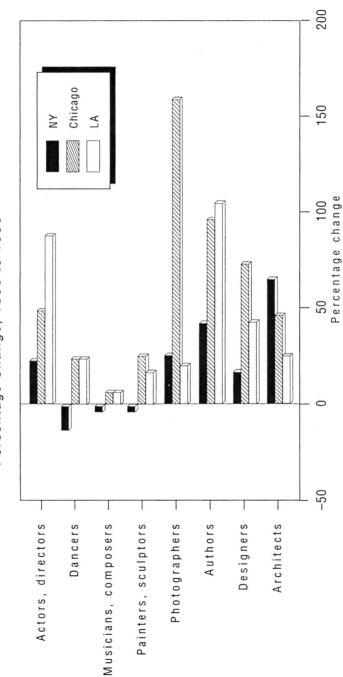

Employed Artists by Occupation:
Major Metropolitan Areas
Percentage Change, 1980 to 1990

Adapted from Port Authority 1993

to sell and display rather than make art. The city is more effective promoting commerce on the basis of its association with high culture than promoting cultural production at the base. The problem is whether promoting the sale of art will take resources away from cultural producers. The reasons why young artists and actors, dancers, and writers come to New York are partly economic - to sell their work - and partly social: to be associated with a variety of cultural communities. But there may be a contradiction between New York's reputation as a site of cultural innovation and as a cultural marketplace.

The art critic Robert Hughes (1990, p. 28) contrasts the "imperialism of the marketplace" regnant during the 1980s with the "imperialism of place" that made New York art so exciting in the mid 1960s. He blames the market for destroying the city's visual culture. "An immense bourse" surrounded by "new galleries, . . . premature canonizations, and record bids, and the conversion of much of its museum system into a promotional machine, the city's cultural vitality – its ability to inspire significant new art and foster it sanely – has been greatly reduced" (p. 33). Whether a city can survive as a bazaar for art, instead of a place where art is produced, is a question that lingers over New York's claim of being unique.

A culture capital cannot just function as an entrepôt of the arts. It must be a place where art is actually produced as well as sold and consumed. The transformation of urban space into "cultural space" depends on developing the two sides of cultural capital. It requires not only the material capital of cheap space and attractive buildings, an arts labor force, and financial investment in culture industries, but also the symbolic capital of vision – a vision of the city as a place where art, culture, and design are in the very air. It is also critical to have a large infrastructure of men and women whose job is to translate the work of cultural producers for a larger public. Both producers and consumers, themselves, they try out and exemplify new trends and then communicate them – in lifestyle and "city" magazines, movies, television shows, and critical reviews – to the rest of the world (Zukin 1991, 202–6).

Any attempt to sustain a vision of the city as aesthetically unique reflects a whole system of global exchanges of cultural products and producers. It also reflects local compromises on the use of space, from the establishment of historic and artists' districts to the expansion of art museums. But the really basic requirement of a culture capital is to have a large concentration of cultural producers. If vision is a source of power in the symbolic economy, it is impossible to ignore the collective power of cultural producers.

The notion of art as a public good also raises problems about a city's ability to maintain its identity as a culture capital despite demands to share the benefits cultural strategies bring. Since the 1970s, there has been both a democratization of urban politics and an aestheticization of the physical aspects of urban space. Democraticization suggests decentralization, recognition of community identities, satisfaction of popular will if not also popular tastes. But the cultural institutions, volunteer groups, and professional associations that mobilize around issues of visual culture are often elitist in their membership and assumptions. To the degree that the agenda of these groups and institutions has been adopted by other communities, it has influenced both architecture and public culture. But the hegemony of vision cannot improve the quality of life for most of the city's population. Groups cannot guarantee that their idea of aesthetic quality will limit future real estate development. Neither can they always persuade other cultural communities that aesthetics is the best measure of the public good.

Planned or not, a culture capital thrives in the intersection of the business, nonprofit, and arts economies. Conflicts are bound to occur over whose vision dominates objects and space: that of real estate markets or cultural communities. Even if cultural strategies of economic revitalization succeed, it is not inevitable that the economic value of the space overwhelm the cultural power of the symbols.

■ Artist and immigrant in the restaurant kitchen: Waiter picks up dish from cook before returning to dining room.

Photo by Alex Vitale.

5

ARTISTS AND IMMIGRANTS IN NEW YORK CITY RESTAURANTS

(with Louis Amdur, Janet Baus, Philana Cho,
Dalton Conley, Stephen Duncombe,
Herman Joseph, Daniel Kessler, Jennifer
Parker, and Huaishi Song)

For some years, the restaurant industry has been a favored
source of jobs for out-of-work artists, actors, and musicians.[9]
One reason they come to such culture capitals as New York
and Los Angeles is the size and reach of the city's symbolic
economy. Through a cross-pollination of markets, actors who
do not get theater jobs seek work in television, feature films,

9. This chapter is the result of an extraordinary collaboration with students
in a research seminar in urban sociology at the City University Graduate
Center. We wanted to do a one-semester research project that would combine
culture and political economy; I convinced the students to study restaurants. In
slightly different form, the chapter was published as "The Bubbling Cauldron:
Global and Local Interactions in New York City Restaurants," in *After Modernism: Global Restructuring and the Changing Boundaries of City Life*, volume
4 of *Comparative Urban and Community Research*, edited by Michael Peter
Smith (Transaction Publishers, 1992). Reprinted by permission of the publisher. We all acknowledge the participation in seminar discussions of Julia
Butterfield and Ramona Hernandez.

commercials, and "industrials." There is easy access to art galleries and record industry talent hunters. But artists, actors, and musicians often survive in the big city by earning money as waiters or bartenders. While a dramatic increase in eating out since the 1970s led all types of restaurants to expand their hiring across the board, the emergence of various types of "new wave" restaurants in major cities during the 1980s increased the hiring of artists and performers.

Besides the food itself, a widespread perception of artists' importance to a restaurant's ambiance has helped renew the reputation of restaurants as centers of urban cultural consciousness. Using the arts labor force as waiters has also helped re-present restaurant work as part of middle-class culture in the form of cuisine rather than working-class culture in the form of taking orders and clearing tables. Waiters are less important than chefs in creating restaurant food. They are no less significant, however, in creating the experience of dining out. For many people, oblivious of restaurant workers' social background, waiters are actors in the daily drama of urban culture.

It is possible to see in the restaurant waiter's new persona the inexorable attraction of "cultural capital." Capital in this sense is based on formal education, training in public speaking and the emotional projection of "self," and informal connoisseurship that enables waiters to speak with real or assumed authority about taste and other aesthetic strategies of domination. Being a gourmet does not, in principle, require great wealth. But it is impossible to imagine acquiring the experience of fine food and wine without certain resources of time and money (see Bourdieu 1984).

Much of the cultural capital of waiters, however, derives from their training in the arts. Like Disney World performers, they project an air of knowing or personable authority. They speak proper English, know how to talk to middle-class customers without being either servile or surly, and generally look good. Although the friendly but obtrusive waiter has been much caricatured in recent years – "Hi, I'm Jennifer, your waiter for the evening" – the change in waiters' persona that began in the late 1970s is part of a democratization of high-class restaurants from haughty "French" to accessible "American" style. This opening up of cultural consumption has in turn enabled certain types of restaurants to play a major role in a city's symbolic economy.

These restaurants are linked to the arts and tourism, to the "quality of life" a city offers corporate executives and those who eat out on expense accounts, and to a city's image as a culture capital. Innovative in cuisine, receptive to capital investment: restaurants that offer the latest news in high-class dining suggest an aura of sensual excitement akin to the latest financial information, publishing coup, or fashion scoop. Indeed, restaurants have become the public drawing rooms of the symbolic economy's business and creative elites. The more corporate expense accounts are concentrated in a city, the greater the resource base to support both haute cuisine and nouvelle alternatives (see Brake 1988; Zukin 1991, ch. 7).

Restaurants as a Cultural Site

In a culture capital, restaurants provide a meeting place for corporate patrons, culture industry executives, and artists. They are sites where new trends are discussed, gossip is exchanged, and deals are made. Restaurant staff, especially waiters, who have direct contact with customers, present themselves along with the menu. They may be seen as potential employees or as trendsetters by culture industry executives. The way they talk and dress shapes a large part of the restaurant's ambiance. Waiters not only provide a backdrop for business meetings, they also contribute to the production, circulation, and consumption of symbols. A restaurant's style is both implicitly and explicitly negotiated by waiters and management. The accents and appearance of waiters affirm distinctions between restaurants as surely as menu, price, and location.

Waiters are not the only source of a restaurant's role in facilitating the accumulation of cultural capital. Restaurants indicate social class and other distinctions. Being seen in a particular restaurant, or with a certain person, or occupying a "good" table are all indicators of power and status in both a city and an industry. By the same token, customers establish a restaurant's relative status. A restaurant that attracts social elites, celebrities, or industry leaders in any field gains glamour. Restaurant design also contributes to the production of a city's visual style. Architects and interior designers, restaurant consultants, and restaurant industry magazines diffuse global trends that are adapted to local styles. Owners are amenable to submitting their own vision to these agents' mediation. They even hire publicists to further the presentation of a specific image. Restaurateurs often appear as a cultural synthesis of the artist, the entrepreneur, and the social organizer. The restaurant itself is both theater and performance. It serves and helps create the symbolic economy.

In a curious way, restaurants also synthesize global and local cultures. They receive culinary styles of preparation and trends from other parts of the country and the world and formalize them in their menus. Yet they also adapt strange food to local tastes and eating patterns. "Mexican Food is Rated No. 1 in Ethnic Foods," says a takeout menu from Fresco Tortillas on 42nd Street near my office. "In Keeping with That, all Our Food is Made Fresh without Artificial Spices, Chemical Spices, M.S.G., Lard or Preservatives." Moreover, restaurants form geographical clusters by restaurant type, which then become such neighborhood institutions as Little Italy or Chinatown. In New York restaurant cuisine, the local reterritorializes the global.

Restaurants similarly bring together a global and local labor force and clientele. The restaurant industry's labor market mobilizes immigrants and natives whose networks, both cultural and economic, influence a restaurant's style. Restaurants in New York and other large cities with immigrant populations may have always been "global" in their hiring patterns. But the rapid increase in immigration in recent years has drawn attention to immigrants and where they serve in restaurants, relative to other groups. It makes people who eat in restaurants more conscious of an ethnic, as well as a social, division of labor. In New York delicatessens, authoritarian old Jewish waiters have been replaced by younger women and Latinos, and sandwiches are made by Latino and Asian men. In the espresso bars owned by a large gourmet food store, many of the counter servers are Asian and busboys are African. In elegant, French-style restaurants, waiters are Europeans or Americans, and the busboys are

■ "We can do anything": Chinese workers prepare tacos at Fresco Tortillas.

Photo by Alex Vitale.

Mexicans or Dominicans. Many Korean owners of fast food franchises hire Mexicans.

With the exception of high-status chefs, the division of labor in restaurants along ethnic and national lines generally parallels the division into "front" and "back" regions with higher social status in the front and lower social status in the back. Overall, a restaurant's status is influenced by the cultural style of its work force and the cultural style, ethnicity, and economic level of its clientele. While some restaurants serve the tourist trade, and are appropriately déclassé, others develop a specific social status because they become meeting places of an international business class or sites to maintain ethnic contacts. When we say that restaurants are "transnational" social institutions (see Smith and Feagin 1987), we mean that they bring together global and local markets of both employees and clienteles (see chart of labor force and clientele).

Analyzing these connections requires a new perspective on the restaurant's social role. While it seems to be among

▪ A restaurant's labor force and clientele: From local to global institution.

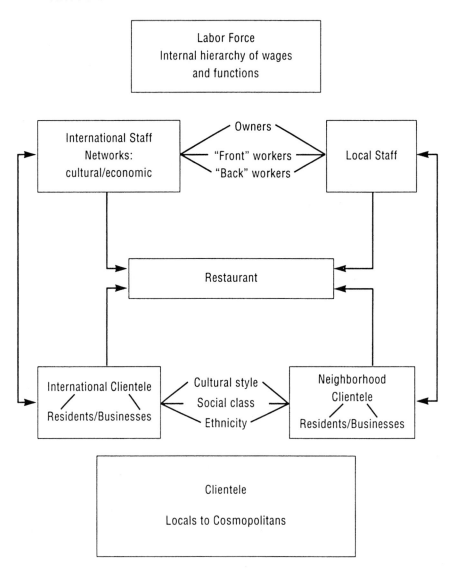

the most "local" of social institutions, a restaurant is also a remarkable focus of transnational economic and cultural flows. As an employer, a restaurant owner negotiates new functional interdependencies that span local, regional, and global scales. Moreover, a restaurant, as a place where cultural products are created and reproduced, affects the transnational diffusion and eventual fusion of cultural styles.

▓ Immigrants and Global Trends

The development of the restaurant industry in New York is inextricable from global processes of change. Not only does it correspond to the development of the symbolic economy and the general growth of services, especially high-level business services, it also reflects the movement of investment capital around the world and a steady supply, since the U.S. immigration laws were changed in 1965 and 1986, of "new" immigrants.

Restaurants generate a large number of low-wage and "dead-end" jobs that are often filled by immigrants who lack English language skills and U.S. educational credentials (Bailey 1985). These factors, and the restaurant industry's traditional barriers to unionization, make this a pliable labor force. Immigrants' lack of attachment to labor unions, their acceptance of unusual work hours, and their willingness to work hard for a subminimum wage – especially if they lack a green card – are somewhat like artists' pliability as workers. But while hotels and restaurants are an employer of first and last resort for both groups, artists, particularly those with a Euro-American background, are employed in jobs requiring more contact with clients (see Waldinger 1992).

Low-wage restaurant jobs support the kind of social inequality described as polarization, which divides haves from have-nots in the urban economy by work, wages, and prospects for advancement. Yet it is possible for immigrants in the restaurant industry to accumulate enough savings and on-the-job training to open restaurants of their own (Bailey 1985; Waldinger 1990). They may live as bachelors or single women in crowded dormitory apartments and pool their savings with family members'. No matter how low their wages are, they often send a large portion of their earnings to their home

countries and return to live there. Regardless of harsh conditions, immigrant restaurant workers still nourish dreams of
upward social mobility. Restaurants offer both owners and
employees a good chance to accumulate economic and cultural
capital.

For some reason, restaurants have not attracted scholarly
attention as major sites in the "new international division
of labor." Researchers have looked, on the one hand, at the
internationalization of manufacturing rather than services
(e.g., Sassen 1987; Perry 1987; Scott and Storper 1986; Hill
1989). On the other hand, small firms in the services seem
less dramatic than either garment or electronics factories,
often depicted as sweatshops, or informal labor in domestic
situations (home care, child care, housekeeping, gardening),
sidewalk peddling, and semi-legal activities. But the services,
which account for a greater proportion of job growth, even
among unskilled workers, are a logical site of inquiry. Small
service firms such as restaurants relate even more directly
than manufacturing or informal work to the simultaneous
processes of global and local social reproduction that characterize many urban populations today. They are places of interaction with a wider public, incubators of multiculturalism,
agents of socialization to dominant norms or what remains of
acculturation. Jobs in such services as the restaurant industry
may also contribute to the differential social experiences of
native-born and immigrant minorities (see Bailey and Waldinger 1991). African Americans have been replaced by European immigrants in hotel and restaurant jobs since the turn
of the 20th century (Ovington 1911) and by West Indian and
other immigrants since the 1980s (Waldinger 1992). Small
businesses, particularly in the service sector, may escape regulations associated with affirmative action policies. The face-
to-face nature of work in retail sales and restaurants may lead
employers to hire applicants from certain racial and ethnic
categories and exclude others strictly on the basis of the way
they look and talk.

These issues shift our focus from spaces to people, from
views to interviews, from the world of high culture to food.
Yet restaurants are also public spaces where social diversity
is negotiated and designed. They provide a stage and a scenario for acting out a public culture, from the moral "incivility"

or superficial social relations of dining out (Finkelstein 1989) to the development of socially acceptable personae. Moreover, by linking immigrants and artists in labor markets, restaurants indicate some of the ways men and women of different social backgrounds find a place in the symbolic economy.

▓ New York Restaurants

The restaurant industry is one of the fastest growing industries in the United States. It employs over 5 million people nationwide, including 130,000 at more than 5,000 restaurants in New York City (U.S. Department of Labor 1989). During the 1980s, the New York restaurant industry alone added 20,000 jobs. Over 33 percent of the work force in New York City restaurants are foreign born, not including increasing numbers of undocumented immigrants (Winnick 1990). There are no data on the number of artists in restaurant jobs.

Despite growing numbers of jobs, average wages in the restaurant industry have continually fallen below average weekly earnings across all industries. Both "front" and "back" employees earn low wages. While "front" employees typically earn more than "back" employees, excluding chefs, most of their income comes from tips. "Back" employees rely only on their wages. Average weekly earnings of restaurant employees increased by only about $130 from 1978 to 1988, at a time when average wages in all industries increased by more than $400. Therefore, restaurant employees earn a steadily decreasing portion of wages paid to workers in all industries in New York City: 51.4 percent in 1980, but only 39.7 percent in 1988 (see graph). To some degree, this decline can be explained by the dramatic increase in a small number of high-paying jobs in financial services, which skews the total average wage (New York State Department of Labor 1986, 1988a, 1988b, 1990).

To examine artists and immigrants in the entire range of New York City restaurants would require a huge research effort. Working together with fewer than a dozen graduate students in a research seminar in urban sociology, I persuaded the class that we could do an interesting preliminary study. One of the students had worked for a year as a hostess in a restaurant in Queens and had good relations with the owners

■ New York City wages and employment, 1980s.

Top line: % of NYC average wages earned by restaurant workers
Bottom line: % job growth in restaurant industry of total NYC job growth

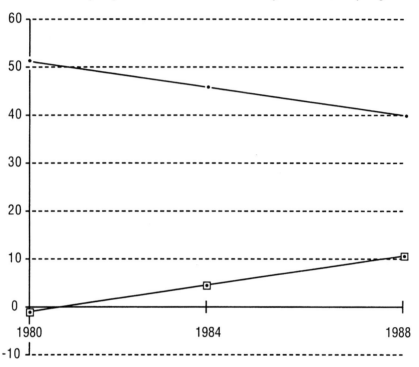

Sources: New York State Department of Labor 1986 and 1990.

and staff. Another student often ate in a Chinese restaurant in Manhattan, not in Chinatown, where he chatted with the waiters. A third student liked a Brazilian restaurant near his home and made it his business to start talking with the owner. It turned out that the restaurant owners from Queens owned another restaurant in Manhattan. On the basis of these contacts, we made up a sample of four restaurants to study. We spent a lot of time discussing whether these restaurants were likely sites of the symbolic economy. Our guidelines were that the restaurants should be neither too "haute" nor too "ethnic," and while the students could not necessarily afford to eat there frequently, they should not feel out of place hanging around. We were guided, in general, by three main criteria: price, location, and "local character." We wound up with three restaurants in Manhattan and one in Astoria, Queens.

Working mainly with immigrants and with owners who may pay workers off the books, we knew it was crucial to establish a rapport with our respondents. We reassured both groups that we would not share our interviews with government authorities. Nevertheless, a small number of employees refused to be interviewed. None of the owners refused.

We made up around 20 questions for both owners and employees. These included questions on the national origins and recruitment of the restaurant labor force, their education and occupational background, their expectations and real conditions of work, the organization of work, employers' hiring preferences, means of access to jobs, living and commuting arrangements, earnings, and career aspirations. The owners were also asked about the sources of their investment capital. All interviews were done at the restaurants, in English, Spanish, and Chinese.[10]

The first restaurant, Aperture, is designed to be an "artsy" place where its clientele, drawn from the photographic, graphic arts, advertising, and publishing industries in the Flatiron district of lower Fifth Avenue, can feel at home. Larry, one of three co-owners, designed the restaurant himself. Theatrical track lighting with colored gels casts warm hues on the white walls. Jazz, Motown, and Europop tapes, mixed by Larry, create a musical backdrop to conversation. The restrooms are built into hollow false columns that imitate the area's loft structures. A "curator" who is not on the restaurant staff chooses monthly art exhibits, and there is an "opening" for each show. Larry is in his early 30s, a native New Yorker, born in Astoria and raised in a solidly middle-class area of Queens. He and his father own the Queens restaurant in our sample. Although Larry has been a co-owner of that restaurant with his father for several years, he exercises control over most daily aspects of Aperture. His two co-owners at Aperture are Egyptians, one in his late 20s – the chef – and the other in his 30s – the manager. Aperture seats 62 with 10 more chairs at the bar. The restaurant was opened in 1985.

---

10. All restaurants, owners, and employees appear under pseudonyms. Supplementary information on the restaurant industry comes from interviews conducted by Jenn Parker, Priscilla Ferguson, and me.

Mia, the second restaurant, is a Chinese restaurant near Gramercy Park, the only private square in New York City. This is a middle-class neighborhood just to the east of the Flatiron district, with apartment houses, banks, insurance company headquarters, advertising firms, and a college. Mia's modern exterior and sleek decor create a posh "American" atmosphere. There are none of the stereotypical red tables and dragon paintings of U.S. Chinese restaurants. Instead, Mia has black-top tables with small vases of fresh flowers, black and white ceramic floor tiles, and a slick black bar. The only Chinese references are the menu, which includes Szechuan-style food, the chopsticks on the table, and a sole Chinese among the waiters. The owner, Lee, comes from Taiwan. His family has owned a restaurant in Taiwan for many years, and his brothers run several restaurants in New York. Mia seats 60 and 10 at the bar and was opened in 1985. Lee makes all menu decisions and designed the restaurant with his family.

Rain Forest, the third restaurant, was opened in 1987 on the Upper West Side not far from Lincoln Center and the gentrified shopping areas of Broadway and Columbus Avenue. Despite its Brazilian motif and menu, the owner, Don Pedro ("Pete" to his customers), is neither Brazilian nor Portuguese but Spanish. Stylized murals on white walls depict forest scenes from the Amazon. The restaurant attracts a middle- and upper-middle-class clientele of Americans from the neighborhood and Latinos from around the city, as well as members of the Latino diplomatic community. Pete formerly owned another Brazilian restaurant in New York, which he sold when the rent was raised. He then worked as a headwaiter at another Brazilian restaurant, from which he took several waiters and a chef to open Rain Forest. Pete makes all the decisions on decor and menu design as well as management. The restaurant seats 107.

Our fourth restaurant, Neptune's, originally opened as a seafood restaurant in Astoria more than 50 years ago. It seats 60. The present owner, John, bought Neptune's around 1970 after it had closed. An immigrant from Italy as a child, he turned it into an Italian restaurant but kept the original name because of the restaurant's reputation in the neighborhood. John initially had three partners; in 1985, his son Larry bought out the remaining two partners and joined John as co-owner. Neptune's is located on a busy commercial street under the elevated subway tracks, a 20-minute ride from Manhattan. Inside, the restaurant has dark wood paneling, mirrored walls, glass brick partitions, and track lighting, creating a subdued, elegant effect. Fishing nets and seashore objects complement an earlier theme, but Larry is in the process of redecorating with "French country" fabrics, wicker baskets, fresh flowers, and paintings. The new decor is somewhat at odds with the menu of traditional Italian dishes and adaptations of nova cucina. Bottles of mineral water are set out on the tables bearing price tags. Since becoming co-owner, Larry has made all the decisions concerning menu and decor. Astoria is historically an immigrant community. In the past 10 years, however, the Irish, Italian, and Greek populations have been supplemented by new immigrants from Asia and Latin America. Besides new residents who resemble gentrifiers, a new source of Neptune's business has been a lunchtime crowd of people who work at a nearby television production center for film, advertising, and television.

Restaurant Employees

Our 35 respondents come from 17 different countries in North Africa, the Middle East, Asia, Scandinavia, the Caribbean, North America, and Latin America. Ranging in age from their late teens to their mid 40s, except for one owner in his late 50s, they include two busboys and a cleaner from Bangladesh; a bartender and two waiters from Brazil; a delivery man, waitress, chef, and take-out manager from China; a waiter, bartender and two owners from Egypt; a cook from Haiti; a manager from Hong Kong; a waiter from Israel; an owner from Italy; a cleaner, cook, and salad man from Mexico; a busboy from Morocco; a waitress from Norway; a waiter from the Philippines; a waiter from Portugal; an owner from Spain, and an owner from Taiwan. Those who migrated to New York from other states include four waitresses from Ohio, Michigan, and Missouri, and a bartender from California. There are only three native New Yorkers in our sample. They were born in Queens and work in the restaurant in Queens. One is Larry, co-owner of that restaurant.

Common to all these countries is the growing number of service jobs in relation to industrial and agricultural employment. In 14 of these countries, jobs in the services far outweigh any other kind of employment. Only a few of our respondents came with industrial skills and experience – an electrician from Brazil and an engineer from Egypt. However, many respondents did come with experience in service occupations. They include a waiter from Brazil, a chef and busboy from Egypt, two office workers from China, a restaurant worker from Haiti, a dishwasher and other low-skilled kitchen staff from Mexico, a salesperson from the Philippines, a social worker from Israel, an airport host from Morocco, and a dancer from Norway. A few had professional experience, such as a real estate manager from Portugal (now a headwaiter) and an agricultural engineer from Egypt (now a bartender). Eight were students before they came to New York.

Nine respondents expected to find work in a restaurant in New York. They either had restaurant experience, as in the case of a previous restaurant owner from Haiti who now works as a cook, a dishwasher from Mexico who is also a cook, and a waiter from Brazil who is still a waiter; or they had been informed about restaurant job opportunities by friends or relatives from their country who already lived in New York City. The rest of the respondents seem to have gravitated into restaurant work. It is relatively easy to get and keep a restaurant job. The flexible work hours enable employees to support primary interests in the arts or university studies.

Most of the employee respondents, 17 out of 29, got their jobs through personal connections – a friend or relative – or they had worked with the owner or chef before. The second most relied upon method was simply walking in off the street to ask for a job. Seven of the respondents obtained their jobs this way. A few of the immigrants, unlike the native New Yorkers and U.S. migrants, found their jobs through a newspaper ad or an employment agency (see table on access to restaurant jobs).

Looking at the types of jobs employees do and their educational level confirms a polarization in restaurants between those who work in the "front," i.e., the dining room or bar area, and those who work in the "back," i.e., the kitchen. Out of 19 "front" respondents in our sample, 12 are immigrants,

▩ Access to Restaurant Jobs for Immigrants, Migrants, and Native
New Yorkers (*n* = 29)

Geographical Origin	Personal Connection	Newspaper Ad	Walked in	Agency
Immigrants	10	3	4	2
Native New Yorkers	2	0	0	0
U.S. migrants	5	0	3	0

3 are U.S. migrant artists or actors, and 1 is an immigrant
dancer from Western Europe. The majority of those who work
in the "front" and come in contact with customers hold college
degrees or are now college students, while no one who works
in the "back" has any college education. Out of 13 waiters, 4
hold bachelor's degrees, 1 has an acting degree, and 3 have
some college education. Only five waiters have no higher education. One of our three bartenders has a bachelor's degree,
one has an engineering degree, and one has no college education. Out of three busboys, one has a bachelor's degree, one
went to bartending school, and one has no college or restaurant
education. A host has an associate's degree in hotel management. Of the two managers interviewed, one has training in
TV production and the other has no higher education.
Although college graduates in our sample include both immigrants and U.S. citizens, the respondents with no higher education are all immigrants except for one native New Yorker.

Native-born employees who migrated to New York from
out of state generally expect to pursue careers in the arts or
professions. Immigrants and native-born New Yorkers, on the
other hand, expect to make careers in the restaurant industry.

While most of the immigrant employees live in the outer
boroughs of Queens and Brooklyn, the arts employees mainly
live in Manhattan, followed by Brooklyn and Queens. All
employees who live in Brooklyn work in restaurants in Manhattan. Queens residents in our sample work in Queens as
well as in Manhattan. The arts employees and those in professional schools tend to live with friends. However, most immigrants in our sample live with family members, although some
live alone. Owners live in the suburbs; all employees except
one live in the city. A bartender and a chef own their own

homes, but the rest rent apartments, and one busboy rents a room. There is no correlation between immigrants, country of origin, and place of residence (see table).

■ The Social Division of Labor

Differences between immigrants and the arts work force parallel differences between the front and back regions of a restaurant. Four vignettes of respondents who work at Aperture and Neptune's in different positions – the waitress Linda, busboy Hassan, salad man Jesus, and chef Medhat – indicate contrasts in both their expectations of restaurant work and the cultural capital they bring to it. They also suggest contrasts in the labor markets of immigrants and cultural producers who work alongside them.

Linda

Linda is a 23-year-old, Euro-American waitress at Aperture. She was raised in a midwestern suburb. After graduating from college with a degree in theater arts, she moved to New York in 1990 to look for a job in the musical theater. She found work as a telemarketer but was laid off after three months. Linda walked into Neptune's because she lives in an apartment nearby and got a job on the waitstaff despite having no restaurant experience. She was given on-the-job training by the other waitresses. The owner suggested she apply for a job on waitstaff at Aperture, his restaurant in Manhattan.

Linda now has a role in a national touring company production of a Broadway hit that will soon be on the road. She has no plans to continue in the restaurant industry. She has met many theater people at Aperture and finds the job good for making business contacts.

■ Place of Residence of Immigrants and Arts Work Force ($n = 29$)

Place of Residence	Immigrants	Arts Work Force
Manhattan	7	3
Outer Borough	15	3
New Jersey	1	0

Linda lives in Astoria with her boyfriend and has a 25-minute commute to work by subway. She has no health insurance, works 36 hours a week, and makes $400 in a good week from salary and tips. None of her family are in the restaurant business. Her father and brother are "corporate types."

Hassan

Hassan has worked as a busboy at Neptune's for four months. He is unusual there in that he found his job through an employment agency. Moroccan by birth, Hassan immigrated to the United States in 1986. He had worked in "hospitality" at an airport in Morocco and thought of restaurant work as a quick entry into the U.S. economy. "If I can find something better, it will be welcome for me. But the first thing is that you have to earn a living. The fastest way is the restaurant because you don't need too much knowledge about anything." With his recently earned certificate in bartending and improved English-language skills, Hassan hopes to move up in the restaurant industry. He is in his late 20s.

Like the waitstaff, Hassan earns most of his money in tips. Clearly not employed for the minimum wage of $4.25 an hour, he earns only $10 for an eight-hour lunch or dinner shift, and another $250–400 a week in tips. He rents a room by himself in Astoria. He has a sister and brother in France and parents in Morocco. His friends, who are Moroccan, Egyptian, and Brazilian, reflect the ethnic diversity, tolerance, and numerical strength of immigrants that he prizes here. He lived in Florida before coming to New York.

Jesus

A 22-year-old from a small town in Mexico, Jesus has worked in New York City for six years. Now he is a salad man at Aperture, having worked his way up from the entry-level position of dishwasher: "Everybody come don't know English, so started like that." The chef brought Jesus with him from Neptune's, where they had worked together. He has been at Aperture 15 months.

The chef is slowly teaching Jesus how to cook. Jesus believes that in nine or ten years he may become "a chef or a nice cook." He plans to climb the restaurant ladder by degrees. Since his English-language skills are limited and his time is fully occupied with work, he depends on the chef for his advancement. Jesus left school in Mexico planning to work in the restaurant business. He has taken some English classes but is not confident about his ability to converse. Eventually, however, and despite his learning to cook, Jesus "would like to do something out of the kitchen" [in the "front"].

Jesus makes $320 for a six-day week. He has no health insurance. His commute to Manhattan from a suburb in New Jersey takes one hour each way. He lives with his mother and father, who is also a salad man. He plays guitar in his spare time and relaxes "because the work is really hard." Jesus does not like New York and misses home. He is friends with other Mexicans in New York but cannot socialize with them easily because they live far away.

Medhat

Medhat is the chef at Aperture and one of three co-owners. He learned how to cook in a two-year restaurant apprenticeship in Cairo after graduating from high school. He was trained to prepare Continental cuisine and is not familiar with Egyptian recipes. Like other chefs in Manhattan, he reads cooking magazines and attends trade shows in search of new ideas. Medhat designs the menu at Aperture. As executive chef, he is responsible for ordering the food and managing the kitchen. He also has general supervisory duties. The owner brought Medhat with him from Neptune's when he opened Aperture.

Medhat pays for his own health insurance. Although his income and hours vary depending on business, he says that he is not making good money because of the high cost of living. He lives in Astoria with his wife, an immigrant from Central America, and newborn child. He says they would like to move away from there but cannot afford to do so. He has no time for hobbies. Medhat is 27 years old and plans to stay in the restaurant industry or enter another entrepreneurial field. His family in Cairo are professionals. Medhat came to New York hoping to get rich.

These four vignettes illustrate both the precariousness and flexibility of restaurant employment. While job applicants who have cultural capital – approximated by English-language skills and middle-class background – find their way to jobs in the front of the restaurant or at the top of the kitchen hierarchy, it is possible for others to work their way up from entry-level positions. Ultimate career goals, however, differ. For the arts labor force, restaurants are always a temporary job – even though other interviews we have done with waiters indicate that they generally continue working in the restaurant industry for many years. For immigrants, restaurants offer both entry-level jobs and access to entrepreneurial opportunities. As they perfect their language skills and become knowledgeable about the industry, restaurants provide their own ladder for internal promotions. Yet waitstaff and kitchen staff all depend on their personal relations with the chef and owner. They lack health insurance, cannot anticipate promotions, and earn less than the minimum wage.

▨ The Ethnic Division of Labor

It is important to note that all four restaurants hire an ethnically diverse work force, although those that feature an "ethnic" cuisine do tend to hire a large percentage of employees from that ethnic group. Ethnicity does not entirely predict the positions for which people are hired. It is true that American-born whites occupy "front" positions rather than work in the "back." Only two black employees appear in these restaurants, and they are both at the Chinese restaurant, Mia. One, an American-born actress, is on waitstaff in the "front." The other, a man who ran a restaurant in the Caribbean, works as a butcher and cook. At the Chinese restaurant, the owner, manager, take-out manager, delivery man, and chefs are Chinese, as is one of the waiters. The other waiters are native-born Americans or other Asians, and the bartender is from the Middle East. By contrast, at the Brazilian restaurant, the owner is Spanish and the cook is Mexican; both lived in Brazil, where they learned the cuisine. The waiters (who double as busboys) are Brazilian, and the headwaiter is Portuguese, so all the "front" employees speak that language. Hiring patterns at these two ethnic restaurants suggest that cultural experience is necessary to prepare the cuisine, but this experience may be achieved by a learning process as well as ascribed by group membership.

John, the owner of the restaurant in Queens, refers to the staff as a "United Nations." The restaurant hires a large percentage of Middle Eastern employees. The deployment of the staff indicates a de facto ethnic division of labor that is typical of many middle-level restaurants in New York. A host and a waiter are the only native New Yorkers. Another waiter and a busboy are from the Middle East, the bartender is from Brazil, a busboy and two cleaners are from North Africa, Mexico, and Bangladesh, and the Italian-born owner is the chef. The owner states that he does most of his hiring from the neighborhood. According to his son, "In Queens it is easy to find a waiter because they all know each other. When they hear of a job opening they'll come in droves." Nevertheless, he also says that he hires waiters through an employment agency. For his other restaurant in Manhattan, he claims he places an advertisement in the *Village Voice* or the *New York Times*.

In fact, the staff at the Manhattan restaurant is predominantly either U.S.-born arts workers who got their jobs by walking in off the street or Middle Eastern immigrants who knew the owner from working at the restaurant in Queens, or walked in off the street. Both arts workers and immigrants work in the "front." In the "back," there is a Mexican salad man (Jesus) and an Egyptian chef (Medhat).

The owner's son indicates the difference between employees at Aperture and Neptune's by explicitly contrasting Manhattan and Queens. The implicit contrast, however, is between artists and immigrants. "In Manhattan, you have a lot of actors, artists, or those who are aspiring to be. In Queens, you get all kinds who are looking to be in the business." He emphasizes the importance of hiring "front" staff who adequately represent the cultural capital invested in the restaurant. "If a waiter is not what you perceive the restaurant to be, the customer's perception will be completely distorted. So they [waiters] mold the restaurant. They turn the restaurant into what it is supposed to be." For this owner, there is no possibility of exchanging the cultural capital of different groups of workers: "If I had my Manhattan waitstaff in Queens, it wouldn't work. Some of my waiters in Manhattan are gay, but it is okay there, whereas it wouldn't work in Queens. It would be offensive."

Yet workers in the "back" are interchangeable in the owner's eyes. Their lack of skills and English language – and their inability to get other kinds of jobs – enable them to establish a niche in the low-paid positions, at least for a time. "I have a good set of 'boys,' " the owner says of his employees. He is thinking especially of the porters, those who do the cleaning up, the lowest people on the restaurant's staff.

For porter, you get a certain ethnic group that seems to go into that. Maybe five-six years ago it was a different ethnic group. Now we're coming into a Mexican domination of that position. Five years ago, it was an influx of Slavic people. You cannot get an American boy or young man to wash dishes or be a porter. It's beneath them.

One summer we tried the Youth Program, to give a job to a needy youth. They sent a few boys over and as soon as they heard they had to clean or wash dishes, they said, "Oh, we won't do that." Well, what did they expect to do, become a brain surgeon in a restaurant? So you have to depend on one ethnic group. Who knows who it will be after the Mexicans? Lately, a fellow from Bangladesh started working here, kind of out in left field, but he happens to be a very good worker. They all get along very well.

Restaurant industry talk confirms that Mexicans have begun to dominate the lowest-skill kitchen positions, perhaps because most Mexican immigrants in New York come from rural areas and lack urban job skills. The word in the immigrant communities is that Mexicans are hard workers. In addition to Neptune's, the Chinese restaurant Mia also has two Bangladeshi busboys who were students in that country and now live in Queens. We can speculate that Bangladeshi immigrants, like Mexicans, lack English-language skills, "urbane" manners, and the European or culturally "white" appearance that would appeal to owners for positions in the "front." Mexicans and Bangladeshi contrast with Egyptians, North Africans, Brazilians, and Colombians – that is, "Europeanized" immigrants from former European colonies or settlements – who are hired mainly for "front" jobs and as chefs, especially in mainstream restaurants.

Alternatively, as recent immigrants, Bangladeshi and Mexicans lack the contacts and internal entrepreneurs that slightly older immigrant groups have developed. Yet certain Middle Eastern and Latin immigrants have objective or subjective characteristics that other groups lack. On the one hand, Egyptians (but not Brazilians) in our sample have either done apprenticeships in Continental restaurants or attended college before they immigrated. Most come from middle or upper-middle-class backgrounds. On the other hand, they have the culturally "white" persona and middle-class manners that many restaurant owners like. "We have Egyptian waiters," the owner of Neptune's says. "They have class. They're great waiters. They have great table manners. They're all that way."

By the same token, immigrants with cultural capital make up a pool of relatively loyal labor for promotion. Lacking investment capital and family connections in this country, they are dependent on their employers for giving them access to entrepreneurial opportunity. As the owner of Aperture says about his two Arab co-owners, who get a share of the profits, if there are any, "I feel very comfortable with them. I knew they weren't going anywhere when they were working for me before, but they were working just as hard so I knew I could have faith in them." All three derive benefits from the co-owner arrangement. For this owner, "it is good because I have the loyalty and initiative I wanted from them to sustain the business without my having to be there [all the time]. For these two guys, I would say they may be able to save for five or six years and eventually open up their own restaurant."

For potential immigrant entrepreneurs, the restaurant industry is both an easy and a difficult point of entry into the mainstream economy. The failure rate of restaurants in Manhattan is said to be 75 percent during the first year of operation. Rents are high. A decor is expensive and may require periodic changes. Moreover, immigrants who prove successful in mainstream restaurants must already have cultural capital.

Nevertheless, the lure of entrepreneurship is as strong as the dream of return. The Egyptian manager, one of the two immigrant co-owners of Aperture, is an ambitious man who completed three of the four required years of law school in Egypt. He began working in restaurants in New York because he chose to become an illegal immigrant by staying in the city after his visa expired. As he moved from restaurant to restaurant, he was promoted from dishwasher, a typical unskilled entry position, to busboy, waiter, and waiter's captain. He became a manager at Neptune's before moving to Aperture with the owner. He lives alone in Astoria, works six days a week, 13–14 hours a day, and has no social life. He plans to pay off his debts in New York, go back to Egypt, and finish law school.

Similarly, the cook, headwaiter, and a waiter at the Brazilian restaurant all plan to open their own restaurants one day. Another waiter expects to remain a waiter. Although they have lived in the United States far longer than the other immigrants in our sample – 13 to 18 years – they also plan to return to their country of origin. In this they are typical of most new immigrants.

■ Restaurant Owners

Five out of six owners in our sample are immigrants, originally from Italy, Egypt, Taiwan, and Spain. This is a somewhat higher percentage than in the New York restaurant industry, at least as that industry was in the early 1980s (Bailey 1985). The sixth owner is the son of the Italian immigrant owner and was born in Queens. Capital for starting the restaurants has come from personal savings as well as mortgages and loans from local banks. Since New York banks do not generally grant loans to open a restaurant, these loans may have been obtained on other grounds. Except for Lee, it appears capital was not obtained outside New York City. Five of our six owners had extensive job experience in the restaurant industry before becoming owners. Thus restaurants are a primary source for earning and saving the necessary capital to become an owner.

Don Pedro, the Spanish owner of the Brazilian restaurant, first immigrated to Brazil. In 1961, he came to New York City, where he worked as a waiter, engaged in some business ventures, and got mortgages and bank loans to open a Brazilian restaurant. Lee, the Chinese owner of Mia, has family in the restaurant business in both Taiwan and New York City. Three years after immigrating to New York, in 1973, and working at his brothers' restaurants, he decided to open his own restaurant. He relied mainly on bank loans for capital. John, the owner of the restaurant in Queens, immigrated to New York City from Italy as a child before World War II. He was a hairstylist in Astoria for ten years before buying the restaurant with three partners at a very low price. His son, the only nonimmigrant owner, worked for a large restaurant chain and started his own catering business in Manhattan, which provided him with the capital to join in partnership with his father at the restaurant in Astoria. He eventually opened two more restaurants in Manhattan, one of which is Aperture. His two Egyptian co-owners began their restaurant careers in New York City as low-skilled kitchen workers and eventually became waiters at Neptune's. They saved their earnings as restaurant employees and took out bank loans.

Individually owned restaurants are a projection of the owner's personality and family ties. These owners exercise daily operating control over most aspects of the restaurants. They also determine the highest level to which staff can rise. A seemingly individual expression, such as a restaurant's decor or theme, may in fact reflect a collective family decision. Lee says that Mia's modern motif was "designed . . . according to the tradition of my family and my own idea." All the family's restaurants bear the name of a family member; Mia is the English name of one of Lee's sisters. Larry, the co-owner of Aperture and Neptune's prides himself on choosing the menu and decor at both restaurants by himself. He pays equal attention to restaurant trends as reported in industry magazines, seminars, and food shows, his local customer base, and his personal desire for change. He tells us he has to be careful that the people he hires translate without violating his vision of what the restaurant should be. He expects his "excellent cooks" (not "chefs") to cook a recipe the way he gives it to them. The owner wants a certain amount of skill in this job, but he also wants pliability and will not pay high wages. "This position requires someone with not too much talent and not too little talent, so it is a tough position to fill."

In fact, this is the job description that most owners and chef-owners give for a chef's position. Unlike an elite restaurant, however, a moderate-price mainstream restaurant like Aperture or Neptune's will hire new immigrants for chef's positions. Chef's positions in New York's elite restaurants are still dominated by West Europeans (mainly French) and increasingly by Americans of European origin; a small number of Asians, especially Japanese, have begun to work as chefs in top-ranked kitchens. Occasionally, you find a sous-chef in an elite restaurant who is an Asian, African American, or Latin American of European decent. Elite chefs tend to be "professionals"; i.e., they have completed a traditional European apprenticeship or graduated from a vocational cooking school or culinary academy. Alternatively, they have had some college education and "switched careers" by doing apprenticeships in other elite kitchens. This is especially true of middle-class Americans who decide they want to be chefs. By contrast, immigrant cooks in full-service restaurants get on-the-job training in food preparation.

Restaurant owners do not often fire people. Yet they can be harsh taskmasters and do not necessarily command the workers' respect. Because owners do not want a unionized work force, they tread a fine line between paternalism and bureaucratic rationality. "I don't want a union house," the co-owner of Aperture and Neptune's says.

> *If they took a vote and voted in a union I would have to sell the restaurant or just close it down until I could get rid of the union. So what I try to do is run the restaurant as close to a union house as possible without it being a union. Therefore, when we fire someone we give them three warnings – union rules – and we write personal letters after a vocal warning. It's more so in Manhattan than in Queens. People are more transient in Manhattan and thus less "into" the job.*

The personalism that restaurant owners who also work as managers show with their staff carries over to their relations with customers. John and Don Pedro develop a "name" relationship with steady customers. Lee, however, who employs several types of managers, refers to regular customers who eat at the restaurant every day but does not emphasize personal relations with them. Personalistic styles of labor management and customer relations to some degree reflect the long hours owners put in and their face-to-face interactions with both the work force and clientele. As this implies, most

restaurant owners define their business in terms of the surrounding neighborhood. However, they develop different
strategies to service the neighborhood without sacrificing
profits.

Neptune's varies menu and prices to suit four markets:
an older, local customer base in Astoria, steady customers
who drive into Queens from the Long Island suburbs to eat
there, new customers from the neighborhood who work in
high-status white-collar jobs, and culturally sophisticated people who work at the nearby film studios. The restaurant features "traditional Italian" dishes at moderate prices as early
bird specials for the older customers, but it also spotlights
as "specials" newer, lighter preparations with more exotic
ingredients. Unlike an elite restaurant that changes the menu
daily, they offer the same specials two or three days in a row.
The younger owner has learned from trade magazines that
people now prefer "real food" to nouvelle cuisine. So he has
changed the menu to include "a lot of stews, mixed grills,
soups, homemade pasta, a lot of cheeses, goat cheeses, a lot
of oils in my sauces." Without eliminating the original seafood
theme – for health-conscious customers – or the Italian theme
that according to industry magazines has "soul," Neptune's
offers an amalgam of culinary traditions. The menu seeks to
appeal to both a local clientele of ethnic customers and a
cosmopolitan clientele of knowledgeable consumers.

The Chinese and Brazilian restaurants are somewhat
different. Their product is a single ethnic cuisine, and their
owners believe in not changing the restaurant. (Lee is ada-
mant on this point.) Yet their menus are not strictly "ethnic."
Mia's dishes are sophisticated and light preparations, including salads of Chinese dishes over greens, that appeal to American palates. They have no stews, dim sum, or inexpensive
traditional ingredients like chicken feet. Unlike Chinese restaurants in New York that cater to Chinese, the menu lists
dishes only in English. The Brazilian restaurant offers a weekend brunch for its Upper West Side customers. The restaurant's appeal is international rather than specifically
Brazilian or Latino, and it draws a high-status Latino clientele
rather than low-income Latino immigrants.

While most restaurants serve a mainly local clientele, owners interpret this function in different ways. They are influenced by the cosmopolitanism or traditionalism of those local residents who can afford to eat in the restaurant and the economic conditions that affect different parts of their customer base. If the neighborhood changes, the owner must decide whether and how to adapt to the change (see Wheaton 1990). The clientele at Neptune's, for example, has become more diverse ethnically, culturally, and economically over the past few years. As the younger owner describes these changes,

> *we started with the people in the neighborhood, typical Queens middle to lower middle class. They were very* New York Post *[a tabloid] type of people,* Daily News *[another tabloid] people, the type of people that were only interested in what is happening on a daily basis in and around the neighborhood. . . . Now what we have evolved to is what the neighborhood has evolved to. A lot of people that are* Times *readers, affluent people, people who read the* Wall Street Journal *for financial purposes. A type of people who are much more educated, [who live here] because of what is affordable. We get a lot of people from [Long Island], New Jersey, and Manhattan who travel to come here. I see a lot more doctors, professionals in general. I know that is what my customer base is because when we got hit with the 1988 recession, [after] Black Monday [when the stock market crashed in October 1987], we got hurt.*

An overextension of cultural capital – in terms of menu and decor that reach toward a global, cosmopolitan clientele – may force a restaurant to scale back to a local market. Nevertheless, local differences are important in deciding which cultural capital to use. A restaurant owner in Queens plays a different role in the local social and professional community than a restaurant owner in Manhattan. The Queens owners describe Manhattan restaurant owners as engaging in cutthroat competition. They see Queens owners as more cooperative, especially in their neighborhood and on their shopping street. Restaurant owners in the borough exchange information rather than withhold it as a trade secret. Further, with the interest in food that has developed in the past few years, a restaurant owner can engage in "outreach" activities that help mold the local community's tastes. Neptune's younger owner writes articles for the weekly neighborhood newspaper; most recently, on the nutritional value of fish. Partly this extends the local merchant's community functions. Partly, too, it expands the restaurant's potential local clientele. "A guy from Queens who goes into Manhattan and is [served] buffalo meat is going to eat it and say it is great, but if they eat the same thing [in Astoria] they are going to say something is wrong with it," Larry says.

Among our owners, only Lee brings investment capital transnationally into the New York restaurant industry. The aspirations of immigrant employees, however, both to open restaurants and return to their country of origin, suggest it is important to trace capital flows from the U.S. restaurant industry to other countries.

■ Symbolic Economy and World Economy

As my students never tire of reminding me, a brief exploratory study using qualitative techniques can only be tentative. Nevertheless, our interviews and observations in four New York City restaurants indicate important issues for further study. These topics range from the macroeconomic implications of capital flows among immigrant workers in restaurants to the microcosmic role of the services in creating global cultures.

Restaurants are not considered important sites in the global economy compared to such basic activities as auto plants or software developers, because they do not create capital. But tourism, of which restaurants are a part, is a large and growing industry. Moreover, the size of the work force, the countries of origin of participants, and the volume of monetary transactions that pass through restaurants do make restaurant work an important transnational activity – and one that is mainly undocumented. Because many restaurant workers are hired off the books, this economy is often untaxed and remains outside the Social Security system. It may thus have an effect on the fiscal crisis of local governments, as well as on government transfer programs and social services. It would be interesting, moreover, to trace the formal and informal institutions that aid immigrants in investing and sending money overseas: Urgente Express, Western Union, South American Express, American Express, check-cashing services, travel agencies that provide a multitude of services, and many other organizations. Perhaps the Quiet Sector of immigrants and their social networks is more important economically than most people think.

The conditions under which immigrants work in restaurants raise questions about the welfare and future of unskilled immigrants. We need a better conception of the impact of such work on immigrants' quality of life, as well as upon the broader public. American society and the urban economy may suffer the costs of neglecting human capital investment by underemploying highly skilled and educated immigrants in both secondary and informal labor markets. Immigrant access to jobs and mobility rely on both social networks and employment agencies that specialize in undocumented workers and nonpermanent residents. Interfirm mobility, as shown by Jesus the salad man and the Egyptian co-owners of Aperture, depends on personal ties through work experience. These issues are significant not only to domestic and transnational monetary flows, but also to understanding how immigrants join the labor force.

We also have many further questions on the nature of employment and entrepreneurship in the restaurant industry. Opportunities offered to immigrants and artists clearly contrast in terms of permanent employment and "front" or "back" responsibilities. But immigrant groups that have developed into successful restaurant entrepreneurs must nonetheless adapt to continual changes in the labor supply both within and outside their own group. We noted that the Chinese restaurant Mia already departs from labor recruitment within the Chinese ethnic group because it employs non-Asian cultural producers as waiters. A year after we finished our study, the owner posted a sign in the window announcing job openings for hostesses and waitresses. When we asked, we learned that the owner was opening a new restaurant. He clearly wanted to continue hiring "front" workers through nonethnic channels, since the odds of finding Chinese would be much greater if he advertised in a Chinese-language newspaper. But there could also be another reason that has to do with the specific skills of recent Chinese immigrants to New York City. The Chinese restaurant owners'association in New York now offers training to the many new Chinese immigrants who arrive in the city with very low skills (*Sing Tao Daily* [*Jih Pao*], June 6, 1991, 26).

Another constraint on immigrant entrepreneurs is the cost of opening a full-service restaurant in Manhattan. Investment in a lease, equipment, advertising, and decor can rise as high as $250,000 to $1 million, which prevents many immigrant entrepreneurs from moving beyond the immigrant sector into the mainstream of the industry.

Rigidities in the ethnic and social division of labor in the restaurant industry raise questions about the industry's continued strategies of labor recruitment as well as the polarization of job opportunities in the city. The lack of interchangeability between groups of "minority" employees (immigrants, teenagers, women) that predominate in different sectors of the industry (Bailey 1985) does not apply to some groups of immigrant men. The objective and subjective conditions in which groups do become interchangeable (Mexicans and Bangladeshi, Egyptians and Brazilians) should be explored. This is especially important in light of the continued underrepresentation of American-born blacks in full-service restaurants, which researchers attribute to job expectations, institutionalized racism, and weak ties to entrepreneurs and labor markets. Special training programs that target blacks and others in prison populations and drug treatment programs are very new and depend on employers' willingness to change existing hiring patterns (*New York Times,* June 12, 1991, C1). Networking among African-American chefs, as among women chefs and indeed, American chefs in general, is still in its infancy.

At any rate, what is going on in the restaurant industry is important as a cultural phenomenon. Restaurants have become incubators of innovation in urban culture. They feed the symbolic economy – socially, materially, and spiritually. For cultural consumers, moreover, restaurants produce an increasingly global product tailored to local tastes. Full-service restaurants like Mia, Rain Forest, and Neptune's, all owned by immigrant entrepreneurs, offer an intermediate menu between "ethnic" and "American" cuisines. It is not easy to define an American cuisine, especially in New York City, with its strong immigrant contributions to urban culture. But immigrant owners are clearly capable of conceiving a menu and decor that appeal to American tastes outside their ethnic group. This suggests that the division between immigrant-sector and full-service restaurants may not be so distinct as we assume (see Bailey 1985).

Moreover, a full-service restaurant's menu and decor demonstrate an interesting interaction between a local and global work force, market trends, and clientele. Restaurants bring exotic foods into an American mainstream. This process differentiates transnational cuisines by the cultural capital invested in their presentation rather than by the national origins of their primary consumers. Eventually, restaurants diffuse the culinary amalgam they develop if and when members of their work force return to their countries of origin and establish their own restaurants. We hesitate between calling this process "acculturation" or "globalization." Yet an immigrant work force also learns English in the restaurant as well as an organization of work, recipes, and – as far as their positions permit them to observe – strategies of dealing with clientele.

At the same time, the need to supply certain kinds of restaurant food encourages immigrant entrepreneurs to cross traditional ethnic boundaries. This is especially true for fast food and ethnic products that the public prefers. Fresco Tortillas, the Mexican take-out restaurant, is owned and staffed by Chinese immigrants. When one of us stopped by to ask how this was possible, a worker said, "We can do anything, this is New York."

We do not know what the demands placed on the personae of "front" workers in hotels and restaurants portend for either the arts labor force or service work as a whole. As at Disney World, actors, artists, and models are clearly preferred for the qualities of "face" and deference toward customers they can show. Yet the instability of restaurant employment makes them more vulnerable to employers' control.

> *"Ian tends to stay away from hiring people who have hotel experience," said Nancy Assuncao, the publicity agent for Ian Schrager. Mr. Schrager owns the Paramount, . . . in Manhattan, and its sister hotels, the Royalton in New York and the Delano in Miami Beach [and is a former owner of Studio 54]. "Ian says that people with hotel experience are too cynical. They have too many ideas"* (Servin 1993).

It remains to be seen whether low-wage work in the services will replace artistic aspirations or whether a new division of labor will develop as artists remain in the restaurant industry, accumulate savings, and join with, work for, or compete against immigrant entrepreneurs.

> *"Right now I work for a textile company on Madison Avenue," said the first candidate [interviewing for a job at the Paramount Hotel], . . . a tall man with long blond hair and a Banana Republic air about him. "I got an agent for modeling. I'm interested in becoming a bartender or a bellhop"* (Servin 1993).

The underrepresentation of native New Yorkers in New York City restaurants emphasizes the industry's dependence on continued migration and immigration. If New York loses the dynamism of a culture capital, the industry risks losing a labor supply of artists, actors, and other creative producers and performers who migrate to New York from other parts of the country and the rest of the world. And if the restaurant industry falters in a continued economic recession, the city risks losing an arts work force that will either leave New York for smaller, less expensive cities or will not move to the city at all.

At any rate, restaurants are always changing. Several weeks after we interviewed him, Medhat, the 27-year-old Egyptian chef and part-owner of Aperture, who came to New York to get rich, died of a heart attack. A year later, the Chinese manager of Mia put a sign in the window asking for waitresses to apply. In Queens, one of Neptune's long-time customers hired away two of the restaurant's chefs and opened his own restaurant. Rain Forest went out of business two years after our visits, but Don Pedro reopened by converting to an Italian menu and representing his Latino waiters as Italians. That restaurant folded within two years.

125th Street Day Parade, Harlem, June 13, 1947.

6

WHILE THE CITY SHOPS

I think it is altogether reasonable to consider shopping in a book about the cultures of cities.[11] Women, and increasingly men, spend a great deal of time shopping. We shop to supply ourselves with necessities and luxuries and to feel at home in the city, a part of its whirl of business and pleasure, its grand displays, its serial social transactions. As shopping has consumed more leisure time, and become a major preoccupation, it has drawn more criticism. Some make a social critique of commodity fetishism; some make a personal critique of "ladies who shop." Shopping is taken to be a case of egregious consumption, a conspicuous example of emptyheadedness, a moment of alienation and anomie. Yet for many people, lacking the intensity and immediacy of a public culture, the shopping experience is a means of overcoming alienation, of connecting action with dreams, of choosing and producing an identity. Moreover, from a crass commercial point of view,

---

11. This chapter began as a rejoinder to Richard Sennett's romantic interpretation of 14th Street in *The Conscience of the Eye* (1990, 163–68). It took preliminary form in some remarks on the vitality of neighborhood shopping streets that I put into a larger paper for a conference on Re-Presenting the City, organized in 1992 by Tony King at the State University of New York at Binghamton. Although I am not a "shopper," I see this chapter in certain ways as returning to my roots. Many thanks to CUNY graduate student Danny Kessler for walking the streets and Brooklyn College students Barbara Hill and Sharon Kettrles for some historical research and interviews with shopkeepers.

retail shopping is one of the modern city's greatest cultural attractions.

In recent years urban social and literary critics have written a great deal about spaces of commercial culture, especially the late 19th century arcades of Paris and the department stores of other great cities, as archetypal public spaces of modernity. At the same time, late 20th century shopping malls have captured the attention of both social theorists and the media as primary public spaces of postmodernity. We are led to assume the importance of consumption to the public culture of modern cities – consumption of a specific kind, in which the eye monopolizes sensory appetite and people sample among superficial sensations, the better to hide the stark loneliness and misery of the city under a facade of novelty, luxury, and neon lights. This view was shaped by the rediscovery of Walter Benjamin in the 1970s by English-speaking readers, followed by research into the roots of modernity by a generation of historians. The secondhand viewer – the urban critic – now tries to unpack the previous unitary perception of urban spaces to get to the roots of ethnic, class, and gender difference in urban cultures.

Under the guise of deconstructing urban experiences, shopping areas have been analyzed – or challenged – in terms of their architecture and technology, their association with safety and danger, and the patterns of behavior they reportedly inspire. While the cast iron buildings of the arcades and the plate glass and electric lighting pioneered by department stores made fantasy accessible in city streets, the climate control and interior streets of shopping malls made consumption a more individualistic experience. Women were "liberated" both to work and shop in 19th and early 20th century consumption spaces, but the conventions of shopping and serving limited their participation in public life and created oases of gentility for the middle class. Perhaps the most celebrated pattern of behavior in the late 19th century literary description of urban culture is that of the *flâneur* – the independent yet impecunious young man, an artist or writer, who wanders the streets and cafés, dreaming, desiring, devouring the city with a cynical, yearning hunger. There is no such contradictory figure in the malls. In malls, those who "resist" – yet also participate in – the public culture of mass consumption may be browsers, elderly joggers looking for a safe place to exercise, or teenagers who hang out in malls because they are suburbia's only public spaces. While we cannot tell what they are thinking just by looking at them, we know the space is important to them, to framing their social identities. The public space of shopping connects them to society (Shields 1989, 1992b; Morris 1988).

Going back to Baudelaire, Manet, and the Bon Marché or forward to Inner Harbor, West Edmonton, and the Mall of America, this view of consumption spaces conforms to a certain critical way of looking at cities. It connects the act of looking to its social context, putting viewer and viewed, subject of social action and object of desire, in a socially conscious frame. Thus the *flâneur* is almost never a *flâneuse* (Wolff 1985), and the artists or writers who are most indebted to women for knowledge of the city always describe a shadow life of sexual adventures with prostitutes, actresses, and models. In earlier pastoral images, relations between men and women were shaped by property.

In cities, relations between women and men are conditioned by commodities. What, after all, is the act of shopping or prostitution in a standardized market society, but an exchange of labor in terms of price? The *flâneur,* by the same token, is an imperialist. As he walks among the displays of new products, many of which are imports, his consuming gaze assimilates the disembodied exotic symbols into the city's rich variety of retail shopping (Shields 1994). However, he is not entirely comfortable with these unfamiliar foreign goods – and the intrusion of the immigrants who market them. The bazaar of foreign goods expands the *flâneur*'s horizons – while destroying his complacency in being a "native." Just so, contemporary city dwellers complain about the "Third World" quality of urban streets.

Commodities, as Walter Benjamin pointed out, embody dreams (Buck-Morss 1989). So city dwellers are dream walkers, too. They are Georg Simmel's abstract materialists, compelled to calculate their social relations by distance, by money, and always by some sort of cost, a dream deferred. Almost 100 years after Simmel wrote about the city, public space still shows the impact of time and money. And urban public cultures are still cultures of the streets – and malls, of the interior streets – where sociability follows the common pursuit of commodities and the risky exposure of difference.

But which streets? And which differences? Despite their many contributions to historical consciousness, quests for the roots of modernity in urban consumption spaces have focused too much research on hegemonic forms of centralized investment and standardized display and spent too little time on populist shopping cultures of the streets. Blame it on the lure of the fancy shops of Paris, on the pervasiveness of mass consumption, or on a reader's preference for the mystical Walter Benjamin of the arcades project instead of the neurotic Benjamin of "A Berlin Chronicle." Blame it on the ubiquity of the malls.

The central spaces of downtown shopping districts and suburban malls are not the only site of lived experience – the *espaces vécus* – where identities and communities are formed. With their constant streams of immigration and markets to supply the daily needs of large populations, great cities create more complex, diverse, ambiguous consumption spaces. In great cities today, as in the past, ethnic shopping streets thrive with imported goods, street vendors, music, political debates: signs, in short, of urban public cultures. Although they are equally devoted to "consumption," these streets certainly differ from the archetypal spaces of arcades and malls. Only a zealot would describe them in terms of commodity fetishism, for they are sites of more important everyday social practices. They owe more to the unmediated theatricality of medieval and early modern markets than to the calculated stage settings of merchant princes of mass consumption.

As Robert Venturi and his associates point out, the bazaar, in contrast to the modern commercial strip, is basically *unsigned.* "In the bazaar, communication works through proximity" (Venturi, Brown, and Izenour 1972, 9; see Agnew 1986: ch. 1): the constricted space, the contestations of exchange, give rise to the social practices of talk, the sensual practices of touch. In some ways, at some times of day, these spaces speak to women's shopping experience. But these *espaces vécus* are also at the center, with the home, of a child's cartography of the city, and thus at the center of a social world. Neighborhood shopping streets, especially when they are connected with ethnicity, social class, and gender, are sites where identities are formed.

Perhaps I am bound by having always lived in centralized older cities – Philadelphia, New York, Paris, Belgrade – to exaggerate the importance of neighborhood shopping streets. Moreover, living for many years in New York, I may see signs of vitality in ethnic markets that are lacking on Kensington Avenue in Philadelphia or in the Maxwell Street market of Chicago. New York has many more immigrants than Philadelphia, which may increase their visibility on the streets. But I am not talking about the touristic ethnic markets of the Chinatowns and Little Italy's that draw visitors to historic areas of settlement.

Despite differences in physical layout, politics, and transportation, I am convinced that the ordinary shopping districts frequented by ordinary people are important sites for negotiating the street-level practices of urban public culture in all large cities. And they are everywhere: the mainly immigrant-run indoor flea markets of New York City are like the "swap meets" of Los Angeles, and the remapping of the Lower East Side by Asian-run garment factories and vegetable stores is not entirely unlike that of London's Brick Lane. A commercial street is nearly always the "heart" of the modern city. Too banal for historical research, neighborhood shopping streets are etched into our memories even when they signify nostalgia for a community lost, an identity abandoned. "The old urban working-class community: the delights of corner-shops, gas lamps, horsecabs, trams, pisstalls: all gone, it seems, in successive generations" (Williams 1973, 297). Memory often begins, is stimulated and provoked, by the neighborhood shopping streets of our childhood.

My generation straddles a childhood memory of wearing white gloves and carrying a little purse to shop downtown (see E. Wilson 1991,1; Beauregard 1993, ix) and an adult marketing boom of gentrification and suburban malls. As I get older, my reveries of childhood are more consciously bound up with "worlds we have lost." It is typical of modernity that many of these worlds are delineated by commercial culture, and typical of an urban childhood that much of the loss is due to the self-imposed exile from their neighborhoods of a white middle class. Memory is highly selective. Yet autobiography often makes these points more clearly than social theory.

■ A Child's Cartography

Sometimes at night I dream about the shopping street in the neighborhood in North Philadelphia where I grew up in the 1950s. It was an older middle-class and lower-middle-class neighborhood, all white, with both synagogues and churches. Tall sycamore trees lined both sides of the street. The houses were undoubtedly smaller than I remember them. Many were six-room rowhouses, but all had lawns and porches in front and fenced gardens in back. Our house was built in the 1920s; my parents were the second owners. As in even older neighborhoods that stretched northward from center city, our garden faced an alley.

Every morning the city sanitation workers wheeled their carts through the alley, clanging the metal lids of garbage cans as they picked up the garbage. From time to time, a knife grinder called his way up the alley. I remember the dairy delivering milk to our front door in glass bottles, and a fruit and vegetable peddler and a large, regional bakery sold food from trucks that parked on our street once or twice a week. The shopping street my mother favored was two blocks away. I realize now it was an outpost of urban Jewish culture – not that we thought of it as either urban or Jewish in the 1950s, or that the children were even conscious of being "European" Americans and white. To us, it was just Eleventh Street: a compact assortment of two-story brick houses, with store-fronts at street level and apartments on top.

Among the stores were three "Jewish" delicatessens that sliced red salty lox from big sides of salmon and sold silver herrings and sour pickles from deep barrels of brine. There were three bakeries that sold their own bagels, challah, rye bread with caraway seeds, onion rolls, and salt sticks, as well as coffee crumb cakes and the spirals of butter pastry I called pigs' ears until I went to France and learned to call them *papillons*. The baker's daughter was my classmate in elementary school. Her mother worked behind the counter. Mrs. Fox sold butter, eggs, and cheese next door. She spoke with an East European accent that I could not identify even now and wore a white apron and brown cardigan over her housedress. She always gave me a taste of Emmenthaler, which we called *schweitzer* cheese, or the sweeter domestic Munster.

Mrs. Fox and the baker's family and the extended family of the delicatessen owner all lived above their shops. There were also both kosher and nonkosher butcher shops and a fish store where live carp swam in a tank. My T-shirts and jeans came from a dry goods store on one block of the cross-street and my saddle shoes from a children's shoe store on another. While there must have been several greengrocers, my mother shopped at only one. She might feud with Ben for selling her a bad tomato, but we always returned to his store. The same with Meyer the butcher, who kept a cigar stub clenched between his teeth as he split a chicken, his wife Ethel who sat at the cash register, and their son Harvey, who worked in the shop and reminded me of Elvis.

As intimate as we were with our local shopping street, we knew it was at the bottom of a cultural and geographical hierarchy. Movie theaters, banks, and supermarkets – outposts of the dominant commercial culture – were farther away but still within walking distance. Near them was the local public library. While there were not yet fast food franchises on Broad Street, we could eat at the counter of a small Horn and Hardart's restaurant and shop at a branch of the Pep Boys auto supplies chain. For serious clothes shopping in department stores and for the treat of lunch and a first-run movie, we took the bus downtown.

Eleventh Street, and many other local shopping streets like it, reflect both the identity and assimilation of an urban, secular, ethnic culture. The social reproduction of this culture is carried out with a certain degree of separation from other groups: to some extent, in our case, from non-Jews, but mainly from non-Europeans and especially African Americans (see Massey and Denton 1993). Yet the intimacy in a public space represented by a neighborhood shopping street reflects more than the insularity of an ethnic community. It also represents the relatively small scale of social life that we associate with neighborhood geography and the coherent social space of gender and social class. Neighborhood shopping streets challenge critical urban social theory because they produce both difference and continuity. Shopping streets make it necessary to understand ethnicity as a negotiated identity made up of a thousand different social interactions in public space, from face-to-face relations to more abstract transactions of commercial exchange (see Harvey 1985a; Sennett 1990, 163–68).[12]

On these streets, ethnicity is in some ways a substitute for intimacy. While we usually did not meet our immediate neighbors on Eleventh Street, we did know a lot about the shopkeepers. And by virtue of the talkative shopping practices of mothers and children, they knew a lot about us. In fact, they were a lot like us. Eleventh Street speaks to the old connection between proximity and survival, when locality excluded strangers (see Shields 1992a), and neighborhood shopping streets rather than regional malls, franchise stores, and home shopping networks satisfied a need for both social community and material goods.

Yet if the neighborhood shopping street of my childhood is quite distant from today's standardized, regional mall, it was also distant from the downtown commercial center of its time. Except for storekeepers, the neighborhood was not a place to work – and has not been, for most Americans, since the middle to late 19th century. On weekdays, especially, the shopping street was a woman's world. Most of the women in my neighborhood when I was growing up were nonworking mothers who prepared lunch each day when their children (the postwar "baby boom") walked home from the local public school. While there were no sidewalk vendors or discount stores, customers could negotiate some prices, within limits, with storeowners, whom they knew by name. Customers also had favorite employees whom they wanted to wait on them. Because stores were small, display space was minimal. Mrs. Fox kept eggs in a back room; her small refrigerated glass case held only a few cheeses and two large mounds of butter, salted and sweet. In the delicatessen, cans were wedged so

---

12. Sociologists will recall the work of the University of Chicago professor Gerald Suttles (1968), whose concept of "ordered segmentation" suggests the importance ethnic groups assign to local territory in their efforts to develop moral communities. My work differs from his because I am concerned less with ethnic differentiation than with public space, I am especially interested in commercial spaces, and I am not limiting the analysis to "slum" communities. I also see both ethnicity and urban space as responding to larger political economic factors.

tightly onto shelves only the owner's grandson could pry them loose. The plate glass windows were large but irrelevant to the display of goods. Except for seasonal fruits and vegetables, the goods never changed. The windows were useful for looking into the stores, reflecting and moving the street indoors.

By contrast, downtown was a fairyland of diversity and display. The long century of department stores (1860–1970) had so balanced rationalization and desire that shoppers, especially women, felt their inner needs were met by an intimacy with the goods (Leach 1993). Display windows reached their apotheosis at holiday times, especially Christmas, when mechanical dolls, blinking lights, and falling "snow" attracted crowds. There seemed no end to the abundance of goods displayed on countertops and in glass showcases, and there were even goods stored away out of sight, which we glimpsed when saleswomen searched through deep drawers for a particular size or color.

One cluster of department stores at Eighth and Market Streets carried a wide variety of clothes and furniture, housewares and toys, at low to moderate prices. Each had a slightly different social status: Lit Brothers' was probably lowest, Gimbel's was higher because the store stretched through the block to the more prestigious Chestnut Street and included a small branch of Saks Fifth Aveue, Strawbridge and Clothier's was higher still because it was associated by ownership and probably clientele with the WASP elite. The larger and grander John Wanamaker store was a few blocks away. Dominating both Market and Chestnut Streets, it competed with City Hall as the true center of the city. A few women's and girls' specialty clothing stores, shoe stores, restaurants, and movie theaters completed our map of the downtown, with my pediatrician's and ophthalmologist's offices, and the theater where I saw my first live stage show, on the western edge of the main shopping district. There were also stores for window shopping only; they were off limits because they were either too expensive or too tawdry.

We shopped mainly in the department stores. I knew the children's floors – toys and clothing – as well as I knew my bedroom, and I savored the separate floors in each store where sheets, lingerie, sofas, and shoes were sold. The escalators were always miraculous to me: little did I think that old John

Wanamaker had to have them for his store when he realized their usefulness in moving shoppers to all the different buying areas (Leach 1993, 73–74). In fact, the vertical stratification of the department stores, from bargain basement to luxury furs and millinery and up to linens, struck me as a natural order. It matched the horizontal stratification of the city from Eleventh Street to Broad Street and downtown, and from our neighborhood to center city through a band of inner city ghettos, of which I gradually became more aware.

Writing about my early life as a shopper confronts both the limitations of childhood memory and the gap between experience (*espaces vécus*) and epistemology (*espaces conçus*). What, after all, despite lives devoted to shopping, do any of us know about the public life of these streets? It seems to me that urban memoirs establish three big historical, method-ological, and theoretical points about neighborhood shopping streets that could well be nursed by social critics: their impor-tance to the social reproduction of different social groups, the distance between them and hegemonic socio-spatial forms of shopping such as "downtown" and malls, and the connections they make between global and local sources of identity, and between ethnic change and commercial decline.

Memoirs suggest, at the very least, that girls develop a rather "domestic" conception of neighborhood shopping streets, while boys experience them as part of a more aggres-sive public life, a public culture of territories and display, and even gangs. Social class also shapes conceptions of the streets: wealth and cultural capital affect whether knowledge of the streets is mediated by hired caregivers and parents, whether a child is – like Walter Benjamin – a *flâneur* or, like Alfred Kazin, "a walker in the city." Another issue concerns the nature of the public in these public spaces. Are shopping streets best understood, as I have suggested, as the moral basis of an insular community? Are they sites of conflict between customers of one ethnic group and shopkeepers of another, often blacks and Jews, or are they sites of integration? After all, the postwar Jewish immigrants who bought stores on Eleventh Street were integrated with their American-born Jewish customers. African street vendors today sell their goods outside shops owned by African Americans.

The easy slippage between "neighborhood" and "ethnic" shopping streets raises questions about time and space, as well as about social identity. Does neighborhood refer only to the scale, while ethnicity refers to the character, of public life? To what degree does the social reproduction of difference depend on the negotiation of sameness? Does identity depend on defining oneself with or defining oneself against the city?

Let us take the urban memoirs of three members of my ethnic group: the European cultural theorist Walter Benjamin, the American travel writer Kate Simon, and the American literary critic Alfred Kazin (the only one of the three who is still alive). Despite the differences in space and time – their childhoods were spent in Berlin, Brooklyn, and the Bronx either before or after World War I – I am always astonished by the likeness between their experience of the modern city and mine. Yet the difference in social class between Benjamin and Kazin, and the difference in gender between Kazin and Simon, shape differences in their child's cartography of the city. Benjamin and Kazin are "white European males." Benjamin was raised in a bourgeois Jewish family in Berlin and so "represents" a burden of modern European history that includes ethnic assimilation, political and artistic leftism, a cosmopolitan palette of urban crowds, cafés, and patrician architecture. Kazin is, like Benjamin, a Jew. But he was born in Europe and raised in a working-class Jewish neighborhood in Brooklyn. His family spoke Yiddish at home and practiced the socialism of Jewish labor unions and immigrant politics. Kazin grew up to "represent" modern American literature, a representation of eternal conflicts between nature and cities, art and politics.

Almost the first words of their early memoirs – of Berlin and Brownsville, respectively – introduce the city seen through the filter of social class. "Now let me call back those who introduced me to the city," Benjamin so evocatively begins "A Berlin Chronicle" (1979, 293). "For although the child, in his solitary games, grows up at closest quarters to the city, he needs and seeks guides to its wider expanses, and the first of these – for a son of wealthy middle-class parents like me – are sure to have been nursemaids." From there he plunges directly into the central pleasure spaces of the city, spaces that he, by his social class and class culture, inherits: "With them I went to the Zoo . . . – or, if not to the Zoo, to the Tiergarten." Kazin, by contrast, begins his early memoirs in Brownsville, a neighborhood so distant from the central spaces of Manhattan that its residents identify going to Manhattan with going to "the city." And his memories are acrid ones: "From the moment I step off the [subway] train at Rockaway Avenue and smell the leak out of the men's room, then the pickles from the stand just below the subway steps, an instant rage comes over me, mixed with dread and some unexpected tenderness" (Kazin 1951, 5). Kazin's rage, so immediately identified with the neighborhood shopping street, springs from his neighborhood and ethnicity, which stand in turn for the status of being an immigrant of the lower social class. Benjamin (1979, 294), quite differently, directs his rage against his mother, whom he so unwillingly accompanied on her mercilessly efficient shopping expeditions downtown that he could not for years (so he says) distinguish between his right foot and his left.

Benjamin does not write about neighborhood shopping streets. In addition to cafés and apartments, his memories of Berlin are all "downtown." From childhood, he is the true *flâneur,* disdainful yet appreciative of novelty, money, and designer labels:

> *In those early years I got to know "the town" only as the theatre of purchases, on which occasions it first became apparent how my father's money could cut a path for us between the shop counters and assistants and mirrors, and the appraising eyes of our mother, whose muff lay on the counter. In the ignominy of a "new suit" we stood there, our hands peeping from the sleeves like dirty price tags, and it was only in the confectioner's that our spirits rose with the feeling of having escaped the false worship that humiliated our mother before idols bearing the names of Mannheimer, Herzog and Israel, Gerson, Adam, Esders and Madler, Emma Bette, Bud and Lachmann. An impenetrable chain of mountains, no, caverns of commodities – this was "the town."* (1979, 327)

Kazin's shopping street in Brownsville is made up of scant displays of bare commodities and their representations of repetition and defeat. Memory of the street is joined with memory of the fear of not being able to escape living close, in all senses, to the margins:

The early hopelessness burns at my face like fog the minute I get off the subway. I can smell it in the air. . . . It hangs over the Negro tenements in the shadows of the El-darkened street, the torn and flapping canvas sign still listing the boys who went to war, the stagnant wells of candy stores and pool parlors, the torches flaring at dusk over the vegetable stands and pushcarts, the neon-blazing fronts of liquor stores, the piles of Halvah *and chocolate kisses in the windows of the candy stores next to the* News *and* Mirror, *the dusty old drugstores where urns of rose and pink and blue colored water still swing from chains, and where next door Mr. A.'s sign still tells anyone walking down Rockaway Avenue that he has pants to fit any color suit.* (1951, 6)

We see already the intimations of postwar racial change. The hopelessness, the degradation of his class Kazin also projects onto the first blacks who moved into the most dilapidated tenements. But even in the ordinary wares of the stores and their immigrant Jewish owners, Kazin finds little to attract and less to fascinate him.

Yet Kate Simon, who immigrated to a working-class neighborhood in the Bronx with her Polish Jewish parents around the same time, after World War I, still remembers the shopping streets with the pleasure – dare I say? – of domestic attraction, of identification with a woman's domestic role.

Bathgate, moving southward from Tremont toward Claremont Parkway, was the market street where mothers bought yard goods early in the week, as well as dried mushrooms and shoelaces. On Wednesdays they bought chickens and live fish to swim in the bathtub until Friday, when they became gefilte fish. Most women plucked their own chickens. . . . On the next block, Washington, was the public library, and a block north of it, on the corner with Tremont, the barber shop where I went for my Buster Brown haircut. Tremont west of Third also held the delectable five-and-ten, crisscrosses of rainbows and pots of gold. (1982, 3)

Removed in time and space from us, Benjamin's, Kazin's, and Simon's memoirs teach us much about the actual production of difference in urban streets. Benjamin inherited entry into a central, affluent space of the city; Simon and Kazin earned their way into the city by getting a university education and choosing an intellectual career. They all escaped their childhood homes: Benjamin, moving easily through the streets of Paris; Simon and Kazin, moving to Manhattan. All came to different ends. Simon died, Kazin has written his memoirs, and Benjamin, unwilling or unable to escape from the Nazis, killed himself in Europe during World War II. Yet their memoirs still speak to me. There were no kosher chicken pluckers on Eleventh Street, but the ethnic identity of Simon's and Kazin's neighborhoods resonates with the sameness-in-difference, or the difference-in-sameness, of my own, more secular shopping street. Downtown Philadelphia also has the patrician architecture and bourgeois interiors that Benjamin wrote about. While our experiences differ, our subjective maps of the city are more or less the same. Benjamin's memories of downtown evoke the social ambitions I remember of shopping on Chestnut Street and strolling through Rittenhouse Square.

African-American urban memoirs, roughly contemporaneous with those of Kazin and Simon, emphasize many of the same neighborhood sites: home, school, church (rather than synagogue), public library, and sometimes early jobs. Yet there are crucial differences, differences born of exclusion rather than insularity. Black authors remember being excluded from racially segregated schools in midwestern and northern cities or being the only African American in their classes. They remember the paradox of neighborhood shopping streets where stores were owned and staffed by whites, a situation that practically prohibits the easy intimacy I found on Eleventh Street. Their experience of downtown was shaped not only by differences of social class and wealth, but also by racial segregation. African Americans had limited opportunities to get summer jobs – compared to whites – and few opportunities to enter stores as customers. As far back as the 1820s, some streets in black neighborhoods were marked by danger, crime, the "low life" that other groups had created and patronized.

The novelist Chester Himes, although born into the middle class, lived for years in his young manhood as a hustler, thief, and pimp. He was introduced to city life as Walter Benjamin was, by the commercial exchanges and romantic alliances of prostitution. He chose the life of the streets. Unlike Benjamin, however, Himes is unable just to be a *flâneur*. Himes constructs his identity by emphasizing an inability to escape the streets in a way Benjamin cannot experience or perhaps even conceive of. Neither does his rage permit him Kazin's rejection of neighborhood streets: he is compelled to identify with other African Americans and with the streets. In 1926, he remembers (1990, 18), when he was a teenager in Cleveland,

> *Scovil Avenue ran from 55th Street to 14th Street on the edge of the black ghetto and was the most degraded slum street I had ever seen. The police once estimated that there were 1500 black prostitutes cruising the 40 blocks of Scovil Avenue at one time. The black whores on Scovil for the most part were past their thirties, vulgar, scarred, dimwitted, in many instances without teeth, diseased, and poverty-stricken. Most of the black men in the neighborhood lived on the earnings of the whores and robbed the "hunkies." They gambled for small change, fought, drank poisonous "white mule," cut each other up, and died in the gutter.*

Several years later, Himes did research on the history of Cleveland and discovered the complicity of whites in creating this neighborhood street. Unskilled East European immigrants, called *hunkies,* or Hungarians, were recruited by white employers to work in the steel mills. They came to the United States without their wives and children, often patronizing African-American prostitutes, creating a base of local employment for black women when black men were hired only as strikebreakers. While knowing this history helps Himes put Scovil Street in perspective, it does not remove the hurt of experiencing Scovil as your neighborhood shopping street.

No matter how mean the streets, or how extensive the cultural capital of some individuals, it is the black ghetto where all blacks "belong," or are relegated, by their exclusion from other social sites. When Himes was a college student at Ohio State University in Columbus, also in 1926, he saw "all the black musicals on Warren Street, which was the next street over from Long and ran through the worst of the black slums. So many soul brothers killed each other for one reason or another on Warren Street, that it was known as the Burma Road" (1990, 26). So why did a college student withdraw to the ghetto? "All the movie theaters in downtown Columbus and the white neighborhoods either segregated blacks in the upper balconies or did not receive them at all. And no white restaurants served blacks anywhere in the city, not even those near Ohio State University. I always tightened up inside whenever I passed one of them" (1990, 26).

These exclusions complicate neighborhood shopping streets in black ghettos, making them both "lower class" because they sell low-price goods and "ethnic" because they cater to a specific cultural group. For the same reasons, these streets are both "regional" commercial centers for blacks from all over the city and the metropolitan region and "local" shopping streets. Seventh Avenue or 125th Street in Harlem, South State Street in Chicago, and Pennsylvania Avenue in Baltimore are African-American downtowns. They become places to see the latest and best in "black" entertainment as well as centers of political information and organization. They attract tourists from white areas of the city and overseas. The diversity of uses explodes boundaries between upper and lower social classes among blacks, between entertainment and danger, between day and night. "South State Street was in its glory then," Langston Hughes writes in his autobiography about this area near the Loop in 1916 (1940: 33),

> *a teeming Negro street with crowded theaters, restaurants, and cabarets. And excitement from noon to noon. Midnight was like day. The street was full of workers and gamblers, prostitutes and pimps, church folks and sinners. The tenements on either side were very congested. For neither love nor money could you find a decent place to live. Profiteers, thugs, and gangsters were coming into their own.*

Even a more mundane, local shopping street – 145th Street on the west side of Harlem – was much more heterogeneous than similar streets in Jewish memoirs – even Brownsville's Pitkin Avenue. The Caribbean American poet Audre Lorde remembers (1982, 50) walking on 145th Street with her two sisters, "three plump little Black girls, dimpled knees scrubbed and oiled to a shine, hair tightly braided and tied with threads," in the late 1930s:

> *We trudged up the hill past the Stardust Lounge, Micky's Hair-Styling – Hot and Cold Press, the Harlem Bop Lounge, the Dream Café, the Freedom Barber Shop, and the Optimo Cigar Store. . . . There was the Aunt May Eat Shoppe, and Sadie's Ladies and Children's Wear. There was Lum's Chop Suey Bar, and the Shiloh Mission Baptist Church painted white with colored storefront windows, the Record Store with its big radio chained outside setting a beat to the warming morning sidewalk. And on the corner of Seventh Avenue as we waited for the green light arm in arm, the yeasty and suggestively mysterious smell issuing from the cool dark beyond the swinging half-doors of the Noon Saloon.*

The mix of store names speaks to corporate identity (the Optimo cigar) and individual ownership (Aunt May, Sadie), to African-American history (the Freedom Barber Shop), to the links between ethnicity and exclusion (the beauty shop and Baptist church), and to the neighborhood Chinese restaurant more typical of Manhattan in the past than of most other American cities. But the diversity also suggests a different pattern of "going out" from that of old Jewish neighborhoods. This is less exclusively a "shopping" street for daily goods, and it speaks of a strong male presence: of men who are unemployed during the day because of night jobs or no jobs, of men who go to church, listen to popular music, and drink in bars.

There is less of a male presence in Jewish shopping streets, at least, outside the neighborhoods of Hasidic Jews. In my neighborhood, during the postwar years, most mothers did not work outside the home. In Kazin's and Simon's time, many Jewish women worked at home on the "putting out" system of garment factories. Black women, by contrast, worked in other people's homes as domestic workers, in stores and restaurants, and eventually in offices. They could not shop on the street during most weekday hours. Yet black women are also important customers of neighborhood shops. Audre Lorde is impressed by her mother's aura of authority, an identity established partly by her bearing and partly by her acting out a domestic role as food gatherer in the local context of a neighborhood shopping street.

> *Total strangers would turn to her in the meat market and ask what she thought about a cut of meat as to its freshness and appeal and suitability for such and such, and the butcher, impatient, would nonetheless wait for her to deliver her opinion, obviously quite a little put out but still deferential. Strangers counted upon my mother and I never knew why, but as a child it made me think she had a great deal more power than in fact she really had.* (1982, 17)

Perhaps this was an exchange made on neighborhood shopping streets: as women assumed their domestic roles, and girls identified with their mothers, so they established an authority outside the home, in public space, in shopping (see also Ewen 1985). Perhaps this memory brings Audre Lorde closer to Kate Simon and, in a way, to Walter Benjamin's mother and to mine.

Yet Lorde also experiences neighborhood shopping streets through a dual exploitation: as a girl and a black.

> *In 1936–1938, 125th Street between Lenox and Eighth Avenues, later to become the shopping mecca of Black Harlem, was still a racially mixed area, with control and patronage largely in the hands of white shopkeepers. There were stores into which Black people were not welcomed, and no Black salespersons worked in the shops at all. Where our money was taken, it was taken with reluctance; and often too much was asked. (It was these conditions which young Adam Clayton Powell, Jr., addressed in his boycott and picketing of Blumstein's and Weissbecker's market in 1939 in an attempt, successful, to bring Black employment to 125th Street.) Tensions on the street were high, as they always are in racially mixed zones of transition. As a very little girl, I remember*

shrinking from a particular sound, a hoarsely sharp,
gutteral rasp, because it often meant a nasty glob of grey
spittle upon my coat or shoe an instant later. My mother
wiped it off with the little pieces of newspaper she always
carried in her purse. (1982, 17)

As in Kazin's memoir of Brownsville, there are strong sensual
memories of revulsion in Lorde's memoir and also intimations
of racial change. Yet both the degradation and the change are
different for a black woman than for a white man. While for
Kazin the transition from Jews to blacks suggests sinking
into deeper defeat, for Lorde it is a means of liberation.

Lorde also describes repeated sexual molestation by a
white storeowner in Washington Heights, not far from her
home in Harlem, which sets new parameters to the dangers of
neighborhood shopping streets – when the customer is young,
female, and black. The storeowner was "a fat white man with
watery eyes and a stomach that hung over his belt like badly
made jello" (1982, 49). He sold secondhand comic books, both
fascinating the author by his stock and repulsing her by his
body and his cigar, offering her the usual sexual trade:

"Lemme help you up, sweetheart, you can see better." And
I felt his slabby fingers like sausages grab my ribs and
hoist me through a sickening arc of cigar fumes to the
edge of the bins full of Bugs Bunny and Porky Pig comics.
. . . By the time he loosened his grip and allowed me to
slide down to the blessed floor, I felt dirtied and afraid,
as if I had just taken part in some filthy rite.

In return, she got an extra comic for free, no small treat for
a child whose parents counted the pennies.

Even for my near contemporary, the novelist John Edgar
Wideman, who grew up, as did his mother, in Homewood, an
historic black ghetto in Pittsburgh, the specific configuration
of neighborhood shopping streets in black areas is a source of
cultural identity in an otherwise alien environment. When
Wideman came to Philadelphia in 1959 as a freshman at
the University of Pennsylvania, he and one of his few black
classmates "would ride buses across Philly searching for
places like home. Like the corner of Frankstown and Bruston

in Homewood. A poolroom, barbershop, rib joint, record store strip with bloods in peacock colors strolling up and down and hanging out on the corner" (1984, 32). Finally, they "found South Street. Just over the bridge, walking distance if you weren't in a hurry, but as far from school, as close to home, as we could get. Another country." Thirty and forty years after Chester Himes and Langston Hughes, Wideman renegotiates their experience, and to some degree also that of their contemporaries among Jewish immigrants. Finding himself in the city is based on finding "home"; an identity of difference is reproduced by both exclusion, or the feeling of being excluded, and the reproduction of sameness on an ethnic shopping street.

Around the same time I moved away from Philadelphia, away from Eleventh Street, Wideman's mother became aware of the "decline" of Homewood. Decline there did not reflect racial transition so much as the denigration of a once stable, working-class black community. While the small shops of neighborhood shopping streets must have shown clear but gradual signs of the net closing in, as Wideman says, he chooses the example of a supermarket, part of a national chain, supposed to be one of those hegemonic forms of shopping – standardized, centralized, clean. "Some signs were subtle, gradual. The A&P started to die. Nobody mopped filth from the floors. Nobody bothered to restock empty shelves. Fewer and fewer white faces among the shoppers. A plate-glass display window gets broken and stays broken. When they finally close the store, they paste the going-out-of-business notice over the jagged, taped crack" (1984: 75).

This memory, too, voices regret at a "world we have lost." No matter what kinds of goods were sold on ethnic shopping streets, or how deep the ethnic group's exclusion from other shopping sites, since the 1960s, shopping experiences in the ghetto have been degraded. "This used to be the downtown of the Southeast Side," says Curtis Strong, a professional boxer, Illinois state champion, and subject of a video made by the sociologist Loïc Wacquant, talking about 63rd Street in Chicago. "This used to be a hot spot in the 60s. You could get anything here. . . . [There was] an A&P, Buster Browns [a national brand of children's shoes], McDonald's burgers."

These memories bring us to our recent history. In the 1960s, we enter a different period, the period of the postmodern city – or what from a different view appears to be the abandonment, the reshaping, and the selective revitalization of the modern city. This happened in a context of long-term suburbanization and a shift of capital investment, white-collar employment, and cutting-edge industries away from older cities. But the central change that occurred in public discourse about American cities at this time was a connection between race and economic decline, an equation of "the urban problem" with "the Negro problem" (Beauregard 1993, ch. 7). This change was embedded not only in demographic movements and housing markets, but also in the transformation of neighborhood and downtown shopping streets. Following the urban riots of the middle to late 1960s, white store owners and shoppers fled many of the neighborhoods that a generation or two of immigrants and their children had called their own. Whether they feared arson, reprisals, or theft, loss of social status or simply physical contact, people left. Many shopping streets abruptly changed their ethnicity. The "ghetto" spread to my neighborhood of North Philadelphia. Eleventh Street receded – like Marshall Street, where my parents had shopped in their youth – to a childhood memory.

▦ Ghetto Shopping Centers

The nightmare that haunted urban renewal in the 1940s and 1950s came true in the 1960s and 1970s: many downtowns and neighborhoods were ghettoized. It was not only that more shoppers were black. They now had equal entry to white-owned shops, theaters, and restaurants where they had been unwelcome. But downtown also changed in another way. Stores that had been landmarks, pillars of merchant society, and beacons of social aspiration were gone. Many moved out to shopping malls in the suburbs; some went out of business, leaving their cast iron facades and plate glass windows empty. By the same token, blacks and the neighborhoods in which they lived were ghettoized. As low-income blacks moved into a neighborhood, shopkeepers offered cheaper goods, took less care with maintenance and display, and followed white customers to the suburbs. The element of choice that distinguishes a neighborhood from a ghetto was diminished even

further in the 1960s and 1970s; the voluntarily assumed ethnic character of many urban neighborhoods was inescapable
for blacks.

Cities were no longer what they seemed to be. The downtowns that had so enchanted children of my generation were,
in fact, suffering from a long downturn in business and new
investment that began in the 1920s (Teaford 1990). After
World War II, the paradox of their occupying expensive land
downtown, as they did less business in those locations, grew
sharper. By the 1980s, the nationwide mania for corporate
mergers and leveraged buyouts led department stores to bail
themselves out by selling their prime real estate. Like many
manufacturing companies, department stores eliminated
their core business – selling goods – and merged with other
stores, moved entirely to the suburbs, or became holding companies for their properties. Between 1970 and 1990, many
declared bankruptcy and tried to reorganize; others disappeared. They were often replaced by small shops specializing
in low-price jewelry, sneakers, and electronic goods: downtown
returning to the bazaar. At the same time, suburban malls also
changed. The concentration of stores and people encouraged
buildings for more diverse uses, including post offices, hotels
and offices, schools, and community centers. It became common to speak of suburban malls as "new downtowns."

In the 1980s, marketing analysts and social critics agreed
that the clearest product of modern times was a shopping
culture. Yet, by that time, the homogeneity and abundance
of mass production and consumption, represented by the
simultaneous horizontal and vertical stratification of urban
shopping streets, were only an image of the recent past. Shopping cultures were more fragmented than they had been for
at least 100 years. The middle classes, no longer growing in
size, failed to support the middle range of goods and stores
that had made cities a virtual landscape of consumption.

As Barbara Ehrenreich (1989, 228) has sharply noted,
polarization of incomes divided consumers between a few sta-
tus-conscious high-price stores and many low-price bargain
outlets. The "revitalization" of downtown shopping districts,
organized around thematic shopping centers, malls, and atria,
competed directly with the suburbs for high-income corporate
managers and professionals. For their part, the leveraged

buyouts undertaken by new corporate department store owners drove up debt and drove out old-time managers. The depth and variety of goods in each store so typical of the long post-World War II economic boom were reduced as stores hustled to pay interest on loans; the sales staff so much a part of the early 20th century white-collar expansion was replaced by self-service.

The death throes of the downtown department store took about 20 years. Of the major department stores in downtown Philadelphia, Gimbel's and Lit Brothers went out of business and Strawbridge and Clothier focused on their stores in the suburbs. John Wanamaker, which filed for Chapter 11 bankruptcy protection in 1994, was by that point a regional chain owned by Woodward & Lothrup, a department store based in Washington, D.C., with many suburban locations. The very image, around 1900, of the modern department store, Wanamaker's "had fallen prey to image problems, as well as increased competition" (*New York Times,* January 18, 1994). In New York, Macy's filed for bankruptcy protection around 1990 and struggled against merger with Federated, the large department store chain that owned Bloomingdale's, Macy's arch-competitor.

But this is a troubling image of both urban revitalization in the center cities and late 20th century commodity production. Even on the outskirts of the city, where they have parking lots to lure mobile consumers, department stores are disappearing – their buildings empty palaces, subdivided into indoor flea markets, or donated to local governments and turned into colleges, libraries, and government offices. Remaining downtown stores are policed by security guards and merchants fearing thefts. More expensive goods are chained to the racks; customers are permitted to try on only one sneaker at a time. Customers with cars flee to shopping centers in the suburbs, where surveillance is pervasive but often less felt by individual shoppers as directed toward them.

In addition to the ghettoization of downtown and the decline of department stores, shopping practices have been greatly changed by the economic recession that began in the 1980s. Households for whom bargain shopping is no longer a hobby but a way of life are attracted to various kinds of distribution "outlets" selling goods at discounted prices, discount warehouses where "generic brand" goods are sold in large quantities without special packaging, and "odd lot" or "99 cents" stores that sell assorted goods at very low prices. Just as department stores were undone by Americans' decreasing reliance on standardized pricing and traditional commercial images, so was Woolworth's undercut by stores that promised to slash prices and offered special deals.

Competition among retail forms has led to their multiplication in a dizzying spiral of adaptation. In the 1970s, department stores renovated their gridlike selling floors into specialized, designer-label boutiques. Specialty clothing shops flourished during the "affluent" 1980s and languished during the 1990s recession. Mail order houses and home shopping networks took consumers away from the stores. The crucial point, however, is that paying attention to price has encouraged customers to be more mobile than ever before: moving among brands of goods, and sites, forms, and social practices of shopping. While this is often associated with specialized, "niche" marketing, the general idea is that retail shopping is a fluid, changing field. The identity of the "thing" itself – the retail good, the store, or even the shopping experience – changes meaning according to who does the shopping, when, and where.

While retail shopping has been changing, new waves of immigration from Asia, Africa, and Latin America have been bringing new consumers and entrepreneurs to urban markets. Because most new immigrants tend to settle in the largest cities, and have little money, they crowd existing "ethnic" neighborhoods, both white and black. They create new spaces of ethnic identity (Little Havanas, Odessas, and Cambodias and suburban Chinatowns) and place new people in existing ethnic divisions of labor. Korean and (East) Indian shopkeepers often replace Jewish merchants in low-income neighborhoods, and buy from Jewish and Italian wholesalers before establishing their own suppliers' networks. Immigrants from all parts of the world swell the ranks of street vendors. West Africans sell knock-off designer scarves and Rolex watches on Fulton Street in downtown Brooklyn and on Fifth Avenue in midtown Manhattan. They sell African art that resembles museum art on 53rd Street, down the block from the Museum of Modern Art, and "tourist" art on 125th Street in Harlem.

Chinese sell frozen shrimp and dried mushrooms on the sidewalk outside grocery shops on Canal Street. Central Americans dispense hot dogs from vending carts all over the city.

Hardly tolerated by local store owners on ethnic shopping streets – many of whom are, themselves, Italian, Chinese, African American, or "Arab," usually Syrian Jews – immigrant street peddlers recreate a bit of the experience of Third World street markets and stalls. They also engage in less sanctioned, informal markets. They join a street economy in legal and illegal goods already flourishing in poor areas of the city. Some sell stolen or pilfered goods. Poor Russian immigrants stand around on Brighton Beach Avenue with shopping bags of their household goods and personal possessions, hoping to barter or sell. Individual blocks and whole shopping streets are in flux between stable ethnic identities, diversity, and change.

This does not occur without political conflict. In New York and Los Angeles, boycotts and demonstrations have been ignited by Korean storeowners who antagonize African-American customers.[13] Passions are inflamed by language differences, mutual suspicions, and resentment against yet another group of alien ethnic shopkeepers – who tend to hire other immigrants, either Asian or Latino. Peddlers, in turn, infuriate the storeowners, who press the police to enforce local ordinances against selling goods on the street. Revitalization threatens to "upscale" the neighborhood shopping street and becomes as big a bogey as gentrification. Even in poor and working-class neighborhoods, merchants' associations use design guidelines to strengthen their control of the shopping street. Like the owners of more expensive downtown property, they see the establishment of business improvement districts (BIDs) as a means of restoring security and civility. The negotiation of their property rights on the street is connected, once again, to the negotiation of ethnicity, social class, and the public cultures they represent.

---

13. Everyone in New York remembers the months-long boycott in the early 1990s of a Korean-owned grocery store on Church Avenue in Brooklyn, sparked by the owner accusing a black customer of shoplifting. Everyone in Los Angeles remembers, as a prelude to the police attack on Rodney King and the riots of 1992, the jury's failure to convict a Korean grocery store owner who shot and killed a black girl in his store – over another accusation of shoplifting.

No amount of immigrant entrepreneurialism negates the history of disinvestment in areas that have a large African-American and Puerto Rican or Mexican presence. Since the 1970s, commercial revitalization of ghetto shopping centers has proceeded together with continued abandonment. Every major shopping street in American ghettos looks the same, with cheap shoe stores next to discount drugstores next to liquor stores next to vacant lots next to burned out and boarded up stores next to local low-price chain stores next to more vacant lots and more burned out stores. The visual culture is unmistakable: plastic signage over the stubbled shadows of older, larger signs . . . the iconic orthography of Dealtown, Sav-Mor, "Dr. J's" and "Dee's" . . . big billboard ads for cigarettes and liquor featuring the appropriate ethnic models. Even sociologists have noted, in Chicago, that blacks prefer to shop outside their neighborhoods, because visible signs of decay are connected to a lack of quality and brand-name goods (Taub, Taylor, and Dunham 1984, 60).

In New York, several major ethnic shopping streets are in transportation hubs outside Manhattan, in the outer boroughs. Many African Americans shop on Fulton Street in downtown Brooklyn; Caribbean Americans shop on Jamaica Avenue in Jamaica, Queens; Asians shop on Main Street in Flushing, Queens. The closer they are to the subways, however, the less these streets attract middle-class consumers – white, black, or Asian. Except for Flushing, each of them has been scheduled for revitalization for so long that grass has overgrown the empty lots. Government agencies and utility companies – the core of the urban "growth machine" – have built new offices or converted old buildings and relocated their agencies, but most private-sector plans have been postponed over and over again. Developers find it hard to attract tenants to speculative office buildings in these areas. It may be difficult for them to get financing, and even if they do, employees may resist relocation to the outer boroughs. Instead of branches of commercial banks, ghetto shopping streets have income maintenance (public welfare) centers, surrounded by check cashing services and sidewalk vendors.

Peddling, a lost art in other areas of the city, dominates the street in ghetto shopping centers. According to New York City's local regulations, storeowners may extend their displays four feet out onto the sidewalk. Many open windows to the street or rent this space to other vendors, but the liveliest commerce is at curbside tables, on blankets spread on the pavement, and around food carts. Peddlers sell sweatshirts, jeans, bootleg videos, electric batteries, socks, handbags, Afrocentric books, African jewelry, incense. West African peddlers sell cloth both handwoven and mass produced in the Côte d'Ivoire. A shopper on 125th Street, not too far from City College, can find books and pamphlets from the reading list of an Afrocentric professor known to be an anti-Semite. Sidewalk tables display religious books and posters for Jehovah's Witnesses, Black Israelites, Muslims, and smaller groups. With proselytizing on the street, ghetto shopping centers provide public space for the discussion of religious as well as political ideas – a reminder of the streetcorner political debates of Jewish shopping streets in the past and a contrast to the privately regulated public space of suburban malls.

There is still a great distance between the department store and the bodega. But ethnic change in urban populations, as a whole, and the fluid symbolic economy of retail shopping suggest that we take another look at shopping streets and what they say about public culture. Were Walter Benjamin alive and living in New York today, I would advise him to head for Harlem and the outer boroughs. In the ghetto shopping centers where African Americans and immigrants sell and shop, he would find a different set of urban dreams, dreams arising from the intersection of ethnicity and class, posing a challenge to both multiculturalism and economic revitalization.

▨ Downtown Brooklyn

Although it has not been an independent city since annexation by New York City in 1875, Brooklyn still has the historic downtown functions of transportation hub, civic center, and major shopping district. It has been ghettoized in two senses: first, by a colonial relationship with Manhattan, the financial center of the city, and second, by industrial decline and racial change, leading to a predominance of lower-income and minority-group residents.

Brooklyn is the second-poorest borough, after the Bronx, in New York City. This reflects such long-term changes as

▨ Once upon a time, a hegemonic downtown: Abraham & Straus, Fulton Street, Brooklyn, in the 1920s.

Photo courtesy of Fulton Mall Improvement Association.

manufacturing decline, the phase-out of the commercial port, and the shutdown of the Brooklyn Navy Yard by the federal government, all of which have wreaked havoc on working-class jobs. It also speaks to the movement of many white ethnic, middle-class residents, to suburbs on the southern shore of Long Island. First, the Irish and Germans left, and after 1960, Italians and Jews. Since the 1960s, the social geography of Brooklyn has been altered by the expansion of African-American ghettos in central and eastern Brooklyn, the investments of Caribbean homeowners, the growth of a new Chinatown, and the gentrification of several brownstone neighborhoods surrounding the downtown.

Since Brooklyn is huge, any attempt to characterize its neighborhoods would be exhaustive. But several neighborhoods have become code words, since the mid 1960s, for singular events of urban resistance and transformation. These are often identified with conflicts between blacks and Italians or blacks and Jews. In 1968–1969, Ocean Hill–Brownsville was the site of an early experiment in school decentralization following a community strike against the public schools. The community was mainly black; the teachers' union, mostly Jewish. In 1989, a young black teenager was killed in Bensonhurst, an Italian American neighborhood, when he came to buy a car on a street with some racial tension. In 1991, riots broke out in Crown Heights, a neighborhood shared by the Lubavitcher sect of Hasidic Jews, Caribbean Americans, and African Americans, after a black child was run over and killed by a car in the Lubavitcher rabbi's entourage and a young Hasidic man from Australia was stabbed to death by someone in the crowd.

Downtown Brooklyn bears most of the stigmata of economic decline, racial change, and stop-and-start urban renewal typical of ghettoized downtowns. Its initial misfortune was to be located so near to Manhattan – one of the world's, and certainly the region's, premiere centers of both corporate offices and retail shopping. But it is also a gateway to the suburban shopping malls of Long Island and, by way of Staten Island, offers easy access to factory outlets in suburban New Jersey.

Yet, by any standard, downtown Brooklyn is livelier and more diverse than many urban centers. It actually contains several different districts, each an artifact in miniature of urban public cultures. Courthouses and lawyers' and dentists' offices cluster around the borough's administrative offices. Nearby are the office buildings of utility companies and government bureaucracies, both local and federal; several colleges, universities, a law school, and high schools, as well as proprietary trade schools such as business colleges and beauticians' academies. Also in the area are the Atlantic Terminal, where trains disgorge commuters from the suburbs of Long Island, the Gothic skyscraper headquarters of the Williamsburg Savings Bank, the tallest building in Brooklyn, and the Brooklyn Academy of Music.

All three historic destinations are surrounded by parking lots. New buildings are recent fruits of the city's policy of encouraging decentralization of jobs outside Manhattan: the back offices of Morgan Stanley, a financial services firm, and a new, mixed-use commercial complex called MetroTech, a $1 billion, 4-million-square-foot corporate and educational complex that is anchored by the Chase Manhattan Bank. MetroTech was conceived in the 1980s to save jobs that would otherwise move to New Jersey, and produce a synergy between high-tech firms and Brooklyn's Polytechnic University. It is not quite as scientific an environment as a French or Japanese technopole, but it was intended as a more coherent expression than anywhere else in the city of New York's interest in businesses oriented toward new technologies.

At the center of all these sites, not far from the Brooklyn Bridge, is Fulton Street, downtown's major shopping district. The street cuts a long gash through the borough, but these eight blocks downtown bear witness to Brooklyn's history of economic decline, suburban flight, and racial change. Behind the facades of today's jewelry, electronics, and sneakers shops lie the empty shells of yesterday's department stores. Now, shopkeepers are mainly immigrants, and most of the customers, especially on weekends, are black.

Efforts to revitalize Fulton Street began at least as long ago as the late 1960s, when the Downtown Brooklyn Develop-

▨ Fulton Street today: Discount stores and sidewalk vendors.

Photo by Alex Vitale.

ment Association was formed to take advantage of the city's, the state's, and the federal government's deep pockets for urban renewal. Without support for a comprehensive plan proposed by the mayor, which would have linked commercial and industrial redevelopment, projects focused on upscaling the existing retail shopping streets and making the area more attractive for eventual office construction.[14] Throughout the 1970s, several plans were proposed to transform Fulton Street into a pedestrian mall. They focused on the outward signs of civility we have come to expect from local merchants' associations: new design criteria for storefronts and signs, canopies, benches, and lights. They also raised an esprit de corps among the shopkeepers and local banking institutions, who formed a Fulton Mall Improvement Association, an early business improvement district. The plans and the organization asserted a common identity, based on a narrative of Fulton Street as an exciting, crowded, culturally diverse urban center. The public culture of the street was supposed to represent a heterogeneous population in a homogeneous shopping culture.

But these plans were, and continue to be, confronted by the negotiation of different identities and a more conflicted public culture. From the 1960s to the 1990s, changes in retail shopping eliminated all the department stores but one. Abraham & Straus, a major retailer founded in Brooklyn in 1885, proudly clung to its flagship store (see diagrams on Fulton Street from 1950s–1990s). Between 1978 and 1993, when Toys "R" Us signed a lease, retailers with name brands and national reputations were unwilling to rent space in a special enclosed space, Albee Square Mall, across the street.

In 1969, local minority groups affiliated with a national movement called Operation Breadbasket, led by the Rev. Jesse Jackson, demanded information on minority hiring from Fulton Street storeowners and held demonstrations in front of the stores to emphasize their demands. Again, in 1978, a coalition of local minority groups – including Black Economic Survival, Fight Back, South Brooklyn Construction Workers, and Free at Last – picketed construction on the mall, claiming

14. Plans to transform downtown Brooklyn into an office center, and completely eliminate the manufacturing economy, date back to the 1940s, with the construction of the civic center and the regional vision of Robert Moses (see Schwartz 1993).

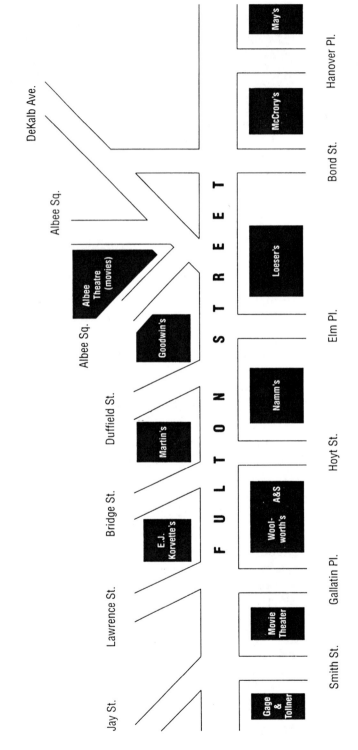

■ Declining hegemony or ghettoization: Disappearance of department stores on Fulton Street, 1950s–1990s

Declining hegemony or ghettoization: Disappearance of department stores on Fulton Street, 1950s–1990s

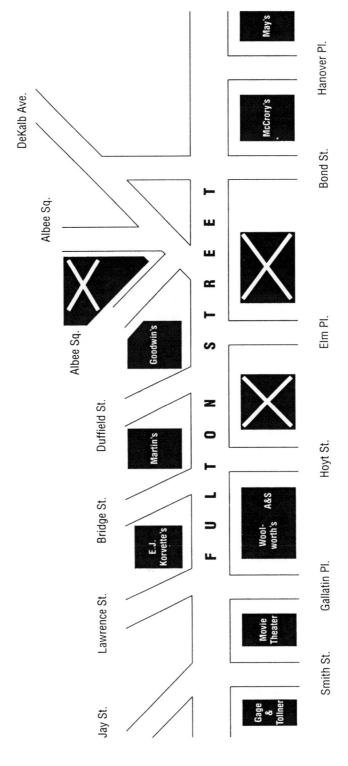

1960s

■ Declining hegemony or ghettoization: Disappearance of department stores on Fulton Street, 1950s–1990s

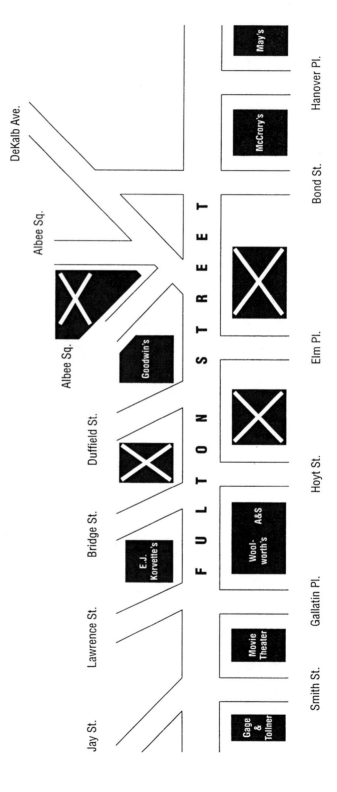

Late 1970s

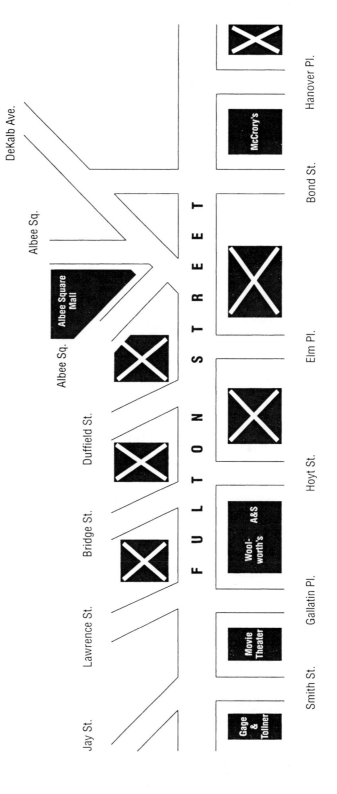

■ Declining hegemony or ghettoization: Disappearance of department stores on Fulton Street, 1950s–1990s

■ Declining hegemony or ghettoization: Disappearance of department stores on Fulton Street, 1950s–1990s

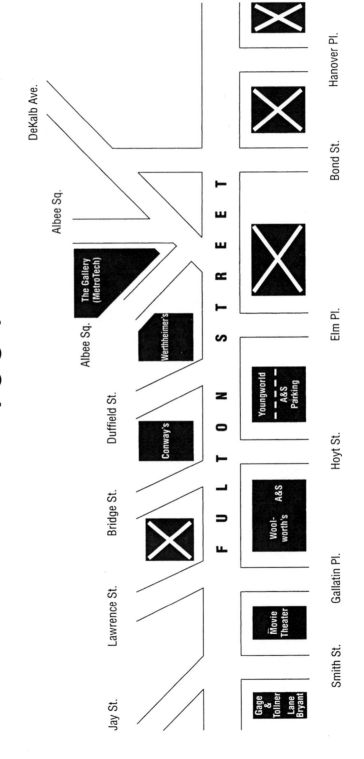

that few minority workers from Brooklyn were working on the site (Van Slyke 1978). While storeowners were confused and divided by these protests, the Fulton Mall Improvement Association mobilized them to negotiate the demands as a group. But these negotiations, which lasted for days, created specific problems of representation. As a local reporter noted, "If '80%' of the Fulton Street consumers are black, then a hefty portion of the 80% are women" (Van Slyke 1978); yet no women sat on either side of the bargaining table. The specter of riots lurked all around the new construction. The reporter says, almost as an aside, "Downtown Brooklyn has, after all, enjoyed several peaceful 'summers' and its luck could be running out."

After the major construction work was finished, criticism focused on the quality of goods available in the shops. " 'It's Schlock Mall right now,' a veteran shopper says sourly [in 1982], referring to the string of wig parlors and discount electronics stores on the street" (Henry 1982). While some planners and merchants blamed the national economy for a one-two punch of inflation followed by recession, others emphasized the predominance of low-income and minority-group shoppers, who suffered from severe unemployment (Kappstatter 1981a; also see *Daily News,* August 23, 1982).

The dialectic of inclusion and exclusion continued to focus on how to define the target public of shoppers and on who would get – as the minority coalition put it – a share of the corporate pie. From a middle-class shopper's point of view (Kappstatter 1981b), the ghettoization of Fulton Street was represented by incense peddlers, sidewalk wig merchants, disco music blaring outside a baby clothing store, jean stores and more jean stores, chain snatchers, people selling stolen goods, and the replacement of department stores by indoor flea markets. From an African American's point of view, however, Fulton Street was represented by A&S, the sole remaining department store, and "the wealthy, successful and mainly white commercial pie" (Van Slyke 1978).

This language was hard to sustain in the 1980s, which was both the affluent decade and the decade of homelessness. More shoppers than ever shopped in the suburbs. After May's, a low-price department store, filed for bankruptcy protection and then closed its doors, Fulton Mall remained bereft of any major anchor store besides A&S (Rangel 1986). Even A&S faced a shaky financial situation. Owned by Federated Department Stores, a national chain, A&S risked being shut down – like other large department stores in major American cities – as Federated struggled to pay off the billions of dollars of debt it incurred on its junk-bond-financed buyout by Canadian entrepreneur Robert Campeau. A&S actually expanded into Manhattan in 1989, as the anchor of a new "vertical" mall near Macy's. This brought to 18 the number of A&S stores in the metropolitan region. Although the board of directors proclaimed a continued commitment to the flagship store on Fulton Mall, in 1995, Federated merged all 18 A&S stores into other retail divisions and changed the name of the flagship store to Macy's.

In contrast to the weakness of corporate retailers, the number of immigrants in Brooklyn soared. Many worked in or near Fulton Mall and also shopped there. So there was a continual need for goods that appealed to low-income shoppers, both working and unemployed, and immigrants with specific tastes and desires. Among the discount and outlet stores, a reporter counted "39 stores selling women's wear, 23 shoe stores, 32 fast-food outlets, 30 jewelry shops, 14 stereo and electronic[s] stores, 4 banks, and a scattering of other stores" (Rangel 1986).

At the same time, the city government tried desperately to interest private developers in building MetroTech. As private-sector initiatives took the lead on redevelopment projects from Ellis Island, site of the Statue of Liberty, to Times Square, conflicts over Fulton Street began to shift toward the question of which forms of shopping would be represented in the stores downtown: name brands and national chains oriented toward middle-income shoppers or more discount, knock-off, and gray-market goods.

When the first buildings of MetroTech finally opened in the early 1990s, they had a highly visible impact on the Fulton Street area. Brooklyn Union Gas, the investment firm Bear Stearns, Chase Manhattan Bank, and the Security Industries Automation Corporation moved more than 10,000 jobs to the site. Chase alone accounted for 6,000 employees. Employees of all the firms were offered discounts and special shopping nights at A&S. On one level, the companies set up "outreach"

■ A selective view of Brooklyn's symbolic economy: Sites of Fulton Mall, West Indian-American Day Carnival Parade, and Caesar's Bay Bazaar.

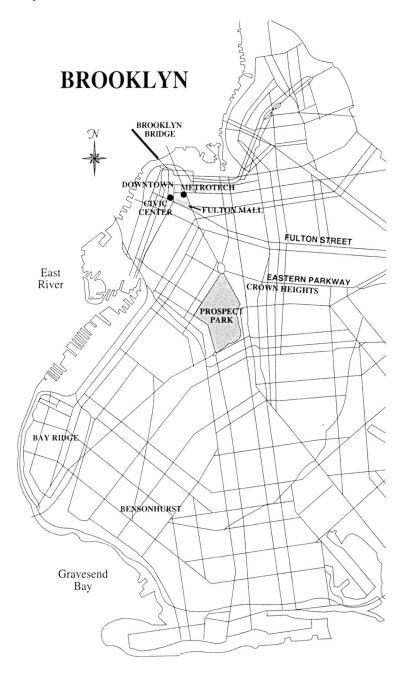

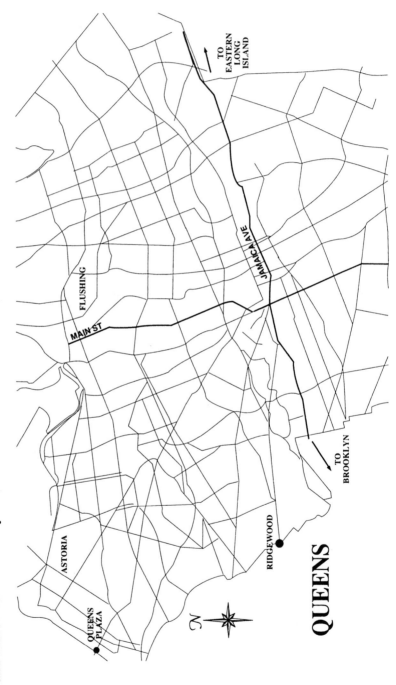

■ A selective view of Queens's symbolic economy: Sites of Asian and Caribbean shopping centers, Neptune's restaurant, and indoor flea markets Q.P.'s and StoreWorld.

▩ A new hegemony in downtown Brooklyn: Plan of MetroTech.

(Drawing is reproduced from a brochure from MetroTech.)

programs to employ local residents and use the facilities or enrich the programs of local schools. On quite a different level, uniformed Chase security guards began to patrol the area around MetroTech, including the railroad and subway stations, and visit downtown stores.

But MetroTech has the potential to isolate itself from downtown Brooklyn as well as to inundate Fulton Mall with affluent shoppers. Chase operates a shuttle bus from its offices in Wall Street, and many employees who commute from the suburbs prefer to park their cars there and take the shuttle bus instead of the subway. Other employees resisted relocation from Manhattan to Brooklyn and took early retirement or requested transfers instead. Those who work in MetroTech – who are mainly white, especially at the upper levels – are afraid to go out to lunch or shop on Fulton Street. They order lunch sent in, or buy their meals from food carts that are wheeled around the floors. Many of the higher-level employees prefer to socialize after working hours at the South Street Seaport in lower Manhattan. Employees who do shop in Fulton Mall are like most other shoppers there. They are mainly black and Latino and live in Brooklyn. As clerks and secretaries, they are a relatively low-income group.

Moreover, as a speculative development project, MetroTech was built with its own shopping plaza and food court. The shops on the plaza there – a café, a deli, a flower and gift shop, and Au Bon Pain – could just as well be found in midtown Manhattan or a suburban mall. They represent a broad, moderate-price, mass-market experience of blond wood, clean design, and nationally recognized names quite unrelated to Fulton Street as it still appears today. In the middle of MetroTech is a tree-lined court, Myrtle Promenade. Yet two blocks from this oasis, near the public housing projects on Myrtle Avenue, stores sell marijuana. Some office workers are said to go there to "get Myrtl-ized": an unanticipated cross-cultural shopping experience.

Indeed, the forms of shopping around Fulton Street challenge both the BID's image of civility and the image of the sleek office buildings that have slowly been built in downtown Brooklyn since the 1970s. At Flatbush Avenue and Nevins Street, one edge of downtown, vendors line the front of the Consolidated Edison building. A table offers incense and "Mohammed Speaks," "How to Avoid the Fall of America," and "How to Eat to Survive" by the Messenger Elijah Mohammed. (The salesperson asks my research assistant Danny, a white guy with a notebook, if he "ha[s] a problem.") The next table sells candy and nuts. Inside the Con Ed building are a commercial bank branch and a bargain toy store. Across the street, a Kansas Fried Chicken restaurant stands next to the Nyabingh Gift Shop, "selling African arts and crafts from the mother country."

Around the corner, on Livingston Street, a block from Fulton Mall, shops display their goods on the sidewalk, while many of the upper floors of the two- and three-story buildings display For Rent signs. Two Indian men with yardsticks stand guard outside a fabric store with six-foot-long fabric rollers displayed on the sidewalk. Inside "Brooklyn Bargain Plaza," a small indoor flea market, large, uniformed security guards are posted at either end of the shopping floor. Korean, Afghan, and black merchants work in booths that offer children's haircuts, ear piercing, African clothing, and mismatched clothes, a current inner city style. The sign of the J.K. Coffee Shop is surrounded by barbed wire. The old McCrory's, a five and ten cent store that closed in 1994, is empty now, its boarded-up building running through the block to Fulton Mall.

A major presence on the mall, Abraham & Straus fills eight interconnected buildings built from 1885 through 1935. The store is an archeological pastiche of ornamental details covered by layers of modernization. While it is the only store outside MetroTech with a substantial percentage of white customers, in front of it on the mall is an Afrocentric bookstand selling tracts, novels, histories, and self-help books, and the owner's poems and essays. Across the mall is "Dr. J's," a shop for sneakers, jeans, and sportswear – one of many shoe stores and discount shops. The commerce is not limited to storefront displays. Hawkers call out goods in front of the jewelry stores and a loan shop. People try to sell things they carry around in bags. A man approaches Danny with belts draped over his shoulders: "Ten bucks, you can't beat the price."

There are 15 stores on Fulton Street near the Flatbush Extension. Most are only 15 × 20 square feet in size. Five sell jewelry, one sells sneakers, one is a small booth selling watches and gadgets, one is a hair styling salon, and the others sell clothing, children's clothing, and beauty supplies. The employees are mainly African American, and the owners include five Koreans, two Iranians, two Jews (who employ black managers), two Italians, two American blacks, and two who would not be identified. Some stores have been there as long as 11 years; some as little as four months, with the average at three years. For half the shopkeepers, this is their first store. Half are the first generation in their family to own a store.

The conflicted identity of Fulton Street is fought out in the quality of goods in the shops, in the politics of the local BID, and on the street itself. Black teenagers who want the enchantment of downtown but feel uncomfortable and unwelcome in both Manhattan and suburban shopping malls that are still mainly white can find that enchantment at Fulton Mall. But the sources of enchantment – in both the image of the commodity form and the image of race – are constantly changing. Corporate finance and suburban competition have almost completely eliminated downtown department stores. Immigrants keep trying to achieve the American Dream as shopkeepers. The "Arabs" are so successful at running cheap shops on Fulton Street that they fight the upscaling strategies of MetroTech's representatives on the board of the Fulton Mall Improvement Association.

Conditions have changed the downtown that represented, by catering to working- and middle-class whites, a European-American immigrant experience and a hegemonic department store culture. Yet the corporate investment represented by MetroTech is strongly challenged by a representation of ethnicity that includes African-American shoppers and Afrocentric goods, as well as by a history of protests over jobs and business ownership. Most of the current customers can hardly know this history. They see shopkeepers and sidewalk vendors of their own ethnic background and assume Fulton Street is their shopping street, a street of incense peddlers and fast-food franchises, discount shoestores and racks of clothes. Is there any chance that a ghetto shopping center could represent the Other of a corporate, white America?

125th Street

While downtown Brooklyn lives in the shadow of MetroTech and plans for new low- and middle-income housing, Harlem faces no such prospect. The eight crosstown blocks of 125th Street that make up the heavily traveled, commercial center of Harlem remain surrounded by ghettos. From Eighth Avenue east to Madison Avenue, 125th Street is an almost entirely black shopping street, with a large African presence, in the center of dilapidated, renovated, and abandoned apartment houses, with a mainly black, partly Latino, population.

From the late 1970s through the mid 1980s, four major public-private commercial projects were announced. Through most of the 1990s, however, none of them broke ground. The Commonwealth Shopping Center, the Harlem International Trade Center, the headquarters of Inner City Broadcasting Company, and "Harlem on the Hudson" – a mixed-use development along the river to be financed by Japanese investors – mutely represent the street's, and the community's, unmet aspirations. The only hints of their construction are signs, scaffolding, and vacant lots. The street's two office towers, both built in the aftermath of the 1960s urban riots, house government agencies and nonprofit groups. Unlike Fulton

▓ View of 125th Street, 1943. Blumstein's Department Store,
opened in 1896 and target of a community boycott during
the Great Depression, is on the south (left) side of the street.
The Apollo, Victoria, and Harlem theaters – all with live
stage shows – are on the north (right) side.

Photographer unknown. Photographs and Prints Division, Schomburg
Center for Research in Black Culture, The New York Public Library,
Astor, Lenox, and Tilden Foundations.

Mall, 125th Street lacks even a memory of large, corporate-
owned department stores. Its narrative is that of a low-income
shopping center, with fast-food franchises, empty land, and
local and national chains of low-price stores.

But this is Harlem. Memories, like the street itself, are
long and deep. The Apollo Theater, declared a New York City
landmark in 1983, is the only black theater left in New York
that can claim performances by all the great African-American
artists of jazz, bebop, and rock and roll. Like some of the old
stores, it had a "whites only" policy until 1934. After live stage
shows were abandoned in the 1970s, the Apollo was completely
modernized in the 1980s with facilities for recording and television production. Live shows were resumed in the 1990s.
Nearby, the Hotel Theresa, where Fidel Castro stayed during

■ 125th Street, 1995. Blumstein's has been divided into smaller stores. Does anyone remember the "whites-only" policy?

Photo by Alex Vitale.

a visit to the United Nations in 1960, was converted to offices in the early 1970s.

Long a center for the sale of Afrocentric literature and soapbox orations, 125th Street has a score of sidewalk tables where posters, books, and newspapers are sold. On a Saturday afternoon, Jehovah's Witnesses walk toward shoppers holding open copies of The Watchtower. Black Israelites stand in a large group around a man denouncing white people over a public address system. (Here Danny is challenged to step on a White Jesus image on the sidewalk. When he does, and offers a comment, the leader calls him a "white faggot" and he is told to move along.)

A couple of local department stores still bear the names of the German Jewish merchants who opened them around 1900, when Harlem was still a predominantly white community. The owner of one of these stores sold it in 1930 rather than admit black customers (Osofsky 1971, 121); the building now houses medical services. Other stores, such as

125th Street as a crucible of African-American identity: Sidewalk vendors display their wares while Nation of Islam militants spread the word.

Photo by Alex Vitale.

Blumstein's, resisted the hiring of black employees, but gave in to community boycotts in the Great Depression. Wertheimer's is still in business on 125th Street, as it is in Jamaica, Queens, and downtown Brooklyn. But most of the white storeowners gradually disappeared after the riots of 1964 and 1968. Reminders of those times – when "Soul Brother" painted on a window identified black-owned stores – are now iconic business emblems. Stores bear names derived from African history and geography, and their windows are emblazened with African statues, posters of Marcus Garvey, the Rev. Martin Luther King, Jr., and Malcolm X. Posters along the street urge people to "Buy Black. Boycott non-black-owned businesses. Pool resources, create jobs." The Studio Museum, the city's main African-American art museum, and the National Black Theater are both on 125th Street. If you are white, walking along 125th Street is a constant reminder that the Other is you.

Also if you are Korean. From September 1988 to December 1989, several years before a notorious black boycott of a Korean-owned grocery store on Church Avenue in Brooklyn, Harlem residents boycotted Koko's, a Korean-owned grocery store on 125th Street, where a Korean employee had mistakenly accused a black shopper of theft and assaulted him with a knife. The storeowner criticized bias against her by the community and the police: "I think if a *white* policeman had come on Sunday morning, my employee would not have been arrested" (Picard and Cates 1990, 11; emphasis added).

Despite periodic rumors of economic revival, many storefronts, and second and third floors, are empty.[15] Rents do not approach the level of 14th Street in Manhattan or Jamaica Avenue in Queens, streets with similar stores and many black shoppers. "It is difficult being a business person here," says the [black] owner of a full-service office equipment store, the

---

15. "The concentration of development activity on 125th Street stems from the belief that the economic health of the two-mile-long street, the commercial center of Harlem for more than 90 years, is a key to the revitalization of the entire Harlem community. It also reflects the view that Harlem, by virtue of its location just north of Central Park and its basically sound and relatively inexpensive housing stock, is on the verge of extensive redevelopment" (L. Daniels 1981). Ten years later, journalists were still sounding the same optimistic tone (see Traster 1990).

Riots in Harlem in July 1964 protested against the police and white-owned stores. Here, the shopwindow announces, "THIS IS A BLACK STORE."

Wide World Photos.

only one on 125th Street. "... I think we have to work harder to stay in business than people in other areas do" (Kennedy 1992). In 1990, the Federal Deposit Insurance Corporation shut down the only Harlem-based bank, Freedom National Bank, after community groups failed to raise $6 million to bail it out. A number of important properties are owned by nonprofit corporations. The Apollo went nonprofit, as an educational facility, in 1991, after several years of business losses. The National Black Theater is another nonprofit organization, and a parking garage and multiscreen, first-run movie theater are owned by the Harlem Urban Development Corporation (HUDC). The movie theater was unable to break even financially and closed for a year in the early 1990s.

Problems of business owners on 125th Street indicate the special circle tightly drawn around race and class in American

■ On 125th Street today, a "Harlem USA Boutique" in a McDonald's franchise sells Afrocentric books and toys.

Photo by Alex Vitale.

cities. Harlem was never developed in terms of "good" jobs for community residents, and its economy has historically lacked a financial and wholesale base to support the development of 125th Street as a profitable retail shopping center (Vietorisz and Harrison 1970). Even with large increases in black-owned businesses from the mid 1950s on, blacks for many years owned smaller stores than whites, with fewer employees outside their own families, smaller inventories, less insurance, and less access to credit (Caplovitz 1973). Typical of the ghettoization of black enterprise prior to the 1960s, most of Harlem's black storeowners ran hair styling salons or restaurants (see Tabb 1970, 44–45). And if more white-owned stores were damaged by riots in the 1960s, it was probably because black-owned stores were generally located on the less heavily traveled avenues (Lenox, Seventh, and Eighth) than on 125th Street, where rents were higher (Caplovitz 1973, 110).

Since the 1960s, aging white storeowners have been replaced by black merchants and entrepreneurs. The local development corporation, HUDC, has helped put together groups of investors to increase minority-owned stores. But recent additions to 125th Street carry a complex social message.

In the 1970s and 1980s, many Koreans opened shops on 125th Street, attracted by vacancies and low rents. As early as 1982, before it was generally recognized in midtown and lower Manhattan that the local greengrocer or dry cleaner was likely to be Korean, 125th Street had an estimated three dozen Korean-owned stores, mainly food and clothing shops, alongside 60 black-owned stores. The Uptown Chamber of Commerce thought that two out of three new businesses that opened on 125th Street that year were Korean owned. The Koreans were criticized by the 125th Street Business Association for failing to participate in improvements to the street – a lack of cooperation that apparently was resolved. But they were also criticized by the Universal Negro Improvement Association, a group dedicated to black control over the community's economic life: "The Koreans have come into our community, taking millions of dollars out and not even giving our youth any jobs" (Rule 1982). So the Koreans became the new Other group of merchants on 125th Street, and the representation of ethnicity on the street was no longer seen in strictly black-or-white (or black-or-Jewish) terms. Korean shopkeepers in a black neighborhood created a complicated triangle, in which Asian nationality was incorporated into white, but never into African-American, ethnicity. By the 1990s, according to HUDC, the Koreans' situation had changed. Few new Korean-owned shops were opening up, and there was more competition for vacant space. Some of the older Korean merchants had even lost their stores to such big corporate chains as Fayva Shoes and McDonald's.

There seemed, indeed, to be a new corporate presence on 125th Street. Spurred, perhaps, by the Los Angeles riots of 1992, a large regional supermarket chain and Manhattan-based discount drugstore chain committed themselves to anchor positions in the Commonwealth Shopping Center, first proposed in a 1978 plan for Harlem's economic renewal but never built. In 1992, a new woman owner took over a very

successful McDonald's franchise next to the Apollo and redeco-
rated it with an African theme. Branches of both The Body
Shop and Ben & Jerry's Ice Cream opened several blocks
away. The ice cream store franchise is owned by a black entrepreneur in partnership with a local homeless shelter. Its
employees are men from the shelter, which receives a major
portion of the profits. To honor the arrangement, Ben & Jerry's
waived their standard franchise fee.

Putting these corporate imprints on 125th Street is
intended to neutralize the cultural values of isolation by class
and race without denying the community's need for low-price
goods. But how to infuse the "neutral" forms of corporate
shopping with a memory of blackness? Ben & Jerry's made a
symbolic adaptation by introducing two new flavors: Harlem
Bluesberry and Sweet Potato Pie. The usual posters of black
leaders are hung on the walls. The franchise owners, of course,
are black. Whether upscale brands can be combined with black
ethnicity is a gamble.

Yet plans to revitalize 125th Street aim at making it
attractive to middle-class black shoppers, most of whom would

■ Corporate investment on 125th Street: The Body Shop tries to
  blend in.

Photo by Alex Vitale.

▓ Ben & Jerry's partnership with the homeless: The hand that holds the cone is black.

Photo by Alex Vitale.

have to be drawn into Harlem to shop. Here revitalization implies a huge contradiction, for 125th Street already is the metropolitan region's premiere shopping street for Afrocentric goods and ethnic foods from the African diaspora. Ironically, while the black middle class has greater resources than ever before to live in more expensive neighborhoods and shop in the suburbs, 125th Street is one of the places where a new African-American ethnicity is being formed.

These issues shaped a conflict over the removal of street vendors from a large, informal "African Market," that grew in recent years at the corner of Malcolm X Boulevard and Martin Luther King, Jr., Boulevard (125th Street). The vendors were expelled by police in 1994. Until then, they congregated on the very same vacant lot where the Harlem International Trade Center was announced in 1979. At that time, local black politicians, led by Rep. Charles Rangel, envisioned an import-export bank that would aid a trilateral trade between the United States, Africa, and the Caribbean, but the project was never funded by the federal government. Instead, trade with Africa soon took a different form. During the 1980s, as political repression and economic crisis in their countries grew more severe, an increasing number of West Africans emigrated and wound up selling goods on the streets in major cities of the world, such as London, Paris, Florence, and New York. Some were connected to established, though informal, distribution networks; others brought over goods made by family members and neighbors. The African trade, then, that was finally set up on 125th Street was in mud cloth and kente cloth; in vests, robes, and jackets; and in sculpture and jewelry. Vendors came mainly from Mali, Senegal, Ghana, and Liberia.

While the African Market seems to have been recognized as a coherent, though unofficial shopping space around 1986, the number of vendors and shoppers increased dramatically in the early 1990s. At least on the vendors' side, self-employment and political oppression contributed to the latest wave of Afrocentrism.

Before Mayor Rudolph Giuliani sent police officers to clear the peddlers from 125th Street, in 1994, we spoke with Yadda, a Liberian woman who was described as the Queen of the

■ Ghetto shopping center or Third World bazaar?: African Market on 125th Street, Harlem, 1994.

Photo by Alex Vitale.

Market. She said the market reminds her of Africa. "The
market is an open place, not controlled; you sell what you
want to sell. Each vendor has a designated spot, and all the
merchants look out for one another. People know better than
to steal from us." Yadda claimed the vendors had permission
from HUDC to sell at this site. But the peddlers on 125th
Street – and it is estimated there were 500 to 1,000 of them
– had no legal status. Although they belonged to at least one
merchants' association, most were not licensed by the city
government. Even when fully licensed by either the New York
City Health Department, to sell food, or the Department of
Consumer Affairs, to sell other goods, street vendors are not
supposed to sell on such a busy street. Moreover, while some
of them rented storage space in the basements of stores on
125th Street, the storeowners ceaselessly lobbied the mayor
and local officials to force the peddlers to go elsewhere.
(Despite the presence of Koreans and a few remaining whites,
most of the small shopkeepers are black, as are nearly all
local elected officials.) So, from time to time, over a 10 to 15
year period, the peddlers were harassed by the police (see, for
example, *Amsterdam News,* August 25 and October 27, 1990;
December 14, 1991; July 3, July 24, August 7, and August 14,
1993).

Indeed, vendors at the African Market claim that Mart
125, an indoor mall of small stalls developed by HUDC under
a grant from the city government, was created to take them
off the street. There must be some truth to their claim. When
Mayor Edward I. Koch took part in the groundbreaking for
Mart 125 in 1979, local merchants complained that peddlers
created dirt and congestion on the street and "spong[ed] off
the community" (Fowler 1979). And the number of street vendors was probably smaller then, for African emigration had
not yet hit its peak.

Yet this is an old, old story in New York City. Mayors
have periodically waged war against street vendors, especially
in times of mass immigration and economic depression.
Between the 1880s and the 1930s, for example, the informal
street markets of pushcart peddlers, most of them immigrants,
were subject to an increasing number of controls and eventually pushed into indoor public markets (Bluestone 1992).

■ Mart 125, an indoor market with official approval.

Photo by Alex Vitale.

Just when the African Market began to draw more shoppers, in the early 1990s, the Dinkins administration was pressured into enforcing the local laws against peddlers, including those on 125th Street. Merchants on many shopping streets opposed the proliferation of street vendors, the result of a confluence of immigration and recession. As they did on 125th Street in the 1970s, storeowners complained about the crowded pavements and litter street vendors left behind. They claimed they lost business to peddlers selling cheap knock-offs and bootleg goods. They contrasted themselves, as honest merchants, with unlicensed vendors who did not pay taxes. On Grand Street in lower Manhattan, Chinese street vendors had similar problems with storeowners, who were both old Italians and new Chinese. Mayor Dinkins, facing a reelection campaign in 1993, responded by expressing sympathy with local business communities.

But in 1992, vendors on 125th Street held a vociferous protest march, frightening storeowners into shutting their security gates with customers still inside the shops. Since many of the storeowners were black, they were put in the position of defending black-owned businesses against African

▦ In New York, peddlers are an old story. Street vendor, 125th
Street, June 1934.

Photographer unknown. United States History, Local History and
Genealogy Division, The New York Public Library, Astor, Lenox, and
Tilden Foundations.

vendors. Mayor Dinkins, an African American, found it difficult to condemn all street vendors "and admitted he was a
teen-age peddler in his Harlem youth, first hawking shopping
bags and later selling Liberty Magazine" (Sullivan 1993).
Even his Jewish predecessor, Mayor Koch, who presided over
the inauguration of Mart 125, was the son of a man who had
been a pushcart peddler in his native Poland (Fowler 1979).

Through the winter and spring of 1993, the City Council
and various city government agencies, including the police,
tried to settle the problems of street vending, which the *Times*
identified as most acute "in the bustling retail areas of 125th
Street in Harlem and on Fulton Street in downtown Brooklyn,"
by removing unlicensed vendors and proposing revisions in
the licensing system. On 125th Street, vendors who could
afford to pay at least $488 a month in rent (including utilities,
security, and promotion) were encouraged to move indoors at
Mart 125. Talk also circulated about herding the vendors to
another location on another vacant lot.

A year later, in 1994, the peddlers were still an issue. The Republican administration of Mayor Rudolph Giuliani followed the strategies attempted by mayors for the previous 100 years and spoke of moving peddlers to new open-air markets (Hicks 1994). Members of the local community board in Harlem, however, were not unanimously opposed to the peddlers' presence. " 'I see a vendor on the corner selling socks, and we have to chase him down. I see a vendor on the corner selling crack, and I don't hear a word about it,' said one community resident" (Reed 1994). For their part, the vendors claimed they contributed to making 125th Street a tourist attraction, no matter what goods they sold. " 'It doesn't make sense for street vendors to be taken off 125th Street,' said Yussef Abdul Aziz, who sold tube socks and jeans there, in the shadow of the Adam Clayton Powell Jr. State Office Building, for one year. 'People come from all over the country to 125th Street to shop, and we're an important part of 125th Street' " (Hicks 1994; also Reed 1994). Vendors also defended peddling as a stepping-stone for immigrant entrepreneurs and a positive alternative to going on welfare.

In October, 1994, one month before federal, state, and local elections, Mayor Giuliani called out the police (*New York Times,* October 19 and 23, 1994; *Amsterdam News,* October 22, 1994). The peddlers were asked to rent inexpensive space, for $7.50 a day, on two outdoor lots nine blocks away from 125th Street, on land owned by the Majid Malcolm Shabazz Mosque, which is led by followers of Malcolm X. At 7 a.m. on a Monday morning, 400 uniformed police officers arrived on 125th Street to prevent about 300 peddlers from doing business as usual. Clearly prepared for a confrontation like that of 1992, some police officers were dressed in riot gear and some were on horseback. Instead of threatening shoppers, the peddlers protested by chanting and marching up and down the street. Before the crowd dispersed, more than 20 protestors were arrested, including the leader of the 125th Street Vendors Association. That night, locks on some shops were tampered with and filled with glue. A protest meeting was held at Mosque Number 7 of the Nation of Islam (the main group of Black Muslims that Malcolm X left before he was assassinated). Although a Black Muslim leader and a black activist candidate for the U.S. Senate – both from outside Harlem –

called for a boycott of stores owned by "whites, Koreans, Latinos, and Arabs," there was no violent confrontation.

In the following days, protesters continued to picket stores. Vendors mainly ignored the lots at the Mosque Malcolm Shabazz's intended outdoor shopping mall, and African-American leaders were divided by their self-interest. Not only did a black mosque own the land to which the peddlers were moved, but that mosque planned to use the new African market to spearhead commercial development on their street. Moreover, some of the stores targeted by the boycott rented their shops from another black church, which could suffer financially if the stores lost business. Black politicians were divided. Most elected officials did not want to antagonize the mayor or storeowners. Unlike the vendors, many of whom may be illegal immigrants, the shopkeepers vote. The chairperson of Community Board 10 and executive director of the 125th Street BID supported the vendors' relocation. As for ordinary people, black folks supported the vendors. Most white folks did not seem to care. Within a couple of months, the local development corporation that runs the Jamaica Market in Jamaica, Queens – an effort at commercial revitalization aimed mainly at African-American middle-class shoppers – welcomed the peddlers from 125th Street to their site. They hoped the vendors would attract more shoppers and bring the publicly subsidized development to life (*New York Times,* December 23, 1994).

Although the street vendors were forcibly removed from 125th Street, the issues they pose loom over the public spaces of most cities. "Good" and "bad" representations of vendors reflect different notions of public order in the streets, as well as a different sense of social class, ethnicity, and public culture. On the one hand, as an HUDC official says, "Peddling is bad economic development policy. These people don't pay taxes. According to the police, 80 percent of the goods are stolen or illegally produced, with false brand names or bootleg videos and cassettes. . . . The peddlers drive away more people than they attract. It leads to street congestion. People get disgusted and they don't come back." Moreover, he claims that the African peddlers on 125th Street were dumped there from all over the city: "They drove the Senegalese from Fifth Avenue and now they are here."

On the other hand, the street vendors of 125th Street were almost all black. (On two Saturdays, the busiest shopping day, Danny saw only two vendors out of 200 to 300 who were not black.) They sold all kinds of music created in black communities, from jazz and reggae to rap, blues, soul, and slow jams. At the height of a Saturday market, a black torso displayed leopard skin underwear at a sidewalk table. A poster at a jewelry stand announced it was black owned. Food peddlers sold cakes and pies, Southern fried chicken, beef sausages, and West Indian-style fried whiting. This was, in all senses, a bazaar. People stopped and talked with the peddlers. Conversations ranged from haggling over prices to street gossip, politics, and discussions of business prospects. When no customer was at hand, the vendors called out descriptions of their products and prices. Most vendors were men, and they called out compliments to women shoppers, telling them how great they would look in the products they sold. Several vendors dealt in posters and smaller framed photographs and prints, including pictures of black families, jazz collages by the artist Romare Bearden, photographs of black leaders, and village scenes in Africa. It could fairly be said – allowing for differences of gender, social class, and national origin – that the street vendors represented ethnicity on 125th Street.

But this is not the representation desired by local political leaders and HUDC. They want black culture *and* economic revitalization. They want 125th Street to look like shopping streets in other neighborhoods. Mart 125 is their model of retail shopping – accessible to the street but not outdoors, a midpoint between bazaar and shopping mall. Indeed, Mart 125 has two floors of small stalls, each 60 or 120 feet square, that are fully rented and draw a lively crowd of shoppers. Their goods are not easily distinguishable from those sold on the street. Restaurants on the second floor serve Caribbean food, soul food, and health food. On the ground floor are two bookstores, one owned by the Nation of Islam. An African tie-dye stall sells fabrics and clothing. African fabric stalls have sewing machines where the proprietor sews while waiting for customers. One of two hat stalls offers name brands next to "personalized" hats on which buyers can design their own messages. But while the goods may be similar, the mart is organized differently from the street. HUDC provides a security staff and a mart manager, and runs educational courses and small business training seminars for the merchants who rent stalls.

HUDC also supports the expansion of Harlem as a tourist attraction. Since the 1980s, a number of tour companies have brought busloads of tourists to view 125th Street and eat at Sylvia's, a well-known restaurant with a varied clientele. German, Italian, and Japanese tourists visit the jazz clubs at night. A street photographer with a Polaroid plies his trade, taking pictures of visitors with jazz musicians, attaching himself to tourists with the same tenacity as his confrères in Paris or Rome. A specific form of black culture, as well as the distance from a hegemonic downtown, continues to distinguish 125th Street from Fulton Mall.

Clearly, 125th Street is a complex representation of race, class, and ethnicity. With the newest source of its Afrocentrism in post-1985 immigration from Africa, it negotiates an identity that is at once global and local. With older sources of Afrocentrism in religious and Black Nationalist literature, the street is typically African American, separatist, aggressively Other. Moreover, 125th Street is not only a site but a means of reproducing difference, exclusion, and "ghetto culture." It is half in the mainstream economy, with both corporate products and their bootleg imitations, and half bazaar. The African Market has to be seen as a form of shopping that both challenges and affirms a ghetto culture. It remains to be seen whether the shopping street will be changed by tourism and the corporate identities of new retail stores or remain submerged in poverty.

▣ Indoor Flea Markets

While the shops of Fulton Mall and the African Market of 125th Street are very distant from Walter Benjamin's experience, I suspect they would not be so strange to Alfred Kazin, Kate Simon, Langston Hughes, Chester Himes, and Audre Lord. The public culture into which they were initiated, as children, combined the ethnic bazaar and downscale goods, the disorder of selling in the streets, the fusion of cultural difference and common ground that marks the bittersweet experience of children of a diaspora. Moreover, the shopping spaces I have described so far are fairly traditional for the modern city.

The shopping street, with its indoor-outdoor division indicating the different sources of legitimacy of merchants and peddlers; the department store, pillar of a modern urban civility; the pedestrian mall, an attempt to restore the remembered civic order and social homogeneity of the arcades – all these would be familiar to those who preceded us in the early 20th century. In our time, a new form of urban shopping space is represented by the indoor flea market. This is a somewhat bewildering hybrid of junk shop and off-price store, of shopping mall and discount mart, of independent entrepreneurs and *hondelers* and totally standardized goods typical of a mass-market economy. Here, too, however, the congeries of tiny "stalls" reflects the constant negotiation of social class and ethnicity that we find in the city's other shopping spaces.

The major reason for the indoor flea market is economic. During the 1980s, because of the crisis in retail trade and the economic recession, indoor flea markets became a popular shopping concept. A varied assortment of small shops, really only stalls, were gathered under a single roof by a management company that leased a vacant warehouse, movie theater, or department store for this purpose. If the building was far enough from the center of the city, it was probably located in a suburban-style shopping center with its own parking lot. The indoor stalls sold the same sorts of goods that are sold on neighborhood shopping streets – jeans, jewelry, shirts, shoes – but these goods were more like street vendors' wares than the name-brand merchandise sold in stores. While some of the merchandise carried designer labels, the presumption was that much of it was either "seconds" or gray-market goods that "fell off a truck." At any rate, prices were lower than in department stores, vendors were often willing to bargain, and shopping carried an element of chance or even discovery.

In contrast to department stores and corporate boutiques like The Gap, indoor flea markets are not designed. As at Mart 125 on 125th Street, the stalls are small, many occupying only 6 × 10 square feet, under 12-foot ceilings; fixtures and lighting carry utilitarianism to an extreme. Jeans hang above a stall, shirts are stuffed onto open shelves, shoes are taken out of their boxes and laid out across a table. Most stalls have no name. But owners display hand-lettered signs identifying products and advertising prices and also comparing the products to specific name-brand goods. Unlike the shopping street, which often features huge billboard advertisements for mass-market videos or drinks, these signs are the only representations of corporate identity. The authenticity of the bazaar plays off the legitimacy of corporate identities.

In New York, indoor flea markets are one step up in social status from street vendors. Nearly all, and certainly the biggest, indoor flea markets are in the outer boroughs. Most seem to be managed by Jews or Italians, while stalls are rented by Asians, followed by Latinos, and then by white, European Americans. At Mart 125 and Brooklyn Bargain Plaza, near Fulton Mall, merchants are black; Brooklyn Bargain Plaza also has Korean and Afghani vendors. At StoreWorld, in Ridgewood, on the border between ethnically mixed, working-class and lower-middle-class neighborhoods of Brooklyn and Queens, 12 stalls are owned by Dominicans, 8 by Koreans, 7 by Pakistanis, 6 by Ecuadorians, 6 by Afghanis, 5 by Italians, 4 by Punjabis, 4 by Serbs, 4 by Jewish Americans, 3 by Lebanese, 3 by German Americans, 2 by Colombians, 2 by Indians, 2 by Israelis, 2 by Turks, and 1 by an Irish person. Five of these stalls sell jewelry: the vendors are Dominican, Ecuadorian, Serbian, Italian, and Korean. Most of their merchandise is identical.

Often vendors of the same ethnic group lease stalls near each other. Like the street vendors of the African Market in Harlem, they watch each other's booths while they go on breaks. Shoppers carry on conversations with vendors in their native languages, and like the vendors of Afrocentric goods on the street, vendors cater to specific group tastes. Dominican stall merchants in a Dominican neighborhood sell brightly colored clothing for grownups and frilly, gauzy dresses for little girls – all manufactured in New York. Yet other Dominicans sell "American" fashion, and one Dominican vendor displays photos customers bring him, modeling the clothing they have bought. So stalls can be both local and global – by ethnic background of vendors and shoppers, language, and visual display. Vendors can be as intimate with shoppers from their ethnic group as on a neighborhood shopping street.

Many indoor flea markets are extremely popular. On a typical Saturday afternoon, a thousand shoppers might enter the doors. But not all indoor flea markets are successful. Q.P.'s, which opened in 1980 on two floors in two interconnected, unused industrial buildings at the transportation hub of Queens Plaza, was at first a great success. It had an ethnic mix like StoreWorld's, with the same diversity among the vendors. Shoppers from nearby lower-middle-class and working-class areas of Queens flocked to the stalls. For some reason, however, Q.P.'s lost its appeal. By the early 1990s, only 11 stalls out of hundreds were left. The Italian and Jewish owners, who also manage real estate, hired the management of Caesar's Bay Bazaar, a successful indoor flea market in Brooklyn, for advice. According to Caesar's Bay, they did not take it. Did Q.P.'s management lose control in some way over the vendors? Was the ethnic mix of vendors, shoppers, and goods too great for a single shopping space? Or was the specific combination of ethnic groups unable to bridge the distance between social classes?

It is interesting to consider what makes Caesar's Bay Bazaar so successful. For one thing, it looks out over the Atlantic Ocean at Gravesend Bay, 12 miles from Manhattan and a mile from the nearest subway line. This makes it much less accessible to low-income shoppers. Since it is surrounded by middle-class, white, ethnic neighborhoods, a highway, parks, and tennis courts, the relative isolation of its physical site is bolstered by social barriers. Not surprisingly, shoppers and vendors are mainly white. Shopping there appeals to white, middle-class shoppers who have not left Brooklyn for either Manhattan or the suburbs. In its own way, it negotiates ethnicity, social class, and gender to produce a sense of locality that is safer and more controlled than that of many neighborhood shopping streets.

Caesar's management is well aware of the pleasures of the controlled shopping environment. The on-site manager prides herself on managing a "mini-mall" rather than an indoor flea market. Burly security guards, nearly all of whose uniforms have sergeant's stripes, stand in front of the doors. Management requires merchants to sign one-year leases rather than the monthly leases typical of most indoor flea markets and screens the merchandise vendors want to sell.

Management also allows only a certain number of stalls of different types. Prices are supposed to be discounted; indeed, Caesar's own advertising handbill states that there are "over 500 factory outlets." But low prices are not supposed to imply cutthroat competition, false representation, and stolen goods. Management also enforces on all vendors a seven-day, money-back guarantee. Unlike at indoor flea markets, the booths have names, listed in newsprint directories distributed by management throughout the store. The booths' names are also featured in the ceaseless program of music and promotions broadcast by the public address system.

On one visit, most vendors at Caesar's Bay are Italian and Jewish Americans and Russian Jewish immigrants, with a small number of Koreans. The only black workers are maintenance men. There are a few Latino salespeople but no Latino stall owners. While the mainly black neighborhood of Coney Island is not far away, there are almost no black shoppers in the store. Most shoppers are white, probably Jewish and Italian, with some Latinos. The food court on the second floor sells knishes, pizza, eggplant, and bagels. There are 28 ladies' wear stalls, 11 booths selling gold jewelry, 8 selling costume jewelry, 2 selling silver jewelry, 5 offering jewelry repair, and the array of consumer goods usually found in a suburban shopping mall.

In Brooklyn's remaining white ethnic neighborhoods – not the gentrified ones, but Bensonhurst, Bay Ridge, and Bath Beach – the sense of style is not so different from that sold in the indoor flea markets. Personalized clothing, gold jewelry, and customized autos with vanity plates are central features of social life, alternating with the counterstyle of leather and jeans adopted by fans of heavy metal music. Shoppers can find both styles in Caesar's Bay. At a record booth displaying autographed photos of local heavy metal bands, guys wearing clothes favored by heavy metal fans come by to hang out with the vendor. Women socialize in the nail parlors, and everyone hangs out in the food court. Many shoppers know the vendors by name. The public address announcements join local references to well-known songs: following the song "Diamond Girl," the announcer says, "Ray's Jewelry [a booth in Caesar's Bay] – where you can select the gold necklaces that will make you shine as you cruise the Third Avenue scene." (Third Avenue in Bay Ridge is a prime spot for "cruising," teenagers and young adults slowly driving by in their cars to look at others.)

When management says that Caesar's is not an indoor flea market, they emphasize their distance from the "fly-by-night" merchants who pay no sales tax and have an otherwise shady relation with the law. Like indoor flea markets, however, Caesar's is located in an unused department store, an old E.J. Korvette's, vacated when that discount chain went bankrupt in the 1980s. Unlike the flea markets, Caesar's has the physical and social space of suburban shoppping. Together with Toys "R" Us, Caesar's owns the shopping center where it is located. For all these reasons, Caesar's site attracted Kmart's attention. The discount chain bought out Caesar's owner, an Egyptian Jewish immigrant merchant, in 1995.

Several factors put the indoor flea markets of the 1980s and 1990s into perspective. While I have emphasized immigration and recession, this is also the period when flea markets as a genre have been transformed. Originally an outdoor space, like the *Marché aux Puces* in Paris, where bric-a-brac, cheap used goods, and "collectibles" are sold, flea markets are now a generic shopping form for off-price bargains. Some are amateur operations, organized for a short time by voluntary groups to raise money for a cause. But most are professionally managed shopping centers with low overhead costs and rents. Indoor flea markets in big cities with large immigrant populations have stalls selling the new merchandise I have described; those in smaller cities and towns still sell "junk" and collectibles. Other indoor flea markets, specializing in factory outlet shops, may be located in converted shopping malls. Regardless of their specialization, indoor flea markets combine qualities of the bazaar, the traditional flea market, and suburban malls.

So the form itself is heterogeneous and feeds on several different sources. People want to be entrepreneurs, the manager of Caesar's Bay says, and shoppers want a personal relationship with vendors. That being said, indoor flea markets differ from both the historic forms of downtown shopping and neighborhood shopping streets. Their ethnic diversity reflects the city's diversity. Perhaps because they are in secure spaces indoors, they mix genders of vendors and shoppers as easily as suburban malls. And they negotiate a "middle" social status between the populism of the street and the hegemonic capital investment of the department store or the mall.

◼ Remembering Walter Benjamin

I confess that I first found Walter Benjamin alluring because he wrote about shopping spaces. The sensuality of his writing and the pain his memories evoke caution us not to ignore the historicity of shopping forms: their meaning to both the history of societies and individual biographies. Benjamin also made me aware that shopping spaces are not just important ways of seeing – with epistemological implications – but ways of being in the city, with great suggestiveness for the formation of identity. It is not simply that they are central spaces for being-in-society, but that the forms and sites and the very experiences of shopping they engender are part and parcel of what makes groups different.

When I thought about the mundane sites where people shop, beginning with Eleventh Street, I became fascinated by the idea of indoor flea markets. What would Walter Benjamin have made of them? Would he see the exotic qualities of foreign vendors selling shoddy or off-price goods, or would the banality of indoor flea markets be quite outside his field of vision? I then began to think about the specific shopping experiences of low-income people and people of color, the shopping spaces where immigrants meet native-born Americans, and the forms of retail shopping that are historically available to both groups. In contrast to all the writing these days about shopping malls, I was drawn to the street and the flea market as "ghetto shopping centers," just as important as the malls for constructing identity and difference. Thinking this way made me more aware than ever that such "new" structural processes as globalization build on old cultural forms. In this case, shopping cultures are not simply formed by immigration or economic crisis; instead, they selectively adapt – rejuvenating long forgotten features – in response to social pressures.

So shopping cultures are not important simply on the level of individual preferences or even consumption practices. They are an important part of building the spaces of cities, and by virtue of the importance of seeing and being seen, they build public cultures. They offer opportunities for the representation of group identities, and for the inclusion of those identities in a larger, urban public culture. They also pose problems of social integration that transcend simplistic formulations in terms of class or race or economic or cultural analysis. Especially when we consider the persistence of the bazaar and the danger it poses for the aesthetic strategies of relatively privileged groups, shopping streets lead us toward a material analysis of cultural forms (see Stallybrass and White 1986).

Why was the rediscovery of Walter Benjamin so important in the 1970s? Certainly it was because he joined material and cultural analysis. Yet he also touched an emotional core of discontent with urbanism and public culture. Such urban planning critics as Herbert Gans and Jane Jacobs had already demonstrated that demolishing older neighborhooods and establishing homogeneous designs for rebuilding them led to monotony, alienation, and disuse. As the next generation looked at neighborhoods where they grew up, they experienced a similar sense of loss. They associated it with the massive urban renewal programs of the 1950s and 1960s – and felt the impotence of having to pull up short roots, the anger of citizens deprived of their neighborhood streets, the frustration of social reproduction of a social class and an ethnic group that Marshall Berman (1982) describes so well for his neighborhood in the Bronx.

Wrapped up in the layers of territorial and tribal dispossession were a political identification with other "dispossessed" groups – the poor and the blacks – and a disillusionment, made up of equal parts of emotion and intellect, with the promise of modernity that had incited the European immigrants' own Great Migration to the cities of the United States and thence to the suburbs. In Benjamin's sensory evocation of 19th century Paris and early 20th century Berlin, my generation found both the downtown department stores and suburban shopping malls of post-World War II America.

So we were doubly disinherited. On the one hand, as critics of social conformity and "one-dimensional man," we felt alienated from the mass consumer mentality represented by malls; on the other, as white ethnics raised in the city, we recognized that the neighborhoods where we had grown up and the downtowns where we had shopped were no longer "ours." During our childhood, the fantasy and grandeur we saw downtown were, in fact, those of an old urban order whose elites had felt themselves under siege since the early 1900s. But we could hardly have known that. At the very moment of our enchantment by the city, the department stores were building branches in suburban malls. While some eventually went out of business, others would rise again, a phoenix in the rubble, anchoring the meaning of new shopping galleries and downtown malls.

The vitality and permissiveness we felt in the streets are felt again in the outdoor markets and sidewalk stalls whose exotic goods and foreign vendors recall the old immigrant peddlers and open-air markets that were shut down by city authorities and disappeared before our childhoods, from the 1930s to the 1950s. Today, peddlers still threaten store merchants' business and damage the image of the shopping street, making it instantly déclassé. Upscaling, the fervent hope of all merchants' associations, from which we middle-class types benefit, is another form of dispossession.

Despite the economic crises of the 1990s, so favorable to discount shopping malls, some merchants and shoppers want to participate in a hegemonic shopping culture. Yet like the Hollywood studios of the 1920s and 1930s, representations of downtown's old bourgeois culture excluded the secular ethnicity of neighborhood shopping streets even while many department stores were owned, and their commercial ethic elaborated, by immigrants and immigrants' children. By the same token, neighborhood shopping streets have often been both representations of, and vehicles for, reproducing a specific ethnicity and social class. Until the 1970s, downtown and neighborhood shopping streets were quite different landscapes: downtown, still a landscape of power, and Eleventh Street, still a vernacular. Each was constructed by a different mix of corporate and "ethnic" products, a different integration of streets and interiors, a different hierarchy of global and local in the cosmopolitan downtown and the assimilation of Eleventh Street's foreign roots. Those were the days before neighborhood delicatessens discovered Brie.

And before the racial balance in many downtowns and neighborhood shopping streets shifted away from European

Americans. The decades of the downtown department stores' greatest image creation, from the 1920s to the 1950s, were also periods of intensive suburbanization by whites and black migration to cities. The disintegration of a hegemonic shopping culture after 1960 represented the fragmentation of a hegemonic public culture. Since the 1970s, the term *upscale* has indicated more than a shopping culture where money makes a difference. It indicates a certain kind of public culture: a racial "balance" in which each group has its place, a public space that is often secured by uniformed guards, a neutralization of ethnicity by both aestheticism and corporate identities. In the upscaling of shopping spaces we find a vision of the middle-class city.

Partly these changes are taking place in the centers of cities – reclaimed from the bazaar by BIDs and corporate strategies of development – and partly in the neighborhoods, even the suburban neighborhoods, where immigrants and native-born Americans struggle over the ethnic identity of shopping streets. It would oversimplify the whole problem of shopping streets to claim that a universal process of globalization was responsible for new forms of shopping in the city. Instead, immigration and recession and a continual adaptation and reuse in the built environment of retail shopping have revitalized such old forms of shopping as street peddlers and flea markets, while raising the social stakes of revitalization downtown. Yet while many groups claim they support revitalization, it is not at all clear what that means. There is a great deal of disagreement, and actual resistance, over who has rights to the street, what kinds of goods should be sold, and how aesthetic criteria for designing the street may challenge existing forms of identity and public culture.

The proximity of different ethnic groups – their opportunity to occupy the same space and time – has given new urgency to the negotiation of ethnicity by shopping cultures. Korean shopkeepers are integrated, by virtue of setting up stores in black neighborhoods, into a "white" ethnicity. Street vendors on neighborhood shopping streets incorporate African and Caribbean elements of the African diaspora into an "African-American" ethnicity. By the same token, the collapse of physical distance between social classes makes it more crucial for some groups – merchants' groups, the city government, the management of mini-malls – to establish explicit, exclusionary rules for the use of shopping spaces. In this way, shopping cultures renegotiate social class in public space.

Regardless of these structural processes, it is impossible to know the narrative of a shopping street without knowing local history. Whether we look back at the historical absence of new investment capital in Harlem or look forward to the development of new elite identifications in downtown Brooklyn, we see that shopping streets are an important part of a city's continuous past. No matter how diverse their clientele or how greatly they may change over time, shopping streets affirm both difference and sameness, a tendency to identify either *with* or *against* the Other, whether that sameness is one of gender, ethnicity, or class.

Shopping spaces are a valuable prism for viewing public culture. The types of goods that are sold, at what prices, and in what forms – these are the everyday experiences in which physical spaces are "conceived" in the light of social structure. Walter Benjamin still teaches us a valuable lesson. In the shopping streets, vision is power.

■ Historic preservation becomes an inclusive vision: The National Trust tries to represent a socially diverse public culture.

IT'S DISCOVERING WHAT THIS COUNTRY WAS LIKE BEFORE IT WAS CALLED AMERICA.

IT'S BRINGING AMERICA'S MAIN STREETS BACK TO LIFE AND GETTING BACK TO BUSINESS.

IT'S JOINING NEIGHBORS AND FRIENDS TO IMPROVE THE COMMUNITY YOU CALL HOME.

What is historic preservation?

It's your memory. It's our history. It's worth saving.

NATIONAL TRUST FOR HISTORIC PRESERVATION   1 800 289 7091
1785 MASSACHUSETTS AVENUE, N.W. WASHINGTON, DC 20036

Public service announcement courtesy of the National Trust for Historic Preservation.

7

THE MYSTIQUE OF PUBLIC CULTURE

Rereading memoirs of city dwellers of the late 19th and early 20th centuries lets us re-view their subjective maps of urban public spaces. As we compare our memories with Walter Benjamin's, Alfred Kazin's, or Chester Himes's, we are forced to confront the question that is implicit in both the neoconservative and radical postmodern critiques of urban decline: How have the great public spaces of modernity stood up to contemporary challenges? How do they translate today's visions of civility, desires for security, and aesthetics of fear? These are the questions that guide this book from the great public spaces of modern cities – streets, parks, museums, department stores – to their sucessors – theme parks, restaurants, ghetto shopping centers, and indoor flea markets. From Times Square to Bryant Park and Sony Plaza. . . .[16]

Public spaces are the primary site of public culture; they are a window into the city's soul. As a sight, moreover, public spaces are an important means of framing a vision of social life in the city, a vision both for those who live there, and interact in urban public spaces every day, and for the tourists, commuters, and wealthy folks who are free to flee the city's needy embrace. Public spaces are important because they are

---

16. For Bob Viscusi, Lou Asekoff, and George Cunningham: *Nil humani alienum.*

places where strangers mingle freely. But they are also important because they continually negotiate the boundaries and markers of human society. As both site and sight, meeting place and social staging ground, public spaces enable us to conceptualize and represent the city – to make an ideology of its receptivity to strangers, tolerance of difference, and opportunities to enter a fully socialized life, both civic and commercial.

We can understand what is happening to public culture today if we look at what is happening to public spaces. Bryant Park and Sony Plaza, Fulton Mall and 125th Street, are different sides of the same public culture. From the 1970s to the 1990s, American cities, and cities in all the rich, multiracial countries of the world, have reshaped public spaces as they have wrestled with the demons of change.

Since the 1970s, the public's attention has shifted from factory workers, school teachers, and engineers to media stars and profiteers in real estate, finance, and culture industries. These are the true imagineers of the symbolic economy. In cities from New York to North Adams, from Orlando to Los Angeles, economic growth has been thematized and envisioned as an image of collective leisure and consumption. As part of the process, collective space – public space – has been represented as a consumable good. Even when it is not bought and paid for, as at Disney World, public space has been joined with retail space, promoting privatized, corporate values. Sony Plaza re-imagines the Parisian arcades that Walter Benjamin describes, imposing a corporate order on the strolling crowds, transforming the dream experience into a "Sony wonder."

Cities have also shifted from a population historically recognized as homogeneous, after the great immigration waves of the late 19th and early 20th century ended, to a population of far greater ethnic and social diversity. This change in the public has had a great impact on public culture. On-going debates about multiculturalism in school curricula and museum exhibits are just the beginning. The future of American political and economic hegemony in the world is at stake, along with the meaning of citizenship within this country and the future of its cities as economically dependent and ethnically mixed. The combination of fusion cultures and economic dependence is highly volatile. How the great public spaces of modernity absorb and reflect the tensions, and create a more inclusive vision of separate identities, is part of the visible struggle to enter the 21st century.

During the 1970s, crises in the mightiest of cities, and the mightiest of basic industries, made us feel for the first time like a powerless nation. While the Vietnam War undermined the widespread belief in American military might, fiscal emergency in the nation's largest city – New York – created the impression that our cities were built on sand. When the steel and auto industries admitted they could not compete against foreign companies, and laid off thousands of workers, local landscapes of power, built around factories, were transformed. At the same time, some of the poorest people were concentrated in cities. With a sense that the cities were plummeting out of control, governments cultivated their dependence on business. The public-private "partnerships" that were formed in the 1970s yielded in the 1980s to private-sector control, seen in the BIDs' control of public space.

This history illustrates the connections between the issues that define power in the most immediate sense today – and that seriously threaten the look and feel, if not also the survival, of modern cities. These issues are

◆ the design and control of public space,

◆ the symbiosis of vision and power,

◆ the meanings and uses of culture.

Bryant Park, which has posed a challenge to control for most of the 20th century, is a key to these issues. The park is a testing ground of subtle and not so subtle strategies of control; it is a microcosm of the simultaneous development of cultural strategies and security forces as means of negotiating social diversity. It is a space many of us love to hate, like Sony Plaza, and a space we hate to love. Bryant Park forces me to wrestle in my own heart with the demons of change. It shows a public space so deeply changed that we can no longer take it for granted.

Does anyone know, in these days of entertainment, security, and retail shopping, what a park is? When a park was recently proposed for the Hudson River waterfront, neighborhood residents in lower Manhattan protested that the city and state governments supported a Big Money park that would be built to the specifications of real estate developers and commercial entrepreneurs. Official plans did indeed suggest building shopping centers and entertainment complexes on landfill and refurbished piers. "I grew up with parks," a community protestor and civil engineer said at a public meeting. "I know what a 'park' is – open space and trees. Not enclosed space and megastores." Another neighborhood activist said, "Let's begin with the obvious. A park is grass, trees, benches, open space and playing fields. A park is not 10,000 square foot restaurants, 100,000 square foot retail outlets, chain stores, amusement complexes or athletic clubs" (*Villager,* December 7, 1994, 1).

These activists contrast the great public spaces of the 19th century, like Central Park, or the 20th century, like Times Square, with the public spaces shaped by the style of the 1990s. Bryant Park and Disney World and Sony Plaza dominate the collective imagination. They dominate through their control of space and their colonization of time. They have exhausted the imagination of what public space can be: it is a vision of civility, bounded by commercial consumption.

At this moment more than half the U.S. population lives outside of cities. Yet urban public spaces are closely watched, for they are crucibles of national identity. The defining characteristics of urban public space – proximity, diversity, and accessibility – send the appropriate signals for a national identity that will be more multicultural, and more socially diverse, in the years to come. In New York City, for example, average annual immigration has risen from 78,300 in the 1970s to 111,500 in the 1990s (New York City Department of City Planning 1995). Such countries as Mexico, Bangladesh, Pakistan, Egypt, Nigeria, and Ghana, which were never well represented even in New York's polyglot population, are now "emerging players" in the city's immigration mix. How do these men and women form a public? How do all of us adjust to unavoidable contact with strangers in positions of moral authority? Whose face do we trust? Ultimately, these come down to questions of culture. But there are no easy answers. Both common usage of the term *culture* and cultural styles have changed.

▓ The Meanings of Culture

Since 1980 culture has become a fiercely explicit battleground in struggles that used to be considered political or economic. This signals both an ideological and a behavioral revolution – but one without overarching goals, movements, or shifts of power. Judging from their reaction to politicians, men and women feel that the center has fallen apart – whether that center is city, family, or face-to-face communications – and they are left defenseless. The language of equality is stretched by new groups making new claims. As in all modern revolutions, the norms of civility are broken; no one knows how to talk to anyone else. And the spaces of seclusion that used to impose defenses against discontinuity – public schools, art museums, "the neighborhoods," the suburbs – are all under siege. It would be nice if we had the "shared meanings" of culture to help us understand, and maybe even navigate, the crisis. But that is the problem. From feminism to racism, from kindergarten multiculturalism to academic poststructuralism, the rules of culture have changed.

Ironically, the exhaustion of the ideal of a common destiny has strengthened the appeal of culture. Yet this is culture rather than Culture; it is both broader than the high culture of museums and social elites and more specific than the old definition of a society's generally accepted patterns of how to see, think, and act. In common American usage, culture is, first of all, "ethnicity": habits carried through space and time, refined through interaction with church and state, and asserted as a means of differentiation and independence. Culture is also understood to be a legitimate way of carving a niche in society. Now that labor unions and political parties seem powerless to challenge social divisions, culture as "collective lifestyle" appears a meaningful, and often conflictual, source of representation. As something that makes implicit values visible, however, culture is often reduced to a set of marketable images. Instrument, commodity, theme park, and fetish: culture is something that *sells,* something that is *seen.* These understandings of culture are common to both the intellectual fermentation around the notion of postmodern society and the daily struggles of real lives. And they have immediate repercussions on public culture.

The media treatment of the annual Gay Games, held in New York in the summer of 1994, on the 25th anniversary of the Stonewall rebellion, illustrates the lowest common denominator of what culture has come to mean. The games are more than an athletic competition for a special group. They are supposed to exemplify the solidarity and pride of homosexuals, burnished by political organizations and ravaged by AIDS. In the publicity surrounding the games, as well as in their athletic and cultural program, homosexuality is represented as if it were an ethnicity with its own traditions and roots. It is also represented as a lifestyle, with its own entertainment forms and consumption choices. Lifestyle is inescapably linked to marketing, as it is often pointed out that most individual homosexuals in the United States have higher incomes than most households. Thus the Gay Games have drawn the support of large corporate sponsors (manufacturers of consumer goods), feature T-shirts and other commercial memorabilia, and are praised for bringing tourist dollars to the city. The mainstream press covered the multimedia games as a cultural, rather than either a sporting or a political, event.

Culture is, arguably, what cities "do" best. But which culture, which cities? The cultures of cities certainly include ethnicities, lifestyles, and images – if we take into account the concentration of all kinds of minority groups in urban populations, the availability and variety of consumer goods, the diffusion through mass media of style. Cities are sites of culture industries, where artists, designers, and performers produce and sell their creative work. Cities also are a visual repertoire of culture in the sense of a public language. Their landscape and vernacular are a call and response among different social groups: symbols making sense of time. Cities are identified with culture, moreover, because they so clearly mark a human-made sense of place and a human-size struggle with scale. Does all this not suggest that culture is, in fact, a common language? That the divergent and multilayered cultures of cities create a single, overriding identity: a public culture of citizenship?

This may have seemed true in the early 20th century, when ethnic, class, and sexual cultures inhabited separate spaces. Private spaces, under conditions of WASP hegemony, upward social mobility, and working-class movements, made possible the fiction of a common public culture. It is hard to pretend to such unity today, despite an overall language of inclusion and with many groups claiming the use of public spaces. Moreover, outright competition has dramatically changed the public sphere. Chronic fiscal crisis has so weakened public institutions and the members of their work force that their sense of mission has narrowed to saving their own jobs. Groups that interact in the same representative institutions, from city councils to boards of education, have radically different agenda that breed immobilism and distrust. The social practices of a public culture seem outmoded because they are "modern," along with the unquestioned hegemony of downtown and the pretended invisibility of class and ethnic cultures. The very concept of public culture seems old because it requires transcending private interests; it has been replaced by new rules of privatization, globalization, and ethnic separation. If every culture can set the rules – is individually hegemonic – it makes no sense to think of a transcendant common culture.

Yet what cities still do have in common is a "symbolic economy" – a continual production of symbols and spaces that frames and gives meaning to ethnic competition, racial change, and environmental renewal and decay. Despite the power of real estate developers, their architects, and members of public commissions, no single vision mobilizes this symbolic economy. Indeed, like the competing claims to embody "representations" of different cultures, the preeminence of culture since the 1970s has occurred despite the absence of vision. We have seen, in this time, the death of urban planning, the powerlessness of old elites to control the conditions of everyday urban life, and unprecedented debates over what should be built (or unbuilt) and where. A deep chasm lies between the post-1970s appreciation of visual culture and the absence of a master vision to control the chaos of urban life. This gap offers opportunities for both access and exclusion, for both elitism and democratization.

The vitality of the symbolic economy cannot hide the deep gut of fear that underlies much of the fragmentation of public life since the 1950s. As fear of symbolic violation by contact with others has yielded to fear of the physical violence of being raped, mugged, or killed, the aesthetics of public space have been shaped by designing spaces to be "defensible" and hiring armies of private security guards. Even these strategies are not enough to enforce civility. " 'We may have more guards, but they are just not forceful enough,' complained George Tully, manager of a Kinney Shoe Store at the [MetroTech] mall [in downtown Brooklyn], who said he had to hire his own security guards to combat a fresh wave of shoplifting over the last year" (*New York Times,* June 19, 1994). And just when the public is so threatening, so unknowable, there is more clamoring for "public space." Yet there is no single overriding vision of the city's public, no vision of how to balance the needs of the "public" and of "space" in the symbolic economy. The streets, parks, museums, and mixed-use commercial centers are torn between a democratic ideology and a restricted access, both legacies of modernism. While neighborhood groups representing "the people" urge more access to parks, conservancy groups representing "the parks" urge more restrictions on public use. While the developers of mixed-use complexes argue that retail space is equivalent to the public space they promise

▨ Maintaining civility on Fulton Mall: Security booth and uniformed police on the street.

Photo by Alex Vitale.

in return for zoning benefits, the public is poorer and less able to buy its way into the stores.

A look at some of the city's public spaces – shopping streets, restaurants, museums – indicates the importance of artists and immigrants to current processes of defining urban cultures. No one could argue that these are powerful groups. Yet they are so involved in challenging previously conceived ideas about the city's identity that they set a new framework for viewing social life. On the one hand, urban renewal is often heralded by the opening of artists' studios and art galleries. "Call It RedHo?" asks a headline in the *New York Times* (May 8, 1994), about the possibility of making Red Hook, a derelict manufacturing area on the Brooklyn waterfront, into an artists' district like Manhattan's SoHo. On the other hand, in Bay Ridge, Brooklyn, a neighborhood that until recently was almost entirely Italian and Jewish, sidewalk displays of merchandise on one shopping street cause residents to call it the "Oriental Market." In cities with large immigrant populations, immigrants hold so many restaurant jobs – often in franchises – that they frame the experience of eating out in the city.

The density of immigrants and minority groups of all kinds in cities contributes to the confusion of meanings around urban culture. In some commercial markets, such as broadcast radio, urban culture is African-American "ghetto culture." The rapidly changing styles and language of hip hop, the boomerang of imitation between what is criminal and what is cool, constitute an ironic acknowledgment of the ghetto's urban authenticity. Yet the streets are both aestheticized and feared as a source of urban culture. Much of the emphasis placed on identifying cities and culture is an attempt to ensure that the culture of cities is *not* understood as ghetto culture. Art museums suggest that they, not the streets, hold the key to cities' unique cultural role. "Europeans" are the preferred "front" employees in upscale restaurants. The populist culture of such commercial centers as Times Square, the ultimate theater of the streets, is re-presented as offices and showplaces of corporate culture industries. Street markets formed by African, Asian, and Latin diasporas are designed away, into indoor markets, so the streets will be compatible with economic revitalization.

The chapters in this book argue that culture is neither an unimportant adjunct of the material transformation of cities nor a purely symbolic realm for differentiating social roles. Instead, cultural symbols have material consequences – and more important material consequences as cities become less dependent on traditional resources and technologies of material production. Whether the city is Orlando or North Adams, New York or Los Angeles, *culture* is a euphemism for the city's new representation as a creative force in the emerging service economy. Given the survival issues of employment, housing, and social welfare, the question of why culture has become so important is usually not put on the urban research agenda, except in terms of dealing with ethnic and linguistic diversity.

Some researchers, however, associate urban culture with changes in the world economy and social class structure (e.g., Kearns and Philo 1993). They recognize, first, that there is always a general strategy of mythologizing the city to sell it as a site. Developers and elected officials seek investment funds by marketing the cultural values of place. Researchers look specifically at the use of cultural sights, institutions, and events to market cities to tourists. They explain the emphasis on culture by referring to the increasing sameness – or "place-lessness" – of cities, leading to a "consumption of difference," magnified or imagined (see Deutsche 1988; Willems-Braun 1994). In materialistic terms, emphasizing culture is a concerted attempt to exploit the uniqueness of fixed capital – monuments, art collections, performance spaces, even shopping streets – accumulated over the past. In this sense, culture is the sum of a city's amenities that enable it to compete for investment and jobs, its "comparative advantage." Another explanation for the visibility of culture in urban life points to the desire for access to cultural consumption on the part of educated managers and professionals in the "new service classes" whose jobs to some degree are still concentrated in cities (Jager 1986; Lash and Urry 1987). Thus the discussion of gentrification in the 1980s often focused on the cultural strivings of the highly educated, urban middle class.

There has also been a reevaluation of the key role of culture and cities in framing modern identities. It is as if Manuel Castells's challenge that helped inaugurate the "new urban sociology" of the 1970s – There is no urban society separate from the capitalist economy – were reinterpreted as, There is no separation between modernism and urban culture. This new awareness developed in the 1980s in the debate over postmodernism and the meaning of modernity. Studies of late 19th and early 20th century cities, especially the rebuilding of Paris under Baron Haussmann, but also Vienna, St. Petersburg, and Berlin, showed the resonance between cultural symbols, urban space, and social power (see Berman 1982; Harvey 1985c; and translations of Walter Benjamin; cf. Jameson 1984). They also suggested that identity was formed by a combination of spatial and social practices. The reconceptualization of modernity as a contested terrain – and recognition of the city's role in that conflict – revitalized urban studies by infusing them with cultural studies. This reawakened urban sociology's rich empirical tradition.

Not only specific cities but also individual buildings and streets emerged as proper subjects of research. To some degree, this reflected researchers' desire to seek out variations within general social and economic systems – not least, "late" capitalism. It also reflected new directions: a Foucauldian interest in micro-regimes of power, a postfeminist focus on social relations and identities, and a postmarxist interest in visual culture. At any rate, these new directions demanded a new narrative outside either the structural (i.e., political economic) or "configurational" (i.e., individualistic) tradition (Sayer 1989). Some urbanists returned to ethnography. Others, coming from an art or literary criticism tradition, studied written or painted representations, class structure, and gender. Still others incorporated culture into a materialist analysis of the crisis of the world economy. All this led to an embrace of nontraditional subject matter and crossing disciplines. New work focused on subjective interpretations of the city (such as in Peter Jackson's [1989] "maps of meaning") and groups that were absent from central landscapes of power (e.g., women and gays, in Wilson 1991).

There have also been changes in the social context of culture in the late 20th century that account for its instrumental importance. Much service employment involves the creation and management of visual and emotional images. More than ever before in commodity capitalism, culture is a mass market phenomenon. There is hope, moreover, among remaining urban middle classes and elites, that culture as a set of aesthetic social practices can offset the fear that pervades urban life. In their view, inflating the cultural role of institutions and events can restore civility to public culture. At least, cultural strategies of reconstructing the meaning of urban spaces give the appearance of a common public culture. Culture also has a political value. It offers a seemingly neutral language to maintain social hierarchy in a polarized society. These uses of culture create new tensions around cultural politics. Debates over historic preservation, subsidies to cultural institutions, and the uses of public space indicate how hard it is for culture to be both a democratic public good and an elite resource.

New York City may be a special case. In New York, the spectacular post-World-War-II decline of small-scale, traditional manufacturing and the equally spectacular rise of corporate business shaped a planning discourse based on national (and eventually, global) priorities rather than local needs, on intangible products, and on the role of the arts in representing the gains of a mainly symbolic economy. Throughout the 1960s, this planning discourse crystallized the image of the city as a "national center," uniquely nurturant of and yet also dependent upon cultural products and cultural institutions. If the city was to specialize in high-level business activities, then art galleries, performances, and philanthropic museum memberships offered the perquisites and symbols of economic power.

In all major cities, a larger picture of the symbolic economy includes culture industries, business services, and real estate development. Compared to the modern industrial economy, these activities of symbolic exchange offer a much larger formative role to such "nonproductive" factors as design and the organization of consumption. Similarly, compared to the modern industrial city, consumption spaces – from leisure complexes to restaurants and retail shops – play a more important role in people's lives. Such spaces make narratives of the city's complex heterogeneous languages (Glennie and Thrift 1992), constructing multiple histories and identities for both individuals and local communities (Morris 1988).

Cities differ in the ways that elites, and ordinary men and women, are mobilized to intervene in these processes of representation. (Downtown Brooklyn and 125th Street suggest somewhat divergent examples.) At the same time, in all major cities, beginning with New York and Los Angeles, industries that deal in symbolic products have become powerful players on the local scene, whether that power is refracted through real estate development, tourism, or jobs. (Their influence is felt in the 1983 and 1993 Port Authority reports on the arts as an industry and in the redevelopment of Times Square.) Rightly or wrongly, cultural strategies have become keys to cities' survival. But how these cultural strategies are defined, and how we, as social critics, observers, and participants, see them, requires explicit discussion.

Cultural Strategies

There are many different "cultural" strategies of economic development. Some focus on museums and other large cultural institutions, or on the preservation of architectural landmarks in a city or regional center. Others call attention to the work of artists, actors, dancers, and even chefs who give credence to the claim that an area is a center of cultural production. Some strategies emphasize the aesthetic or historic value of imprints on a landscape, pointing to old battlegrounds, natural wonders, and collective representations of social groups, including houses of worship, workplaces of archaic technology, and even tenements and plantation housing. While some cultural strategies, like most projects of adaptive reuse of old buildings, create panoramas for visual contemplation, others, like Disney World and various "historic" villages, establish living dioramas in which contemporary men and women dress in costumes and act out imagined communities of family, work, and play. The common element in all these strategies is that they reduce the multiple dimensions and conflicts of culture to a coherent visual representation. Thus culture as a "way of life" is incorporated into "cultural products"; i.e., ecological, historical, or architectural materials that can be displayed, interpreted, reproduced, and sold in a putatively universal repertoire of visual consumption (see McCannell 1976, 1992; Mitchell 1988). In the process, and with occasional lasting recriminations, alliances are forged over the less contentious area of "culture" than over the more exasperating area of the economy.

I minimize the conflicts involved. We cannot ignore the struggles over particular pieces of real estate, and over who might be displaced by their cultural appropriation, as well as over *whose* representations of *whose* culture are going to be enshrined by *which* institutions. In the United States, however, where localities are responsible for their own economic development, and in Great Britain, where localities are increasingly cut off from the traditional government welfare policies that cushion unemployment, cultural strategies emerged by the mid 1980s as a relatively consensual means of managing economic decline and envisioning possibilities of economic growth. Whether this is a realistic strategy in the long term is another question. But in the aftershocks of deindustrialization and economic recession, an increasing number of local business and political elites look toward cultural strategies to remake their cities. The headline on the lead article in the *Wall Street Journal* of February 1, 1985, is instructive in this regard: "Old New England City Heals Itself; Can One in Midwest Do So Too / Local Consensus That Helps Lowell, Mass., Lure Jobs Is Missing in Akron, Ohio / From Old Mills, New Park."

The story in the *Wall Street Journal* contrasts the apparent resurgence of Lowell, whose textile industry declined in the 1920s, with Akron's continued decline, following losses in the rubber industry in the 1970s. It locates the key to Lowell's success in the creation of a National Historical Park, financed by the National Park Service, in 1984. Not only did the Park Service clean up the derelict and polluted industrial sites of abandoned textile mills, but local bankers and politicians formed a "formidable consensus" that financed redevelopment oriented toward small-scale, "technically innovative" businesses. The park also attracts tourists who want to view the 19th century industrial past, generating new service jobs and a more detached view of industry.

Akron is not so detached from its industrial history. There is no political consensus surrounding the new recreational park, which is sited on land that could be used for suburban housing development for nearby Cleveland. Moreover, since the park prohibits hunting, some local residents oppose it for limiting their recreational opportunities. Most important of all, local industrialists are still in place and do not favor subsidizing new strategies of economic development that exclude them.

The relative fortunes of Lowell and Akron differ now, long after the "Massachusetts Miracle" of high-tech and service-led growth has abated and the southern tier of the Middle West, favored by Japanese implants, has regained auto industry jobs. And no cultural strategy has been able to absorb the workers that have been unemployed since Wang, the computer maker who sparked the economic revival of Lowell in the 1980s, shut down. The general point, however, is the perception, even at the *Wall Street Journal,* that cultural strategies of development are significant.[17]

And why not? Nearly a decade later, tourism (or the hotel and tourist industry, including restaurants) is the country's biggest employer, after the auto industry. Tourism engenders new work, sexual, and other social relations (see Urry 1990b); it fits the transience and image creation of a service economy based on mass media and telecommunications. On a local level, developing tourism works well with real estate interests and absorbs, to some degree, men and women in the work force who have been displaced by structural and locational changes. The "real" cities of Orlando and Las Vegas have developed behind a tourist front. Even in the old steel region of the Monongahela Valley near Pittsburgh, tourism is touted as a development strategy that works in the short term to clean up industrial sites and put people to work (*Architectural Record,* March 1994, 24–27).[18]

So cultural strategies are often a worst-case scenario of economic development. When a city has few cards to play, cultural strategies respond to the quality-of-life argument that encourages flight to newer regions. They represent a weapon

17. Every country must have its own paired comparisons. In Britain, I think of the competition, on the basis of cultural resources, between Glasgow and Edinburgh, and the consensus or lack of consensus among political parties and labor unions in Lancaster (Urry, 1990a), Cheltenham (Cowen 1990), and Sheffield.

18. This is not necessarily an easy process. The National Park Service is not really receptive to integrating abandoned and often polluted industrial sites into a system based on the management of "pristine" natural places.

against the decentralization of jobs from established industrial concentrations. They do not reverse the hierarchies of place that lead to competition for distinctive segments of capital and labor – competition that is often perceived in terms of image. Indeed, cultural strategies suggest the utter absence of new industrial strategies for growth, i.e., the lack of local strategies that have any chance of success in attracting productive activity.

Yet they also suggest new political strategies for managing social diversity. As challenging, and challenged, as multiculturalism has been in its brief history, cultural strategies permit elites to "take the high road" by acknowledging eclecticism and alloting each group a piece of the visual representation of a city or region. To some extent, this avoids ranking groups in terms of the justness of their claims. "Everybody has a culture, so everybody is equal." Every group can have its visible recognition, even a visual acknowledgment of past oppression. The emphasis is on "past" oppression, for establishing a visual order of cultural hegemony seems to equalize by identifying and making formerly "invisible" social groups visible, at least in their previous (sometimes romanticized, sometimes not) incarnation. This interpretation differs from the criticisms of themed developments for making history "fun" (e.g., Harvey 1989b, 88–98) and of "heritage" presentations because they sanitize and homogenize history (e.g., Wallace 1985; Boyer 1992). Instead, cultural strategies that rely on visual representations attempt to create a new public culture that is both nonhierarchical and inegalitarian. Although they are often applied to populist sites – commercial streets, working-class neighborhoods, public parks, city centers – cultural strategies use visual aesthetics to evoke a vanished civic order associated with an equally vanished, or at least transformed, middle class.

While this is painfully clear in downtown Brooklyn, it is true on a much grander scale in downtown Los Angeles. In the wishful rebuilding of Bunker Hill as a cultural center and the creation, practically from nothing, of an international financial district, the city has constructed two downtowns on two quite separate levels of land. Bank City is infinitely more remote from populist, mainly Mexican, Shopping City than the financial districts of most older places. You find Bank City up a steep flight of stairs or lonely escalator, landscaped with fountains and trees, offering stores and restaurants to workers who travel from one office complex to another by shuttle bus and drive home to their neighborhoods by nightfall. The utopian vision of the mixed-use commercial complex, with an espresso bar and its own concierge, has been separated from the less regimented dreams of downtown shopping. Shopping City is the open markets and sidewalk displays – no street vendors in downtown Los Angeles – the immigrant shopkeepers, the empty department stores and old movie palaces, the schlock and sleaze, the mingled scents of tacos and danger.

The new design of Bryant Park, across 42nd Street from my office, is a smaller and more humane attempt to use aesthetics to banish fear. The design was calculated to repel muggers and drug dealers and encourage sitting and strolling by office workers, especially women. And it has succeeded in making the space safe for many more users, especially women, as well as recapturing it for adjacent office building owners and tenants. Similarly, the strenuous objections to garish and overbearing shop displays on 34th Street, the persecution of street peddlers in Manhattan and downtown Brooklyn, and the war against sidewalk stalls present themselves as defending an aesthetically pleasing visual order, while also trying to restore a public order consistent with the commercial ambitions of building owners and commercial tenants. It is significant that such visual strategies are often championed by local business improvement districts that have acquired management rights over public space (usually, parks and streets) by taking on quasi-governmental functions. While the financial resources of some of these groups – those located on prime urban real estate – have been criticized, the work they do is nearly always praised in terms of a relation between the visual order of urban design and the social order of public culture.

The notion of "restoration" is both implicit and explicit in this work. On the one hand, architectural designs explicitly restore, on the basis of existing ruins or historical plans, a late 19th century image. Such contemporary designs may, of course, also fabricate a vision of the past out of pastiche, allusion, and imagination (see Wright 1985; Hewison 1987). This is the case with Bryant Park, which for most of its history was unattractive and even an eyesore. On the other hand, the social order that is alluded to – one based on assumptions of public safety, a common level of civility, and *en fin de compte,* citizenship – is more implicit; it is consciously embedded in the design. Such visual strategies adapt a middle-class urban order last seen around 1960 to current realities of social diversity, homelessness, and crime. Each element of danger is assigned its place in the landscape, with the public-private corporation firmly in control of the panorama. At last, many people exclaim, an urban space that works! Or as an admiring editorial column in the usually ironic *New Yorker* (February 14, 1994, p. 8) says, "Now [Bryant Park] is safe, as beautiful as a Seurat, and lovingly used."[19]

By the same token, some public sites that are likely to be incorporated into a new visual order of cultural hegemony are fiercely contested by different social groups. In the early

▨ A vision of civility: Georges Seurat, *A Sunday on La Grande Jatte,* (1884).

Oil on canvas, 207.5 × 308 cms, Helen Birch Bartlett Memorial Collection, 1926.224 Photograph © 1994, The Art Institute of Chicago, All Rights Reserved.

19. Seurat painted la Grande Jatte, of course, when smokestack industries were moving out of Paris into the suburbs and the recreational patterns of the Parisian working class were also displaced.

1990s, in the course of excavating for the foundation of a new public building in lower Manhattan, an old Negro (now African) Burial Ground was rediscovered. This led to acrimonious conflicts over who would control the site, as well as over the processes leading to its historical recuperation. In Houston in the mid 1990s, new cultural strategies of economic development focused on ethno-tourism and historic preservation, leading to struggles to designate historic African-American neighborhoods as landmarks regardless of their value to real estate developers (Lin 1993). The area on Houston's East Side may be declared a landmark, and the area on the West Side may fail to get this designation, because the West Side is more desirable for high-class commercial development.

Despite their reliance on governmental controls, visual strategies nonetheless tend to move the framing of public culture away from government and toward private spheres. The neighborhood groups involved in visual strategies are often "nonpolitical": they do not represent the "material" interests of tenants or homeowners or workers or people of color. Yet visual strategies, especially historic preservation, have impressed nonhegemonic no less than powerful groups with their ability to do something concrete, like raising property values. The combined material and symbolic effects of visual strategies have, then, democratized to some degree the desire to use culture for material or social ends.

Efforts to expand historic preservation in Harlem illustrate this trend. When community leaders from Upper Manhattan pressed the New York City Landmarks Preservation Commission in the early 1990s to designate as a landmark the Audubon Ballroom, where Malcolm X was killed in 1965, they opposed the aesthetic values that have become the most legitimate part of historic preservation with an argument in terms of political significance. This argument also made a rather specific case for using a historic landmark to construct the political culture of a single community, "the" African-American one, rather than for constructing, and certainly not for restoring, an inclusive public culture. Requests by community leaders from central Harlem that apartment houses with no great architectural or historic distinction be designated as landmarks aims at constructing another social community. Their argument is not merely that Harlem and other African-

American areas are underrepresented in the list of New York City landmarks. They insist, with some knowledge of gentrification, that historic preservation would "stabilize" the area and reward the striving for middle-class status of neighborhood residents.

I suspect that some of the minority group neighborhoods in Houston and other places are similarly motivated. This suggests that visual strategies such as historic preservation can be politicized and used as tools of community development. It also suggests that culture, in the sense of the material control of symbolic resources, may eventually be seen as a public good. The point, however, is that cultural strategies now provide significant means for framing disputes over public goods and moving them away from government into private spheres. Communities have always been repositories of powerful visual images whose control depends on expressing and imposing a coherent vision. But now, politics, and the development of the symbolic economy as a real economic frontier, have broadened competition over the control of visual images.

▨ Seeing Visions

The rise of new industries based on cultural consumption seems to justify visual strategies in the crassest material sense. The commercial success of Disney World and its apparent synergy with a low-wage, mainly European-American work force and military technology and service firms in Orlando demonstrate how the pleasures of vision coexist with corporate cultural hegemony. While the failure of Euro Disney, at least in its first years, suggests a counterexample, it may in fact just qualify the sorts of visual strategies, their timing, and placement, that work in different circumstances for different publics. The same can be said about the criticism aimed at Disney's America, the project to replicate Civil War and other historic sites in virtually the same location as the real sites.

In New York and other great cities, where the rapacity and self-interest of past generations of elites created the enormous visual resources of great museums, the professional administrators of these museums take a palpable pride in identifying the visual or aesthetic value of a well-known painting in their collections with the cultural and economic value of the city. The uniqueness of the art is described as part of the city's wealth, and the status of both art and city justify the museums' expansion. There has been, since the 1970s, an explosion in the prices paid for art, as well as in competition among museums for private and government support. Market competition among museums has intensified their strategizing on the basis of visual attractions (and raising revenues by turning more of their unique visual resources into postcards and gifts), but it has also fed into the competition for capital investment and tourist spending among cities and regions. Painting Glasgow as the culture capital of Europe or New York as the culture capital of the world confirms these multiple levels of material and symbolic competition.

North Adams, on the other hand, is not a believable site of avant garde cultural consumption. The failure of the original MASS MoCA plans and their replacement by a more modest, artist-driven conception underlines the social context from which visual strategies derive. MASS MoCA was defeated by the absence of a group of local patrons of the arts and local artists committed to the same forms that were to be displayed, as well as by the strength of other cultural strategies in the Berkshires. It was taken seriously in two contexts: the unemployment crisis of western Massachusetts and the expansion crisis of the Guggenheim Museum. The fact is, however, that a cultural strategy can be revised and scaled down but not discarded. Even in North Adams, economic redevelopment can be premised on assumptions about aestheticizing – seeing art in – the landscape.

Historically, power over a space (or over a body or a social group) determines the ability to impose a vision of that space. Many of Michel Foucault's historical speculations reverse that relation – and it is that standpoint that I have adopted here. Often the power to impose a coherent vision of a space enables a group to claim that space. This is a framing process.

The aestheticization of modern spaces that begins with the City Beautiful movement of the late 19th and early 20th century, and continues with the elaboration of office campuses and business parks in the suburbs in the 1950s and 1960s, contributes to the framing of cities as culture centers. While the purpose of such visions is often to separate the "higher functions" of cities from the chaotic, swirling mass of poverty and decay, the power of framing requires a power to persuade. Few people believe that either planners or developers, and still less public officials, create coherent visions of public life. But visions persuade if they suggest an escape from the chaos of social decay. Therein lies the subversive charm of Disney World, MASS MoCA, and exurbs in "natural" surroundings.

Who can tell where these re-visions begin in our time? Many of the specific facts that interest me about the cultures of New York today are shaped by immigration, ethnicity, and economic crisis. Yet they also relate to the development of a cultural strategy of economic growth that began in the 1960s and that I wrote about some years ago (Zukin 1989 [1982]). Clearly, the related issues of economic decline, of a perceived loss of bargaining power by local communities, and of a common turn to tourism intensified from the 1970s, when people began to acknowledge a structural crisis in the global economy, to the 1990s, when the death of cities and their pervasive privatization appeared to be inescapable by-products of fiscal crises and financial markets. During this time, cultural strategies that initially represented the *results* of economic development turned into strategies aimed at *stimulating* economic growth.

Who can tell where all this leads? When I wrote about loft living, I said that the Artistic Mode of Production was a means of social control, a mechanism to absorb unemployment, an ideological story, along with historic preservation, to cushion the transition from industrial to postindustrial society. From a later viewpoint, however, this analysis has to be more nuanced. As the preservationist ethos and museumification movement have spread beyond an educated elite, culture has been politicized and democratized. Some of this has occurred because of the battles over multiculturalism and social diversity; some has occurred because the arguments about the economic benefits of culture have been accepted by the larger society.

When more social groups are involved in cultural appropriations of space, culture becomes a public good: it is not only a smokescreen for but also a means of clarifying and extending political conflicts over distributive justice. Vision, too, becomes not just a tool of cultural hegemony but a common property.

It represents an opportunity to "restore" a different and more inclusive public culture that predates the 1970s, when downtown was quite distinct from both the ghetto and neighborhood shopping streets. At this point, it is logical to ask *whose* vision informs public culture.

Take, for example, Salvatore Scotto, the president of the Gowanus Canal Community Development Corporation, who lives in a gentrified working-class area near an abandoned industrial neighborhood on the Brooklyn waterfront.

■ Salvatore Scotto's vision: Site of future restaurants, art galleries, and boutiques on the Gowanus Canal, Brooklyn.

Photo by Alex Vitale.

> *He sees restaurants, art galleries and boutiques where now there are auto graveyards, warehouses and assorted rubble. He sees nice apartment buildings rising. Fish will return. And, under Federal legislation now pending, Mr. Scotto, an undertaker in neighboring Carroll Gardens who has fought for a generation to clean up the Gowanus, sees the area around the canal becoming a national demonstration site for dealing with abandoned industrial lands. (*New York Times, *October 11, 1993)*

Is this irony on the part of the reporter? Is it a discursive representation, both highly colored and coloring a special group in the urban population? Or is it a common mode of reorganizing a vision of the city and then fighting to change it? In this latter sense, the aesthetics of vision becomes a moral language.

Even in the eye of the most ordinary beholder, aestheticization is the other side of fear. This is not fear in a great metaphorical sense – fear of the Other, or women, or the end of civilization. No, this is fear in a historically specific sense, in which appreciation of the visual culture of the city seems the only way to save it – to save it from wreckers and builders, from criminals and the poor. If only it worked.

But how can it work, when so many inconsistencies are built into the expectations raised by cultural strategies? Implementing cultural strategies of economic development emphasizes the opposition between upgrading and stabilizing a community, between cosmopolitan and local cultures, and between visual coherence and social disorder. Moreover, culture has the capacity not only to remain a "separate sphere" – a way of avoiding discussion of hard problems of social and economic inequality – it also has the capacity to reproduce differences that are associated with these problems. The issues I have looked at in this book – issues of art, money, and public space, urban design, ethnic divisions of labor – raise questions of principle for nearly all discussions of urban revitalization.

1. How can we make culture more "democratic" when the city itself – as a cultural object, a representation – is being upgraded to appeal to more affluent people?

Despite the increasing poverty of urban populations, business and political leaders persist in using cultural institutions to lead strategies of economic development. The economic benefits that trickle down from cultural strategies are minimal. Cultural institutions themselves provide few high-wage jobs; like the rest of the nonprofit sector, they have also shifted to hiring more temporary and part-time workers. Their financing, moreover, is hardly secure. Even in New York, both the Metropolitan and the Guggenheim Museums have limited their hours of operation, citing financial difficulties. (The Metropolitan Museum subsequently obtained a corporate donation to restore the original hours.) As for the hotel, restaurant, and tourist industry, which has created a great number of jobs since 1980, most of these jobs pay low wages with little career mobility. If urban cultures are to be democratized, which should mean that they are more representative and more participatory, the city's economy should not be polarized between those who work and the unemployed, those who hold high-wage and low-wage jobs. Similarly, the city cannot be praised as multicultural when some agents of culture – for example, street peddlers – are run off the streets because their image does not conform to the goals of economic development.

2. How can we make culture more ethnically diverse when we "cannot understand" the poor?

Appreciation of cultural diversity is limited mainly to ethnic "color" and remains on the level of cultural consumption by eating ethnic dishes and reading stories, especially in elementary school, about countries of origin. While such an appreciation is undoubtedly better than unabashed xenophobia, it has little to do with bringing people into a mainstream economy or understanding their interrelated and often intractable problems in becoming productive citizens. There is a great gap between an appreciative respect of cultural diversity and an inability to understand the social problems – from drive-by shootings to lack of homes for foster children – that are disproportionately concentrated in low-income areas. Multiculturalism has not confronted, and cannot confront, the cultural identities created and reinforced by lack of integration into the legal, mainstream economy.

3. How can we make the city as a cultural object more accessible when cultural institutions still regularly create markers of social distinction?

High culture institutions such as art museums and symphony orchestras have multiplied their efforts to reach out to new audiences. In some ways they have succeeded and in some ways not. Yet while museums and historic preservation groups expand their missions into urban communities more than in the past, commercial culture – no matter how standardized – is based on reproducing social differences. The example of restaurant work shows how ethnic divisions of labor persist in stratifying the city's population and perpetuating notions about which group fits into which slot in the social hierarchy. If we also consider shopping streets as cultural objects, the debate over which kinds of goods and stores belong on the street is also a debate over who belongs in the city. The revitalization of major shopping streets by business groups poses important questions about the right to sell, the right to be in plain sight, and the segregation of shoppers by their social class and ethnicity.

4. Are cultural strategies of economic redevelopment really destroying the conditions for original cultural production?

Artists and performers still gravitate to cities, particularly great commercial cities, to make their careers. They are able to survive by working in other jobs, finding cheap spaces to live and work, and forming artistic communities. Often their very presence puts the seal of cultural innovation on a "hot" area for restaurants, art galleries, and real estate. But the goal of much redevelopment strategy is to upgrade areas so that property values rise and low-rent uses are excluded. This raises the threat of displacing artists and performers, and replacing them with stores and residents that can pay higher rents. By the same token, many jobs for cultural producers created by new culture industries pay so little these artists cannot afford to live in the city. They move away, reducing the city's attraction as a culture capital.

Unfortunately, it is not at all clear that cultural strategies of framing space really reverse a real estate recession or that strategies of enhancing cultural tourism have a great positive effect on the city's economy. The same day that a New York City tabloid trumpeted "[Big] Apple Tops with Tourists," a front-page headline in the *New York Times* sombrely stated, "Economy in New York Region Is Stagnant, Unlike Nation's" (January 6, 1995).

While these questions demand we examine the ends of cultural strategies more critically, we also need to focus attention on the means by which they are put into practice. Neither will government take up the slack. The thinking behind current cultural strategies is to subsidize only the large cultural institutions that bring tourist dollars.

Bryant Park represents the top of the hierarchy of public spaces since it has a geographically central position and access to private funds. Nevertheless, it illustrates some of the general problems of making connections between cultural strategies, public space, and social exclusion. I pass the park nearly every day. It is a joyous place, under public-private sponsorship, and well used. No one would suggest it be used as a campground for homeless people, and the city government has too many parks to be able to lavish special care on this one. That the park is much better maintained than many others is clear. But should it be criticized for that reason? Should it be given back to the city government or turned over to "the people"? It is hard to criticize the efforts of business improvement districts when they so palpably improve the quality of life in the public spaces they command, even when the controls they exercise, from urban design to private security guards, are blatantly aimed at exclusion.

Control over public space is, however, a step toward a larger role in government. Perhaps this was always implicit in the very concept of a BID. Certainly the possibility of issuing their own bonds gives BIDs a greater resource base for launching bigger plans. A large BID with substantial capital resources can supplement or even take over the tasks of individual property owners and developers, and public agencies, in making specific areas of the city more attractive for investment. It is too soon to say whether this will work, but if it does, it will widen the disparity between richer and poorer commercial areas of the city. Without oversight, it also risks extending to other areas the Dickensian scenarios of using criminal offenders and homeless people as a low-cost work force. In New York, the SoHo Partnership and the Union Square Park Community Coalition already use homeless people in outdoor and office jobs.

For most of the modern period, from the late 19th to the late 20th centuries, cities have succeeded in supporting both patrician and ethnic cultures. While the differences between them have been reduced by mass markets, standardization, and culture industries, it is interesting to ask whether cultural strategies of revitalizing cities continue to reduce, or in fact restore, these differences. Neighborhood programs to recapture a historical heritage combine movements for historic preservation and ethnic pride, suggesting a favorable comparison with more elite efforts in wealthier neighborhoods. So they should be a means of overcoming material disadvantages, a reasonable way of rewriting history, a cultural strategy of empowerment. But what does it mean to organize an "old timers' " day in a low-income community that has a high proportion of racial minorities and public housing projects or to set up an exhibit on the ethnic groups that live in a racially tense community? When a low-income group supports a historical project, men and women appropriate the place where they have lived without ever really controlling the space. When an elite group preserves its historical heritage, those men and women control space without any necessary connection to the place. Thus an elite group can disinterestedly defend the architecture, or the look, of a place without thinking about the right of people to live there. A low-income group, or an ethnic group in a contested community, conceives a cultural strategy in terms of their right to be in that place. This is bound to further conflict.

Yet if the media and technology have influenced the way we see, we must view our neighborhoods, and our cities, the way culture industries have trained us to do. Certainly Disney World's connection between visual coherence and social control has shaped the BIDs' visual strategies. Commercial reuse of historic buildings reflects the contextual strategy of finding meaning in a juxtaposition between archaic and modern, live action and instant replay, reading and watching videos. Many of the public spaces that are redesigned to attract shoppers are inspired by old photographs of the most patrician spaces in the city, by paintings like Seurat's *Grande Jatte*. Thus our visual images of cities are filtered through the cultural products that we consume as well as by our memories and daily lives. The dependence on these cultural filters means that cities' visual identities are constantly being smoothed out and equalized by the very groups that aim for "difference." Similarly, the complex realities of neighborhoods are not easily captured by visual images. Yet visual strategies simplify, exaggerate, and in some cases, valorize images of fear. It matters ideologically which strategies are used in different situations to visualize different places. The social consequences of these visual strategies have to be thought through.

And what of those who write about cities? Authors are constantly searching for the right voice, an "authentic" voice, in which a story of modernity and cities can be told. Chastened by feminist and "postcolonial" critiques, they suggest a writer use several different "subject" positions, and perhaps even tell several different stories, since no single voice is adequate, or detached enough, to convey more than a single impression (e.g., Gregory 1994). For this reason, many urbanists were

▓ Visual strategies valorize images of fear. Uniformed police arrest young man on Fulton Mall.

Photo by Alex Vitale.

impressed by the ending of Marshall Berman's (1982) book on modernity, in which he spoke in his own voice about the destruction of his homeland, the Bronx, suggesting an objective and a subjective empathy between his own deprivation and the destruction of communities by urban renewal. Yet, with the exception of Mike Davis (1990), few authors manage to do the footwork that would provide a many-sided view of the city, a view from both the ghettos and the heights, from the outlands as well as the central spaces. Fewer still would renounce the authority of the author's voice, which is, after all, a storyteller's right.

In my case, I have made the city tell my stories. I am interested, first of all, in a centralized city with an historical claim to be a center of culture. Writing in these times, however, I have had to turn the concept of culture around and examine it, looking for those self-conscious negotiations of space and place that define a city's rich tapestry of meanings. In recent years, the process of negotiation has been bounded by aestheticism and fear – by the feeling that what counts in the city is its cultural vitality and the creeping fear that the place itself will not survive. Like me, any city dweller has to deal with this vise of perceptions, and I have tried to suggest the resulting tension and fragility in representations of the identity of the city itself.

As myself in the world at this time, I am also concerned with documenting continuities, and discontinuities, in public space and public culture. If people feel that the city is falling apart, that cities in some of the most economically advanced countries on the earth look like "the Third World," they are expressing historically new complaints that speak to me, my place in the city, and my roots. Should I feel threatened by some cultural strategies and protected by others? All cultural strategies create meaning in the city by relating autobiography and hegemony, and I have tried to identify some of the little voices of autobiography that make up the local hegemonies of urban landscapes. This is my way of looking at multiculturalism in public spaces.

The story I have tried to tell is, above all, a story of how the production of symbols depends on, and shapes, the production of space. I cannot escape what I see as the harsh disparities of power and money in the symbolic economy. Yet there is no easy answer to the questions about public culture that I set out in Chapter 1: How are spaces connected to a vision? Can culture replace political strategies to overcome fear? Is it useless to dream of a public culture? With its democratic discourse and economic disparities, its emphasis on visual identity, and its competing constituencies tied to a myriad of separate little places within it, a city is a complex homeland. For all these reasons, however, it is still a microcosm of the world.

A Word About Theory

Readers may wonder why this book is called *The Cultures of Cities.* The answer lies in the thoughts I have shared, as a reader, for the past 10 to 15 years, and how I place myself, as a writer, in the creative dance of social theory.

In the preface, I offered a straightforward account of where this book fits in my own writing. There is, more or less, a straight line from art and real estate to economic and cultural landscapes, and from landscapes to the cultural strategies now transforming public space. I have also pointed out where my life intersects with these larger-than-life issues. I want to give my daughter not only a sense of the city I know, but a way to question its coherence and continuity. I want to exorcise some ghosts – the ghosts of Eleventh Street – and claim that all of us, children of various diasporas, can find a home in the city. I want to tell the seemingly real, factual story of how cities use culture. But, in fact, this story is shaped as much by my theoretical understanding of cities and spaces as by the empirical materials – interviews, histories, autobiographies, and photographs – I have carefully laid out.

I began this work by assuming that the meanings of culture are unstable. I am not saying that the term "culture" has many meanings. Anthropologists can count as many definitions of culture as the French make cheeses. I mean, rather, that culture is a fluid process of forming, expressing, and enforcing identities, whether these are the identities of individuals, social groups, or spatially constructed communities. Much of the theoretical insistence on fluidity, change, and resistance to control reflects the concerns of the relatively long era of modernity. Much of the focus on identity and multiplicity refers to the anxieties of the lengthening, postmarxist, postpositivist, postmodern *fin de siècle.*

At any rate, we cannot assume culture has a single meaning: it is neither high art, nor an official set of artifacts, nor a language governing social interactions within or across group boundaries. Culture, to borrow Homi Bhabha's (1994) telling phrase, has many locations. From the "inside" to the "outside" of a society, from elites to marginals, from Bryant Park to 125th Street – these sites *together* make a culture; their contrasts are a necessary condition of their speaking to each other in this space and time, and across space and time. If we apply to cities a sense of culture as a dialogue in which there are many parts, we are forced to speak of the *cultures* of cities rather than of either a unified culture of the whole city or a diversity of exotic subcultures. It is not multiculturalism or the diversity of cultures that is to be grasped; it is the fluidity, the fusion, the negotiation.

Whether we come to this point of view from latter-day postmodernism or high modern phenomenology doesn't matter. Except for one thing: postmodern social theories have changed our understanding of society so fundamentally that we can no longer consider only the process of constructing culture a negotiation. The product – culture itself – is a continual negotiation. This position demands a flexible methodology, for both the subject of our research – basic cultural categories – and our analytic categories are constantly changing. Yet I wouldn't like to see us throw out a concern with culture as a systematic reproduction of social hierarchies. Certainly we who write about the spaces and politics and policies of cities must pay greater attention to alternative uses, means, and forms of culture, from street cultures to culture industries. But we must also pay greater attention to the material inequalities that are at stake in cultural strategies of economic growth and community revitalization.

These thoughts lead to my second starting point, a concern with the material basis of cultural representations. Studies of gentrification and urban redevelopment suggest that the politics of representation plays a significant role in conflicts over economic revitalization. This is clear when we look at the advertising and publicity surrounding large-scale projects that produce both symbols of, and spaces for, growth, from downtown Los Angeles to North Adams and Orlando. But the politics of representation is also shaped by concrete questions of who owns, who occupies, and who controls the city's public spaces. Surely racial and ethnic politics are affected by who can sell and buy there, and how each space is represented by certain kinds of goods, or bodies, or special signs. To some extent these questions refer to the usual subjects of urban political economy: property values and the forces that drive them up or down, relations between social classes, and a convergence of interest between the laws of the state and people and institutions with economic power. Yet questions of representation also reshape the traditional concerns of urban political economy. Property values are not only determined economically; they respond to intangible public cultures, cultures of ethnicity and gender as well as social class.

To a degree, these issues suggest a micro-level concern with social worlds. If social class, ethnicity, and power are constructed by interpersonal relations of intimacy in public space, we should look very closely at how people behave. It is useless, however, to look at behavior without looking at individuals' locations in society and without considering the social and historical context of the space itself. The decision to place movable chairs in Bryant Park is very interesting, but would that decision work outside the central business district, and without a phalanx of private security guards and uniformed police officers? Can attitudes toward Korean shopkeepers in black ghettos be understood without recalling the ghettoization of shopping streets in recent urban history? Would the division of labor in restaurants be so significant if immigrants and artists could change places?

Taking a materialist approach compels us to look for structures of power outside the cultural field. At the very least, we must look for structured coherences between cultural and other kinds of power. From this point of view I am fascinated by the power of vision, which I have interpreted as the ability to frame a work of art, a street, a building, or an image of the city in an aesthetically coherent way. Art critics and art historians have written quite a bit in recent years about framing in terms of the power of interpretation and display held by museum curators and by committees that choose public art (see, for example, Tagg 1992, Deutsche 1988, Karp and

Lavine 1991). Students of colonialism and imperialism have made us painfully aware that the colonizers' visual framing of colonial subjects makes it easier to relegate them to an inferior position, both intellectually and politically (see Mitchell 1988). Yet urban political economists and sociologists have not studied the concept of framing as an important strategy of legitimizing political and economic claims. Framing gives us analytic leverage over a wide variety of cultural forms: over cultural institutions such as museums, culture industries such as Disney World, cultural strategies such as historic preservation, cultural sites such as parks, and places of cultural consumption such as restaurants and shopping streets. Moreover, since framing asserts a material claim to space in the city – so obvious in the design of public space, museum expansion, and landmarks designation – it is equally a symbolic and a material power.

These days, when culture industries and cultural institutions are so openly market driven, the power to frame things symbolically is taken to be a form of material power. But we shouldn't jump to the conclusion that the producers of symbols (artists, architects, designers) have much power. As in any other market economy, framers wield more power than producers. Those who deal out the symbols – the Disney Company, BIDs, museums – are in control. Like any hegemonic power, however, the power of vision depends on a dynamic mobilization of fresh talent, new symbols, and different publics. The ability to frame the cultures of cities is most uncertain in economically marginal activities (consider the old immigrant restaurant owner who hires recent immigrants, his "boys", to cook and clean and the Egyptian chef who died of a heart attack while still in his 20s) and among socially marginal groups (the kids who create styles on 125th Street or Fulton Mall but who have no control over either the shops or the street). Nevertheless, most people forget about degrees and kinds of power; they identify cultural symbols with material power. The Van Gogh painting "Wheat Field with Cypresses" *is* as bankable as tourist dollars. The civility of Bryant Park *is* a painting by Seurat. A landmarked apartment house in Harlem *is* a middle-class place to live.

Or is it? Claims about the power of symbols are not independent of claims about political and economic power. Nothing makes this point more urgently than the question of whether New York City can be maintained as a culture capital in the face of massive governmental cutbacks and a diminished public sphere.

In addition to the instability of culture and a desire to appropriate the cultural studies' trope of representations, my third starting point was in Henri Lefebvre's (1991) distinction between spatial practices, representational spaces, and spaces of representation. These terms can be understood in many different ways. I think Lefebvre wants us to feel the difference between physical space as experienced sensually and socially, as intellectualized, and as manipulated both physically and symbolically. Reading Lefebvre – especially his brief evocations of ancient cities or Venice or Modern architecture – makes us feel the materiality of space and yet also awakens us to the intimate relations between space and processes of making symbols. Ideologies, or as Foucault puts it, discursive practices, are created in specific spaces. These spaces then provide the pictures in our minds when we conceive our identities. In turn, ideologies structure, and continue to structure, the ongoing production of spaces: the distinctions between high and low, sacred and profane, gentrified neighborhood or inner city. I wanted to suggest some of the material conditions in which spatial practices are now being transformed, the commercialism that is overwhelming public space, the tacit exclusions and ghettoization that continue despite a language of inclusion and real cultural fusions.

Lefebvre's language made me think about ethnic shopping streets as both *espaces vécus* and *espaces conçus,* resonating with the hopes and dreams of local men, women, and children. I also thought about the new public spaces of Bryant Park, Times Square, and Sony Plaza as embodying a new kind of space: a template of privatization for the whole society, an attempt at combining democratic access with social controls. If we dare think in terms of a single public culture, it is surely made up of these different, and conflicting, locations.

Many theorists today say that urban spaces can only be interpreted from a variety of different viewpoints, none of which is more authoritative, or more correct, than any others. To a degree, this is true. Spaces are experienced by the many different people who inhabit them. What is "culture" to one group may be "repression" to another. We see how ethnic shopping streets enforce both integration and exclusion. We see a museum presented as both a local economic development strategy and an outpost of a global institution. We see restaurants with artists in the front and immigrants in the back — a "reading" made more complicated by artists who continue working for years as waiters and immigrants who move on to become entrepreneurs. Even Bryant Park can be interpreted in dramatically different ways, as both a safe and attractive urban space and one that forcefully imposes a specific vision of security and civility. Theory can reflect this hybrid quality by saying that each of these public spaces creates a variety of public cultures, and that the overarching public culture of the city is a dialogue among them.

All public spaces, however, are influenced by the dominant symbolic economy. And just now, the dominant symbolic economy owes more to Disney World than to the African market of 125th Street. Sony recently chose as chairman an executive with experience in movies and entertainment rather than in technology. The North American distiller Seagram's has become a major owner of MCA, an entertainment company in Hollywood that owns Universal Studios, theme parks, and music companies. Is it any wonder that public spaces from parks to museums are often represented as consumable goods, sites of delectation, and themed experiences of retail shopping? Add to this a widespread fear of crime in public places, and the aestheticization of fear in urban design moves ever closer to the movies, magazines, and advertisements produced by the media corporations.

Even so, the cultures of cities retain a residual memory of tolerance and freedom. The very diversity of the population and their need for cultural and economic exchanges create unpredictable spaces of freedom: the markets, restaurant kitchens, designated landmarks, and parades that become both sites and sights of new collective identities. This is the city that people cherish. It is this transcendant narrative of opportunity and self-respect that lends hope to a common public culture. But if entire cities, led by their downtowns, continue to be ghettoized by public rhetoric and private investment, the dream of a common public culture will fall victim to an empty vision.

REFERENCES

Agnew, Jean-Christophe. 1986. *Worlds Apart: The Market and the Theater in Anglo-American Thought*. New York: Cambridge University Press.

Anderson, Alexandra and Paula Di Perna. 1977. "The Power Aesthete." *Village Voice* (August 22).

Anderson, Elijah. 1990. *Streetwise: Race, Class, and Change in an Urban Community*. Chicago: University of Chicago Press.

"The Arts and New York." 1978. *New York Affairs* 4(4).

Arts Research Center, City of New York. 1993. *The Economic Impact of Major Exhibitions at the Metropolitan Museum of Art, the Museum of Modern Art, the Solomon R. Guggenheim Museum, Fall and Winter 1992–93*. New York: Author.

Asada, Akira. 1991. "Discussion." *Anyone*, ed. Cynthia C. Davidson. New York: Rizzoli.

Bagli, Charles V. 1993. "Cinderella's Walking the Deuce: Disney May Rescue 42nd Street." *New York Observer* (September 20).

Bailey, Thomas. 1985. "A Case Study of Immigrants in the Restaurant Industry." *Industrial Relations* 24: 205–21.

Bailey, Thomas and Roger Waldinger. 1991. "The Changing Ethnic/Racial Division of Labor." *Dual City: Restructuring New York*, ed. Manuel Castells and John H. Mollenkopf, pp. 43–78. New York: Russell Sage Foundation.

Ball, Edward. 1991. "Theme Player." *Village Voice* (August 6): 81.

Baudrillard, Jean. 1986. *Amérique*. Paris: Grasset.

Beauregard, Robert A. 1993. *Voices of Decline: The Postwar Fate of US Cities*. Oxford: Blackwell.

Benjamin, Walter. 1979. "A Berlin Chronicle." *One-Way Street and Other Writings*, trans. Edmund Jephcott and Kingsley Shorter, pp. 293–346. London: NLB.

Berger, John. 1985. "Manhattan." *The Sense of Sight*, pp. 61–67. New York: Pantheon.

Berkshire County (Massachusetts) Regional Planning Commission. 1985. *Berkshire County: A Statistical Profile*, June.

Berman, Marshall. 1982. *All That Is Solid Melts into Air*. New York: Simon and Schuster.

Bhabha, Homi K. 1994. "The Commitment to Theory." *The Location of Culture,* pp. 19–39. London and New York: Routledge.

Biederman, Daniel A. and Anita R. Nager. 1981. "Up From Smoke: A New, Improved Bryant Park?" *New York Affairs* 6(4): 97–105.

Bluestone, Daniel. 1992. "The Pushcart Evil: Peddlers, Merchants and New York City's Streets, 1890-1940." *Landscape of Modernity*, ed. David Ward and Olivier Zunz, pp. 287–312. New York: Russell Sage Foundation.

Borak, Jeffrey. 1994. "The Man Behind MoCA." *Berkshire Eagle* (March 31).

Bourdieu, Pierre. 1984. *Distinction: A Social Critique of the Judgement of Taste*, trans. Richard Nice. Cambridge, MA: Harvard University Press.

Boyer, M. Christine. 1983. *Dreaming the Rational City*. Cambridge, MA: MIT Press.

—. 1992. "Cities for Sale: Merchandising History at South Street Seaport." *Variations on a Theme Park: The New American City and the End of Public Space*, ed. Michael Sorkin, pp. 181–204. New York: Hill and Wang.

Brake, Klaus. 1988. *Phonix in Der Asche – New York Verandert Seine Stadtstruktur*. Oldenburg: Bibliotheks-und Informationssystem der Universitat.

Brecher, Charles and Raymond D. Horton. 1993. *Power Failures: New York City Politics and Policy Since 1960*. New York: Oxford University Press.

Bruun, Erik. 1988. "MoCA Open House a Smash." *Berkshire Eagle* (October 30).

—. 1990. "Krens Says He's Upbeat on MoCA." *Berkshire Eagle* (March 3).

Buck-Morss, Susan. 1989. *The Dialectics of Seeing: Walter Benjamin and the Arcades Project.* Cambridge, MA: MIT Press.

Burgess, Jacquelin. 1985. "News from Nowhere: The Press, the Riots and the Myth of the Inner City." *Geography, the Media and Popular Culture,* ed. Jacquelin Burgess and John R. Gold, pp. 192-228. London: Croom Helm.

Campbell, Robert. 1992. "Architecture View: A Logo of the Past on the Screen of the Present." *New York Times* (August 6).

Caplovitz, David. 1973. *The Merchants of Harlem: A Study of Small Business in a Black Community.* Beverly Hills, CA: Sage.

Caro, Robert A. 1974. *The Power Broker: Robert Moses and the Fall of New York.* New York: Vintage.

Cougan, Tim. 1988. "The Forging of a Small New England Mill Town: North and South Adams, Massachusetts, 1780–1880." Unpublished Ph.D. dissertation, New York University.

Cowen, Harvey. 1990. "Regency Icons: Marketing Cheltenham's Built Environment." *Place, Policy and Politics,* ed. Michael Harloe, C. G. Pickvance, and John Urry, pp. 128–45. London: Unwin Hyman.

Cranz, Galen. 1982. *The Politics of Park Design: A History of Urban Parks in America.* Cambridge, MA: MIT Press.

Cunningham, William C., John J. Strauche, and Clifford W. Van Meter. 1990. *Private Security Trends 1970–2000: The Hallcrest Report II.* Boston: Butterworth-Heinemann.

Daniels, Lee A. 1981. "Amid Uncertainty, Revival of 125th St. Proceeds." *New York Times* (December 3).

Davis, Mike. 1990. *City of Quartz.* London: Verso.

Densmore, Bill. 1989. "Modify MoCA." *The Advocate* [Williamstown, Massachusetts] (August 23).

—. 1992. "Long Distance MOCA Parking OK'd." *The Advocate* [Williamstown, Massachusetts] (May 27).

DePalma, Anthony. 1991. "Booming Orlando Becomes Magnet for Prosperity and the Ills It Conceals." *New York Times* (August 6).

Deutsche, Rosalyn. 1988. "Uneven Development: Public Art in New York City." *October* (47): 3–52.

Drucker, Jesse. 1994. "Thanks for Nothing: Homeless Sue Boss." *New York Observer* (November 21).

Dunlap, David W. 1993. "Rethinking 42nd Street for Next Decade." *New York Times* (June 27).

Eco, Umberto. 1986 [1975]. *"Travels in Hyperreality." Travels in Hyperreality,* trans. William Weaver, pp. 1–58. New York: Harcourt Brace Jovanovich.

Economic Development Commission of Mid-Florida. 1991. *Opportunity Orlando* 2 (1). Orlando, FL: Author.

Ehrenreich, Barbara. 1989. *Fear of Falling: The Inner Life of the Middle Class.* New York: Pantheon.

Ellis, Edwin. 1994. "Return to Sender: Recidivism and Urban Geography." Unpublished presentation, Brooklyn College, CUNY.

"The Entertainment Economy." 1994. *Business Week* (March 14): 58-66.

Ewen, Elizabeth. 1985. *Immigrant Women in the Land of Dollars.* New York: Monthly Review Press.

Ewen, Stuart. 1988. *All Consuming Images: The Politics of Style in Contemporary Culture.* New York: Basic Books.

Federal Writers' Project. 1939a. *The Berkshire Hills.* New York: Funk and Wagnalls.

—. 1939b. *WPA Guide to New York City.* Republished, 1970, New York: Octagon Press.

Feiden, Douglas. 1992. "Midtown Bonds Spark BID Controversy." *Crain's New York Business* (April 6): 1, 30.

Finkelstein, Joanne. 1989. *Dining Out: A Sociology of Modern Manners.* New York: New York University Press.

Fitch, Robert. 1993. *The Assassination of New York.* New York: Verso.

Fjellman, Steven. 1992. *Vinyl Leaves.* Boulder, CO: Westview.

Fowler, Glenn. 1979. "Koch Breaks Ground for a Peddler's Market." *New York Times* (November 24).

Frieden, Bernard J., and Lynn Sagalynn. 1989. *Downtown Inc.* Cambridge, MA: MIT Press.

Gaines, Judith. 1992. "Not a Pretty Picture: City Hopes Museum Proposal Can Spark Dismal Economy." *Boston Globe* (March 2).

Gamerman, Amy. 1990. "Will Blockbuster Museum Get off the Drawing Board?" *Wall Street Journal* (February 27).

Gandee, Charles. 1991. "Gandee at Large: Nick Ashley: Life After Laura." *HG* (April): 212.

Gates, Henry Louis, Jr. 1993. "Culture of Complaint: The Fraying of America." *The New Yorker* (April 19): 113–17.

—. 1994. *Colored People: A Memoir*. New York: Knopf.

Gill, Brendan. 1991. "The Sky Line: Disneyitis." *The New Yorker* (April 29): 96–99.

—. 1992. "The Sky Line: Pure Wright." *The New Yorker* (July 27): 67–71.

Glennie, P. D. and N. J. Thrift. 1992. "Modernity, Urbanism, and Modern Consumption." *Environment and Planning D: Society and Space* 10: 423–43.

Glueck, Grace. 1990a. "Million for Art, a Lot of It Unfinished." *New York Times* (June 12).

—. 1990b. "A New Museum's Bright Future Grows Dim." *New York Times* (April 11).

Goldberger, Paul. 1990. "A Commission That Has Itself Become a Landmark." *New York Times* (April 15).

—. 1992a. "25 Years of Unabashed Elitism." *New York Times* (February 2).

—. 1992b. "A Curious Mix of Versailles and Mickey Mouse." *New York Times* (June 14).

—. 1992c. "The Liberation of the Guggenheim." *New York Times* (June 21).

Golway, Terry. 1991. "Budget Ax Slashing Art Groups in City." *New York Observer* (March 18).

Gregory, Derek. 1994. *Geographical Imaginations*. Oxford: Blackwell.

Griffith, Joseph P. 1992. "Commercial Property: 34th Street Partnership. A Carrot and a Stick to Tone Down the Garishness." *New York Times* (June 28).

Grover, Ron. 1991. *The Disney Touch: How a Daring Management Team Revived an Entertainment Empire*. Homewood, IL: Business One Irwin.

Guilbaut, Serge. 1983. *How New York Stole the Idea of Modern Art: Abstract Expressionism, Freedom, and the Cold War*, trans. Arthur Goldhammer. Chicago: University of Chicago Press.

Harvey, David. 1973. *Social Justice and the City*. Baltimore: Johns Hopkins University Press.

—. 1985a. "Money, Time, Space and the City." *Consciousness and the Urban Experience: Studies in the History and The-*

ory of Capitalist Urbanization, pp. 1–35. Baltimore: Johns Hopkins University Press.

—. 1985b. "Monument and Myth: The Building of the Basilica of the Sacred Heart." *Consciousness and the Urban Experience: Studies in the History and Theory of Capitalist Urbanization*, pp. 221–49. Baltimore: Johns Hopkins University Press.

—. 1985c. "Paris, 1850–1870." *Consciousness and the Urban Experience: Studies in the History and Theory of Capitalist Urbanization*, pp. 63–220. Baltimore: Johns Hopkins University Press.

—. 1989a. "From Managerialism to Entrepreneurialism: The Transformation in Urban Governance in Late Capitalism." *Geografiska Annaler* 71: 3–17.

—. 1989b. *The Condition of Postmodernity*. Oxford: Blackwell.

Heilbrun, James. 1992. "Art and Culture as Central Place Functions." *Urban Studies* 29(2): 205–15.

Henry, John. 1982. "Future of the Fulton Mall." *Daily News* (August 23).

Hewison, Robert. 1987. *The Heritage Industry*. London: Methuen.

Hibbard, George A. 1894. "Lenox." *Scribner's Magazine* 16(4): 420–34.

Hicks, Jonathan P. 1994. "Giuliani Broadens Crackdown to Banish All Illegal Vendors." *New York Times* (May 9).

Hill, Richard Child. 1989. "Comparing Transnational Production Systems: The Automotive Industry in the USA and Japan." *International Journal of Urban and Regional Research* 13: 462–80.

Himes, Chester. 1990. *The Quality of Hurt: The Early Years*. New York: Paragon House.

Hoelterhoff, Manuela. 1977. "A Museum's Scheme for Expansion." *Wall Street Journal* (August 5).

Horowitz, Helen Lefkowitz. 1976. *Culture and the City: Cultural Philanthropy in Chicago from the 1880s to 1917*. Lexington: University of Kentucky Press.

Hochschild, Arlie. 1983. *The Managed Heart: The Commercialization of Human Feeling*. Berkeley and Los Angeles: University of California Press.

Horsely, Carter. 1977. "Museum of Modern Art Tower Endorsed by Community Board 5." *New York Times* (August 12).

Hughes, Langston. 1940. *The Big Sea*. New York: Hill and Wang.

Hughes, Robert. 1990. "The Decline of the City of Mahagonny." *The New Republic* (June 25): 27–38.

Huxtable, Ada Louise. 1977. "Architecture View." *New York Times* (August 7).

——. 1991. "Re-Inventing Times Square: 1990." *Inventing Times Square: Commerce and Culture at the Crossroads of the World*, ed. William R. Taylor, pp. 356–70. New York: Russell Sage Foundation.

——. 1993. "Inventing American Reality." *The New York Review of Books* (December 3): 24–29.

Jackson, Peter. 1989. *Maps of Meaning*. London: Unwin Hyman.

Jager, Michael. 1986. "Class Definition and the Esthetics of Gentrification: Victoriana in Melbourne." *Gentrification of the City*, ed. Neil Smith and Peter Williams, pp. 78–91. Boston: Allen and Unwin.

Jakle, John A. and David Wilson. 1992. *Derelict Landscapes: The Wasting of America's Built Environment*. Savage, MD: Rowman and Littlefield.

Jameson, Fredric. 1984. "Postmodernism, or the Cultural Logic of Late Capitalism." *New Left Review* 146 (July–August): 53–93.

Johnson, David A. 1969. "Museum Attendance in the New York Metropolitan Region." *Curator* 12(3): 201–30.

Johnson, Ken. 1988. "Showcase in Arcadia." *Art in America* (July): 94–102.

Kappstatter, Bob. 1981a. "Bright Future in Stall for Fulton St." *Daily News* (January 9).

——. 1981b. "Downtown and Key Store Need a Bunch of Friends." *Daily News* (May 17).

Karp, Ivan and Steven D. Lavine, eds. 1991. *Exhibiting Cultures: The Poetics and Politics of Museum Display*. Washington: Smithsonian Institution Press.

Kasinitz, Philip. 1992. *Caribbean New York: Black Immigrants and the Politics of Race*. Ithaca, NY: Cornell University Press.

Kazin, Alfred. 1951. *A Walker in the City*. New York: Harcourt Brace and World.

Kearns, Gerry and Chris Philo, eds. 1993. *Selling Places: The City as Cultural Capital*. Oxford: Pergamon.

Kennedy, Shawn G. 1992. "New Momentum Builds on 125th Street." *New York Times* (November 8).

Kernek, Lisa. 1990. "Shouting for the Glen." *The Advocate* [Williamstown, Massachusetts] (February 28).

Kimmelman, Michael. 1992. "After the Guggenheim, Bigger May Be Better." *New York Times* (June 21).

Kramer, Hilton. 1976. "Art: Modern's Tower May Add Pictures at an Exhibition." *New York Times* (February 17).

——. 1990. "The Nuttiness at the Guggenheim: Sell Art Masterpieces, Buy Ideas." *New York Observer* (June 25).

——. 1992. "Guggenheim Takeover Is About Power, Not Art." *New York Observer* (July 13–20).

Kramer, Jane. 1992. "Whose Art Is It?" *The New Yorker* (December 21): 80–109.

Lash, Scott and John Urry. 1987. *The End of Organized Capitalism.* Cambridge: Polity Press.

Leach, William R. 1993. *Land of Desire: Merchants, Power and the Rise of a New American Culture.* New York: Pantheon.

Lefebvre, Henri. 1991. *The Production of Space,* trans. Donald Nicholson-Smith. Oxford and Cambridge, MA: Blackwell.

Lenardson, Alfred R. 1987. "Tanglewood." *Berkshire Magazine* (Summer): 52–57.

Lin, Jan. 1993. "Uses and Abuses of the Minority Enclave: Redevelopment and Postmodernism in Houston." Unpublished paper, annual meeting, American Sociological Association (Miami Beach).

Logan, John and Harvey Molotch. 1987. *Urban Fortunes.* Berkeley and Los Angeles: University of California Press.

Lord, George F. and Albert Price. 1992. "Growth in a Period of Decline: Deindustrialization and Restructuring, Flint Style." *Social Problems* 39(2): 155–69.

Lorde, Audre. 1982. *Zami: A New Spelling of My Name.* Freedom, CA: The Crossing Press.

Massachusetts Museum of Contemporary Art. 1989a. *Feasibility Study and Development Plan.* North Adams, MA: Author.

——. 1989b. *From Mill to Museum: History and Change at the Marshall Street Complex.* North Adams, MA: Author .

——. 1993. *Feasibility Study and Development Plan.* Grant Agreement #4, Amendments to the Phase I Plan, December. North Adams, MA: Author.

Massey, Douglas S. and Nancy A. Denton. 1993. *American Apartheid: Segregation and the Making of the Underclass.* Cambridge, MA: Harvard University Press.

"Mass MoCA Starts Tours of Project." 1990. *Union News* [Springfield, Massachusetts] (July 12).

McCannell, Dean. 1976. *The Tourist.* New York: Schocken.

——. 1992. *Empty Meeting Grounds.* New York: Routledge.

McCunn, Ruthanne Lum. 1988. *Chinese American Portraits: Personal Histories 1828–1988.* San Francisco: Chronicle Books.

McGill, Douglas C. 1989. "A 'Mickey Mouse' Class – for Real." *New York Times* (August 27).

McHugh, Clare. 1990. "Is Krens Spreading His Resources Too Thin?" *New York Observer* (March 12).

——. 1991. "The Transom." *New York Observer* (November 18).

Merry, Sally Engle. 1981. *Urban Danger: Life in a Neighborhood of Strangers.* Philadelphia: Temple University Press.

"The Met Grill." 1988. [Interview With Thomas Krens.] *Metropolitan Home* (April).

Mickey Mouse Movie Stories. 1988. Facsimile ed., intro. by Maurice Sendak. New York: Harry N. Abrams.

Mitchell, Timothy. 1988. *Colonising Egypt.* Cambridge: Cambridge University Press.

Molotch, Harvey. 1976. "The City as a Growth Machine." *American Journal of Sociology* 82: 309–32.

——. Forthcoming. "L.A. as Product: How Art Counts in a Regional Economy." *Los Angeles: Geographic Essays,* ed. Allen Scott and Edward Soja. Berkeley and Los Angeles: University of California Press.

Moore, Charles. 1965. "You Have to Pay for the Public Life." *Perspecta,* nos. 9–10: 57–106.

Morris, Meaghan. 1988. "Things to Do with Shopping Centres." *Grafts: Feminist Cultural Criticism,* ed. Susan Sheridan, pp. 193–225. London: Verso.

Mullins, Patrick. 1991. "Tourism Urbanization." *International Journal of Urban and Regional Research* 15: 326–42.

Munk, Erika. 1990. "Urban Renewals." *Village Voice* (January 30).

Nash, David J. 1989. "Contemporary Art at Auction." *The Business of Art,* ed. Lee Caplin, pp. 303–7. Englewood Cliffs, NJ: Prentice-Hall.

Nash, June. 1989. *From Tanktown to High Tech: The Clash of Community and Industrial Cycles*. Albany: State University of New York Press.

Nathan, Jean. 1988. "New Director of Guggenheim Hints Big Changes Lie Ahead." *New York Observer* (February 22).

——. 1989. "Where the Boys Are." *Art and Auction in America* (November): 212–21.

New York City Department of City Planning. 1995. *Update of Immigration to New York City: 1990–1993*. New York: Author.

New York State Department of Labor. 1986. *Annual Labor Area Report, Fiscal Year 1986*. New York: Author.

——. 1988a. *Annual Labor Area Report, Fiscal Year 1988*. New York: Author.

——. 1988b. *Industry Profile, 1988*. New York: Author.

——. 1990. *New York City Occupational Supply and Demand*. New York: Author.

New York State Urban Development Corporation. 1984. *Draft Environmental Impact Statement, 42nd Street Redevelopment Project*, 2 vols. New York: Author.

"The Nonprofit Sector of the Region's Economy." 1982. *Regional Plan News* 111 (September).

Orlando Business Journal. *1992 Book of Lists*. Orlando, FL: Author.

Oser, Alan S. 1990. "Controlling Scale Near Historic Districts." *New York Times* (October 28).

Osofsky, Gilbert. 1971. *Harlem: The Making of a Ghetto*. New York: Harper and Row.

Ovington, May White. 1911. *Half a Man: The Status of the Negro in New York*. New York: Longmans, Green, and Co.

Owens, Carole. 1984. *The Berkshire Cottages: A Vanishing Era*. Lenox, MA: Cottage Press.

Pearl, Daniel. 1989. "North Adams Rues Renewal." *Berkshire Eagle* (May 21).

Peretz, Henri. 1992. "Le vendeur, la vendeuse et leur cliente: ethnographie du prêt-à-porter de luxe." *Revue française de sociologie* 33: 49–72.

Perry, David C. 1987. "The Politics of Dependency in Deindustrializing America: The Case of Buffalo." *The Capitalist City: Global Restructuring and Community Politics*, ed. Michael P. Smith and Joe R. Feagin, pp. 113–37. Oxford: Blackwell.

Phillips, Susan C. 1990a. "Coalition Hits Glen and MOCA." *Berkshire Eagle* (January 25).

—. 1990b. "Inspector General Says MoCA Plan Illegal." *Berkshire Eagle* (June 22).

—. 1991. "Time to Think Small on MoCA, State Says." *Berkshire Eagle* (September 25).

Picard, Joe and Sharon Cates. 1990. "Clash at Uptown Korean Market." *Village Voice* (June 5).

Pincus, Andrew L. 1989. "As Tanglewood Goes, So Go the Berkshires." *New York Times* (July 2).

Port Authority of New York and New Jersey. 1983. *The Arts as an Industry: Their Economic Importance to The New York–New Jersey Metropolitan Region*, New York: Port Authority of New York and New Jersey and Cultural Assistance Center.

—. 1993. *The Arts as an Industry: Their Economic Importance to the New York–New Jersey Metropolitan Region.* New York: Port Authority of New York and New Jersey, Alliance for the Arts, New York City Partnership, and Partnership for New Jersey.

Porter, Henry. 1992. "London Diary." *New York Observer* (February 2).

Pred, Allan R. 1973. *Urban Growth and the Circulation of Information: The United States System of Cities, 1790–1840.* Cambridge, MA: Harvard University Press.

Rangel, Jesus. 1986. "Two Years After Renovation, Brooklyn's Fulton Mall Seeks an Anchor." *New York Times* (June 14).

Reed, Danielle. 1994. "Board 10/Officials Peddle Vendor Relocation Plan." *New York Observer*(April 18).

Register, William Wood, Jr. 1991. "New York's Gigantic Toy." *Inventing Times Square: Commerce and Culture at the Crossroads of the World,* ed. William R. Taylor, pp. 243–70. New York: Russell Sage Foundation.

Research Center for Arts and Culture. 1989. *Information on Artists: A Study of Artists' Work-Related Human and Social Service Needs in Ten U.S. Locations.* New York: Trustees of Columbia University and Research Center for Arts and Culture.

Richardson, John. 1992. "Go Go Guggenheim." *New York Review of Books* (July 13): 18–22.

Roberts, Susan M. and Richard H. Schein. 1993. "The Entrepreneurial City: Fabricating Urban Development in Syracuse, New York." *Professional Geographer* 45 (1): 21–33.

Rodriguez, Sylvia. 1989. "Art, Tourism, and Race Relations in Taos: Toward a Sociology of the Art Colony." *Journal of Anthropological Research* 45: 77–99.

Rosenthal, Jack. 1992. "Mickey Mousing." *New York Times Magazine* (August 2).

Rosenzweig, Roy and Elizabeth Blackmar. 1992. *The Park and the People: A History of Central Park*. Ithaca, NY: Cornell University Press.

Rudolf, Fredrick. 1947. "Chinamen in Yankeedom: Anti-Unionism in Massachusetts in 1870." *American Historical Review* 53(3): 1–29.

Rule, Sheila. 1982. "Korean Merchants Face Ire in Harlem." *New York Times* (September 11).

Sassen, Saskia. 1987. "Growth and Information at the Core: A Preliminary Report on New York City." *The Capitalist City: Global Restructuring and Community Politics*, ed. Michael P. Smith and Joe R. Feagin, pp. 138–54. Oxford: Blackwell.

Savageau, David and Richard Boyer. 1993. *Places Rated Almanac: Your Guide to Finding the Best Place to Live in North America*. New York: Prentice-Hall Travel.

Sayer, Andrew. 1989. "The 'New' Regional Geography and Problems of Narrative." *Environment and Planning D: Society and Space* 7: 251–76.

Schwartz, Joel. 1993. *The New York Approach*. Columbus: Ohio State University Press.

Scott, Allan J. and Michael Storper, eds. 1986. *Production, Work, Territory*. Boston: Allen and Unwin.

Sears, John F. 1989. *Sacred Places: American Tourist Attractions in the Nineteenth Century*. New York: Oxford University Press.

Seider, Maynard. 1985. "North Berkshire Labor and the Current Industrial Crisis." Unpublished paper, Berkshire Forum Conference on The Crisis of U.S. Industrial Workers (Stephentown, NY).

Sennett, Richard. 1990. *The Conscience of the Eye*. New York: Norton.

Servin, James. 1993. "Enter Bellhop, Stage Right." *New York Times* (November 7).

Shields, Rob. 1989. "Social Spatialization and the Built Environment: The West Edmonton Mall." *Environment and Planning D: Society and Space* 7: 147–64.

—. 1992a. "A Truant Proximity: Presence and Absence in the Space of Modernity." *Environment and Planning D: Society and Space* 10: 181–98.

—. 1992b. "The Individual, Consumption Cultures and the Fate of Community." *Lifestyle Shopping: The Subject of Consumption*, ed. Rob Shields, pp. 99–113. London and New York: Routledge.

—. 1994. "Fancy Footwork: Walter Benjamin's Notes on Flânerie." *The Flâneur*, ed. Keith Tester, pp. 61–80. London and New York: Routledge.

Siegel, Fred. 1992. "Reclaiming Our Public Spaces." *City Journal* (Spring): 35–45.

Silverman, Deborah. 1986. *Selling Culture: Bloomingdale's, Diana Vreeland, and the New Aristocracy of Taste in Reagan's America*. New York: Pantheon.

Simon, Kate. 1982. *Bronx Primitive*. New York: Harper and Row.

Slatin, Peter. 1993. "Al Fresco Dining Facing Grand Central?" *New York Times* (August 22).

Sliwa, Carol. 1994a. "Mass. to Keep MOCA on Track." *Berkshire Eagle* (March 30).

—. 1994b. "MoCA: Slight Glitch, Optimism." *Berkshire Eagle* (March 31).

Smith, Michael Peter and Joe R. Feagin, eds. 1987. *The Capitalist City*. Oxford: Blackwell.

Smith, Neil and Peter Williams, eds. 1986. *Gentrification of the City*. Boston: Allen and Unwin.

Sontag, Susan. 1977. *On Photography*. New York: Farrar, Straus and Giroux.

Sorkin, Michael. 1992. "See You in Disneyland." *Variations on a Theme Park*, ed. Michael Sorkin, pp. 205–32. New York: Hill and Wang.

Sotheby's. 1987. *Sotheby's Art at Auction, 1986–1987*. New York: Sotheby's Publications.

Spear, W. F. 1885. *History of North Adams Massachusetts: 1749–1885*. North Adams, MA: Hoosac Valley News Printing Co.

Stallybrass, Peter and Allon White. 1986. *The Poetics and Politics of Transgression*. Ithaca, NY: Cornell University Press.

Storper, Michael. 1989. "The Transition to Flexible Specialization in the U.S. Film Industry: External Economies, the

Division of Labor, and the Crossing of Industrial Divides."
Cambridge Journal of Economics 13: 273–305.

Sullivan, Ronald. 1993. "Crackdown on Vendors in the Streets." *New York Times* (April 13).

Suttles, Gerald D. 1968. *The Social Order of the Slum*. Chicago: University of Chicago Press.

Tabb, William K. 1970. *The Political Economy of the Black Ghetto*. New York: Norton.

Tagg, John. 1992. "A Discourse (With Shape of Reason Missing)." *Art History* 15: 351–73.

Taub, Richard P., D. Garth Taylor, and Jan D. Dunham. 1984. *Paths of Neighborhood Change: Race and Crime in Urban America*. Chicago: University of Chicago Press.

Taylor, William R., ed. 1991. *Inventing Times Square: Commerce and Culture at the Crossroads of the World*. New York: Russell Sage Foundation.

—. 1992. "The Evolution of Public Space: The Commercial City as Showcase." *In Pursuit of Gotham: Culture and Commerce in New York*, pp. 35–50. New York: Oxford University Press.

Teaford, Jon C. 1990. *The Rough Road to Renaissance: Urban Revitalization in America, 1940–1985*. Baltimore: Johns Hopkins University Press.

"Thinking Big." 1987. *Art News* (September).

Thurow, Lester C. 1989. "Regional Transformation and the Service Activities." *Deindustrialization and Regional Economic Transformation: The Experience of the United States*, ed. Lloyd Rodwin and Hidehiko Sazanami, pp. 179–98. Boston: Unwin Hyman.

Tichenor, Mary-Jane. 1989. "450 Cinderellas Can't Go to the Ball." *Berkshire Eagle* (February 7).

"Tolerance as an Art Form." 1993. *Monographs (National Assembly of Local Arts Agencies)*(May–June).

Tracy, Allison. 1982. "A Celebration of Dance." *Berkshire Magazine* (Summer): 25–27.

Traster, Tina. 1990. "Hope on 125th Street; History, Black Affluence, and Local Initiative May Turn Harlem Around." *American Demographics* (August).

United States Department of Labor, Bureau of Labor Statistics. 1989. *Employment Hours and Earnings, States and Areas, 1972–1987*, vol. 3, bulletin 2320. Washington, DC: Author.

Urry, John. 1990a. "Lancaster: Small Firms, Tourism and the 'Locality.' " *Place, Policy and Politics*, ed. Michael Harloe, C. G. Pickvance, and John Urry, pp. 146–64. London: Unwin Hyman.

—. 1990b. *The Tourist Gaze*. London: Sage.

Van Slyke, Irene. 1978. "Fulton Street – and the Shoppin' Ain't Easy." *The Brooklyn Phoenix* (April 13).

Venturi, Robert, Denise Scott Brown, and Steven Izenour. 1972. *Learning from Las Vegas*. Cambridge, MA: MIT Press.

Vietorisz, Thomas and Bennett Harrison. 1970. *The Economic Development of Harlem*. New York: Praeger.

Vogel, Carol. 1993. "In Times Square, Art Conquers Kung Fu." *New York Times* (July 7).

Waldinger, Roger. 1990. "Immigrant Enterprise in the United States." *Structures of Capital: The Social Organization of the Economy*, ed. Sharon Zukin and Paul DiMaggio, pp. 395–424. Cambridge: Cambridge University Press.

—. 1992. "Taking Care of the Guests: The Impact of Immigrants on Services – an Industry Case Study." *International Journal of Urban and Regional Research* 16: 97–113.

Wallace, Mike. 1985. "Mickey Mouse History: Portraying the Past at Disney World." *Radical History Review* (32): 33–57.

Wallock, Leonard. 1988a. "New York City: Capital of the 20th Century." *New York: Culture Capital of the World 1940–1965*, ed. Leonard Wallock, pp. 17–52. New York: Rizzoli.

—, ed. 1988b. *New York: Culture Capital of the World 1940–1965*. New York: Rizzoli.

Watson, Catherine. 1992. "A Touch of Americana at Euro Disney Resort." *Sacramento Bee [Minneapolis–St.Paul Star Tribune]*(April 26).

Watson, Peter. 1992. *From Manet to Manhattan: The Rise of the Modern Art Market*. New York: Random House.

Watson, S. 1991. "Gilding the Smokestacks: The New Symbolic Representations of Deindustrialised Regions." *Environment and Planning D: Society and Space* 9: 59–70.

Weisgall, Deborah. 1989. "A Megamuseum in a Mill Town." *New York Times Magazine* (March 5): 32 ff.

Wheaton, Dennis Ray. 1990. "The Busy Bee: Homes away from Home." *The Journal of Gastronomy* 6(1): 16–23.

Whitt, J. Allen. 1987. "Mozart in the Metropolis: The Arts Coalition and the Urban Growth Machine." *Urban Affairs Quarterly* 23:15–36.

Whitt, J. Allen and John C. Lammers. 1991. "The Art of Growth: Ties Between Development Organizations and the Performing Arts." *Urban Affairs Quarterly* 26: 376–93.

Whyte, William H. 1980. *The Social Life of Small Urban Spaces*. Washington, DC: Conservation Foundation.

—. 1988. *The City: Rediscovering the Center*. New York: Doubleday.

Wideman, John Edgar. 1984. *Brothers and Keepers*. New York: Holt, Rinehart and Winston.

Wilkinson, Richard G. 1973. *Poverty and Progress: An Ecological Model of Economic Development*. London: Methuen.

Willems-Braun, Bruce. 1994. "Situating Cultural Politics: Fringe Festivals and the Production of Spaces of Intersubjectivity." *Environment and Planning D: Society and Space* 12: 75–104.

Williams, Raymond. 1973. *The Country and the City*. New York: Oxford University Press.

Wilson, Alexander. 1992. *The Culture of Nature: North American Landscape from Disney to the Exxon Valdez*. Oxford: Blackwell.

Wilson, Elizabeth. 1991. *The Sphinx in the City: Urban Life, the Control of Disorder, and Women*. London: Virago Press.

Winnick, Louis. 1990. *New People in Old Neighborhoods*. New York: Russell Sage Foundation.

Wolfe, Kevin. 1993. "Who Saves What and Who Benefits?" *Metropolis* (June): 54–67.

Wolff, Janet. 1985. "The Invisible Flâneuse: Women and the Literature of Modernity." *Theory, Culture & Society* 2(3): 37–48.

Wolfson, Howard. 1992. "New York Bets on BIDs." *Metropolis* (April): 15, 21.

Wright, Patrick. 1985. *On Living in an Old Country*. London: Verso.

Zuber, Martha. 1992. "Mickey-sur-Marne: une culture conquérante?" *French Politics and Society* 10: 1–18.

Zukin, Sharon. 1989 [1982]. *Loft Living: Culture and Capital in Urban Change*, 2nd ed. New Brunswick, NJ: Rutgers University Press.

—. 1990. "Socio-Spatial Prototypes of a New Organization of Consumption: The Role of Real Cultural Capital." *Sociology* 24: 37–56.

—. 1991. *Landscapes of Power: From Detroit to Disney World.* Berkeley and Los Angeles: University of California Press.

—. 1993. "Hochkultur Und 'Wilder' Kommerz:Wie New York Wieder Zu Einem Kulturellen Zentrum Werden Soll." *New York: Strukturen Einer Metropole*, ed. Hartmut Haussermann and Walter Siebel, pp. 264–85. Frankfurt: Suhrkamp.

INDEX

Abraham & Straus, 217, 229
aestheticization of fear, 2, 11, 26,
    39, 49, 53, 259, 267, 275,
    282, 288, 294
African Americans, 21, 42, 43,
    44, 160, 193, 194, 201, 202,
    203, 205, 211, 214–5, 223,
    229, 230, 231, 244, 245,
    277–8; and landmarks, 125,
    277; and tourism, 83, 245; as
    customers, 200, 212, 216,
    223, 230, 234, 238–9, 251,
    256; as employees, 171, 182,
    229, 234; as storeowners,
    228, 229, 234–5, 236, 241,
    242; ethnic culture, 44, 238,
    239, 246, 247, 256, 267, 277;
    neighborhoods, 44, 207, 210,
    214, 215, 251 see also
    Harlem, 125th Street
African market, 239–47, 249,
    267, 294
Africans, 156, 230; street
    vendors, 196, 210, 244–6 see
    also African Market
air rights, 15, 130–1
Akron, Ohio, 272–3
Anaheim, California, 9, 49, 50
Anderson, Elijah, 41
Apollo Theater, 231, 235

"Arabs" (as storeowners), 211,
    229–30, 245
arcades (Paris) 188, 190, 260
architecture, 36, 60, 80, 151,
    188, 293; architects, 148,
    292; critics, 69; design, 2, 77,
    131, 137, 150, 275;
    postmodern, 50n, 69 see also
    historic preservation,
    landmarks
art market, 94, 102, 105, 150,
    279
art museums, see museums
Artistic Mode of Production,
    111, 280
artists, 12–13, 20, 22, 23, 60, 79,
    87, 90–1, 94, 110, 111, 112,
    116, 118, 119, 125, 147–51,
    188, 189, 264, 267, 271, 292;
    as arts work force, 115,
    144–7, 148–50, 284; as
    restaurant work force, 144,
    152, 153–84, 291, 294 see
    also New York City, arts
    economy
arts economy, 23, 116 see also
    New York City, arts
    economy
arts: government funding for,
    110–1, 143–4

Asians, 156, 191, 212, 237
ATMs (automatic teller
    machines), 43
auction houses, 114, 115, 118,
    119
auctions: art, 112, 142
Audubon Ballroom, 126–7, 277
avant garde art, 19, 88, 90, 92,
    103–4, 105

bazaar, 53, 67, 150, 189, 190,
    208, 240, 249, 254
Beaux Arts architecture, 54, 124,
    134
Benjamin, Walter, 188, 189–90,
    196, 197–8, 200, 201, 204,
    213, 247, 253–7, 259, 260
Bensonhurst, 214, 251
Berger, John, 31
Berkshire Mountains, 80, 81
    (map), 84–9, 109, 279
Berlin, 197–8, 254, 269
Berman, Marshall, 254, 288
Bhabha, Homi, 290
BIDs, *see* business improvement
    districts
Biumo Di Panza, Count, 91,
    93–4
Blacks, *see* African Americans,
    African market, Africans
Blackmar, Betsy, 29
Blumstein's Department Store,
    231, 232, 234
boycotts: of Bryant Park, 31; of
    Korean–owned stores, 211,
    211n, 234, 245; of
    white–owned stores, 204,
    231, 234, 245
Broadway theaters: as public
    space, 3, 139; economics of,
    111, 112, 115, 135–6, 145–6,
    147
Bronx, 199, 213, 254, 288
Brooklyn, 213–4, 225 (map);
    downtown, 212, 213–30, 257,
    266, 271, 274; Downtown
    Brooklyn Development

Association, 216–7 *see also*
    Bensonhurst, Brownsville,
    Crown Heights, Fulton Mall,
    MetroTech
Brownsville, 197–9, 205, 215
Bryant Park, 1n, 3, 6, 9–10, 24,
    28, 29–32, 34, 39, 40, 259,
    260, 261, 262, 275–6, 285,
    286, 290, 291, 294, 292, 293
Bryant Park Restoration
    Corporation, 6, 28, 29–30,
    33, 34
Buchanan, Patrick, 46
Bush, George, 10, 144
business improvement districts,
    33–8, 40, 46, 55, 65, 66–7,
    256, 261, 275, 285–6, 292 *see
    also* Bryant Park
    Restoration Corporation,
    Fulton Mall Improvement
    Association, Grand Central
    Partnership, 34th Street
    Partnership, Times Square
    BID

Caesar's Bay
    Bazaar, 250–3
Camden, New Jersey, 22, 83
Caribbean Americans, 20–1, 203,
    212, 214, 215
Castells, Manuel, 268
Central Park, 3, 20, 25–6, 27, 28,
    29, 32–3, 116, 118, 121, 129,
    133, 260, 262
Central Park Conservancy, 28,
    29, 32–3, 36
childhood memory, 191–2,
    196–207
civility, 36, 42, 44, 46, 52, 54, 65,
    160–1, 211, 217, 248, 263,
    266, 270, 276, 292, 294;
    visions of, 31, 228, 259, 262,
    276
Conceptual art, 93–4, 97, 103,
    107
consumption, 13, 81, 187, 188,
    208, 260, 270; commercial,

262; cultural, 2, 10, 11, 13,
19, 117, 182, 268, 278, 279,
283, 292; of symbols, 156;
practices, 253; spaces, 13,
59, 64–5, 188, 189, 190, 270
corporate culture, 74, 267
Crown Heights, 20, 215
cultural capital, 70, 74, 128, 154,
155, 160, 168, 170, 172, 174,
179, 183, 196, 201
cultural hegemony, 119, 121,
274, 276, 279, 280
cultural institutions, 2, 12, 14,
15, 24, 104, 109, 110, 111,
113, 114, 115, 116, 117, 118,
119, 120, 133, 143, 144, 147,
151, 270, 271, 283, 284, 285,
292; and elites, 270; growth
of, 128–33; history of, 116,
120–2 *see also* Broadway
theaters, museums, and
names of individual
institutions
cultural producers: *see* artists
cultural strategies, 41, 261, 270,
271, 279, 284, 285, 286, 288,
289, 292; of economic
development, 12, 14, 23, 31,
51–2, 54, 63, 77, 80–1, 83,
89, 102, 106, 107, 109,
111–2, 121, 126, 151, 271–8,
280, 282, 284, 290, 294
culture: capital, 12, 147–51, 153,
155, 279; industries, 9, 10,
12–14, 19, 51, 110, 112, 119,
139, 146, 147, 148, 150, 155,
260, 264, 267, 270, 284, 286,
290, 292; meanings of, 12,
112–3, 261, 263–71, 289–90;
visual, 54, 265, 269 *see also*
corporate culture; cultural
strategies of economic
development; New York
City, arts economy; New
York City, as culture capital

Davis, Mike, 39, 288
department stores, 42, 118, 188,
195–6, 209–10, 213, 216,

217, 223, 229, 231, 233, 246,
248, 252–3, 255, 259, 275;
buyouts and mergers, 208–9;
hegemony of, 218–22, 230;
reorganization of, 208, 210
see also Abraham & Straus,
Blumstein's, Macy's
Dinkins, David N., 20, 125, 143,
242, 243
Disney Company, 3, 8–9, 10, 19,
49, 50–3, 55, 69, 71, 73, 141,
142, 292
Disneyland, 45, 49, 50, 52–3, 54,
56–7, 58, 72, 76
Disney, Walt, 51, 55–7, 75
Disney World, 34, 37, 38–9,
49–78, 154, 183, 260, 278,
280, 286, 292, 294;
aquaculture at, 73; as public
culture, 52–3, 60, 67, 76, 77;
as public space, 38–9, 49, 53,
59, 61, 65, 67, 69; as service
industry, 55, 69–74; as
symbolic economy, 46, 49,
52, 55, 74–7; as theme park,
50–1, 54, 55, 57, 61, 70, 72,
75, 76; as urban design, 57,
63–4; work force, 52, 55, 63,
69–74, 74–5, 278 *see also*
Orlando
"Disneyitis," "Disneyization",
67–9, 128
Disney's America, 278
diversity, 2, 31, 64, 65, 107, 112,
113, 195, 202, 203, 262, 290,
294; aesthetic, 64; cultural,
217, 283, 290; ethnic, 42,
125, 169, 179, 182, 188, 211,
252, 260, 268, 283; social,
156, 168–71, 260, 261, 274,
276, 280
divisions of labor: ethnic, 10,
156–8, 171–5, 210, 282, 284;
social, 156, 168–71
Dominicans, 157, 248
downtown, 190, 196, 198, 200,
207, 208, 209, 212, 255, 256,

257, 265, 281, 294 *see also*
    Brooklyn, downtown;
    department stores;
    Philadelphia, downtown

Ehrenreich, Barbara, 208
11th Street (shops), 192, 193,
    194, 196, 206, 207, 253–5,
    289
Emmerich, André, 4, 6, 17
emotive labor, 70
"entertainment economy", 8, 51
espaces conçus, 196, 293
espaces vécus, 190, 196, 293
ethnicity, 44, 46, 67, 77, 81, 157,
    171, 188, 198, 203, 206, 207,
    211, 213, 230, 236, 238, 239,
    245, 255, 256, 257, 280, 284,
    291; ethnic cultures, 42, 264,
    265, 286; ethnic identity, 20,
    45, 49, 124, 191, 194, 210,
    211, 255, 256; ethnic Other,
    41–3, 44, 236; negotiation of,
    20, 211, 247, 248, 249, 250,
    256 *see also* African
    Americans, ethnic culture;
    divisions of labor, ethnic;
    Jews, ethnic culture
Euro Disney, 50, 57–8, 65, 278

fashion collections: Bryant Park,
    9–10
fear of crime, 38–9, 41, 42, 43,
    77 *see also* aestheticization
    of fear
fiscal crisis, New York City:
    1970s, 32, 135, 261; 1990s,
    40–1, 114, 143
Fjellman, Steven, 53
flaneur, flaneuse, 188–9, 196,
    198, 201
flea markets, indoor, 191, 209,
    223, 228, 247–53, 255, 259,
    267
Flint, Michigan, 22, 83
42nd Street, 6, 19, 24, 34, 51,
    134, 139, 275; art

installations, 19, 111, 138–9;
    redevelopment, 17–9, 37,
    133–42, 224, 271 *see also*
    Times Square, Times Square
    BID
42nd Street Redevelopment
    Corporation, 134, 135, 137
    see also Times Square
Foucault, Michel, 279, 293
framing, 15, 291–2; by art,
    15–23, 113, 116, 279, 291–2;
    of city 2, 77, 113, 259; of
    public space, 6, 20–2, 25, 42,
    284, 291
Fulton Mall, 216–30, 231, 247,
    249, 260, 266, 292 *see also*
    Fulton Street
Fulton Mall Improvement
    Association, 217, 223, 230
Fulton Street, 216 *see also*
    Fulton Mall

Gates, Henry Louis, Jr., 42
Gay Games, 264
gender, 188, 191, 193, 196, 197,
    246, 291
gentrification, 9, 17, 23, 28, 39,
    81, 111, 122, 124, 191, 211,
    214, 268, 278, 290
ghettos, 9, 39, 42, 43, 46, 196,
    201–3, 205, 206, 207, 281,
    288; culture, 267; ghetto
    shopping, 46, 207–13,
    213–30, 240, 253, 259;
    ghettoization, 207, 213,
    218–22, 223, 236, 291, 293
Giuliani, Rudolph W., 34, 111,
    144, 240, 244
global culture, 46, 59, 80, 91,
    92–3, 103, 156, 180
globalization, 77, 91, 183, 253,
    256, 265
Grand Central Partnership,
    34–6, 38
Grand Central Terminal, 34, 44
Guggenheim Museum, 15, 117,
    129, 132, 133, 279, 283; and

MASSMoCa, 80, 84, 90–2, 96–7, 99–100, 102, 103–5, 279; expansion, 90–2, 104 *see also* Krens, Thomas R.

Harlem, 202, 204–5, 213, 230–47, 257, 292; economic redevelopment, 234, 237–9; historic preservation, 125–7, 277; history, 277; tourism, 247
Harlem Urban Development Corporation, 235, 237, 241, 245, 246
Harvey, David, 67
Held, Al, 4, 6, 17
Himes, Chester, 200–2, 206, 247, 259
Hispanics, *see* Latinos
historic districts, 77, 81, 125, 127, 128
historic preservation, 1, 17, 39, 67, 81–2, 121, 122–8, 130, 132, 137, 270, 277, 278, 286, 292 *see also* historic districts, landmarks, New York City Landmarks Preservation Commission
homeless, homelessness, 27–8, 223, 276; and Grand Central Partnership, 35–6; in public space, 9, 52, 63, 66, 285; low–wage work force, 286
homosexuals, 264
Hudson River Park, 24, 28
Hughes, Langston, 202, 206, 247
Hughes, Robert, 150
Huxtable, Ada Louise, 131, 137–8

identity, 3, 11, 13, 20, 44, 46, 54, 66, 67, 75, 81, 103, 126, 134, 187, 190, 193, 201, 203, 206, 210, 247, 253, 256, 264, 267, 268, 269, 270, 288, 289–90, 293; collective, 3, 53, 113, 217, 264, 294; community,

122, 124, 151, 270; corporate, 247, 249, 256; cultural, 24, 119, 151, 205, 283; local, 36–7, 83, 103, 107, 133, 196, 247; national, 262; social, 19, 55, 59, 189, 197; visual, 287, 289 *see also* ethnicity
immigrants, 2, 20, 22, 44, 112, 153–84, 190, 191, 207, 210, 212, 213, 224, 245, 255, 256, 267, 291, 294; as storeowners, 189, 196, 199, 211, 216, 249, 275, 292; as vendors, 211, 242, 246, 248–55; as work force, 10–12, 159–61; in restaurants, 152, 153–84, 267; recent increase in, 262
Indians, American, 14, 20, 21

Jackson Heights Beautification Group, 127
Jakle, John, 41
Jamaica, Queens, 212, 234, 245
Jews, 196, 198, 199, 203, 205, 206, 215, 229, 249, 267; as storeowners, 210, 233, 250; ethnic culture, 192, 193, 236
Judd, Donald, 93

Kazin, Alfred, 196, 197–9, 200, 201, 203, 205, 247, 259
Koch, Edward I., 137, 241, 243
Koreans, 251; as storeowners, 157, 210, 211, 228, 234, 237, 249, 256, 291
Kramer, Hilton, 92
Krens, Thomas R., 84–5, 90–2, 94, 101, 103–4, 105–6

labor unions, 13, 29, 30, 63, 72, 85–6, 89, 116, 121, 145–6, 147, 159, 177, 197, 215, 263, 273n

LaGuardia, Fiorello, 31
landmarks, 29, 58, 82, 117, 122,
    122–8, 132, 207, 231, 277,
    278, 292, 294 *see also*
    historic preservation
Latinos, 42, 76, 83, 156, 164,
    178, 230, 251
Lefebvre, Henri, 293
Lincoln Center for the
    Performing Arts, 116, 118,
    120, 121
Lord, Audre, 203–4,
    205, 247
Los Angeles, 16, 19, 22, 39, 43,
    44, 45, 47, 61, 271;
    downtown, 274, 291; riots,
    43, 72, 211n
Lowell, Massachusetts, 22, 82,
    86, 89, 107, 272–3

Macy's, 67, 209, 223, 224
Malcolm X, 126, 128,
    244, 277
Manhattan: Borough President,
    144; map, 5 *see also* New
    York City
markets, outdoor, 253–4, 255 *see
    also* African market, street
    vendors
Mart 241, 242, 243, 246–7, 248,
    249
Massachusetts Museum of
    Contemporary Art, 46, 78,
    79–107, 279, 280
Metropolitan Museum of Art, 14,
    15, 44, 91, 108, 116, 117,
    118, 120, 121, 129, 132, 133,
    143, 283
MetroTech, 215–6, 224–8,
    229–30, 266
Mickey Mouse, 50, 51, 57, 59–61
middle class, 39, 97, 116, 174,
    255, 268, 274; as consumers,
    51, 117, 208, 212, 223, 230,
    239, 245; as employees, 62;
    as tourists, 87; culture, 32,
    154, 270; neighborhoods,

121, 122, 164, 192, 214, 249,
    250; space, 10, 19–20, 53,
    64, 188, 292
Mills, C.Wright, 9
Minimalist art, 93–4, 103
modernism, 107, 122, 266, 269
modernity, 191, 254, 269, 288,
    289; cities in, 254; public
    spaces of, 42, 45, 188, 190,
    259, 261
Monongahela Valley, 273
Moore, Charles, 52–3
multiculturalism, 2, 160, 213,
    260, 262, 263, 274, 280, 283,
    288, 290
Museum of Modern Art, 14, 90,
    91, 117, 129–33, 147, 210
museums, 1, 2, 3, 7, 12, 13, 14,
    15, 19, 22, 23, 79–107, 113,
    117, 118, 122, 128–33, 259,
    260, 263, 266, 267, 271, 278,
    292, 294; and framing, 15,
    291–2; branch, 84, 91, 92;
    expansion, 118, 120, 121,
    129–33, 151, 279, 292;
    marketing of, 14, 284 *see
    also* names of individual
    museums
Museum Tower, 130–2

New York City, 13, 40, 268, 270,
    271, 278; arts economy, 23,
    110–1, 113–5, 147–50; as
    culture capital, 110, 111–2,
    115, 118, 122, 128, 134, 142,
    147–51, 153, 184, 279, 293;
    City Council, 43, 124, 144,
    242; community boards, 127,
    131, 244, 245; Department
    of Consumer Affairs, 67,
    241; Department of Cultural
    Affairs, 15, 110, 143–4;
    Economic Development
    Commission, 126;
    Landmarks Preservation
    Commission, 122, 123, 124,
    125, 127, 277; Parks

Department, 29, 30, 32–3,
142; Planning Commission,
3, 131, 136; police
commissioner, 46; Police
Department, 30 *see also*
Bronx, Brooklyn, Queens
New York State Urban
Development Corporation,
135–6, 138
North Adams, Massachusetts,
78, 102, 103–4, 107, 109,
261, 268, 279, 291

Olmsted, Frederick Law, 20, 29,
30, 87
125th Street, 202, 210, 213,
230–47, 260, 271, 290, 292,
294 *see also* African Market,
Blumstein's, Harlem
Orlando, Florida, 9, 48, 49, 51,
57, 61–4, 260, 268, 273, 291

Paris, 50, 58, 188, 190, 191, 200,
240, 247, 252, 254, 269 *see
also* arcades, Paris
parks, 7, 16, 24–5, 26–7, 28,
29–30, 38, 44, 259, 266,
273–4, 292, 294;
amusement, 56–7; definition
of, 261–2; design, 25, 28, 29,
30, 31–2, 36; eating in; 31–2
see also individual names,
privatization
peddlers, *see* African market,
street vendors
Philadelphia, 191, 192, 205, 206,
207; downtown, 22, 191,
194–5, 200, 209
privatization, 46, 66, 77, 265,
293; of parks, 1n, 29–30, 32;
of public space, 38–9, 55 *see
also* business improvement
districts, public–private
partnerships
public–private partnerships, 15,
28, 40, 66, 120, 261, 275,
276, 285

public culture, 10–1, 45–6, 128,
151, 160, 247, 254, 259–62,
270, 288–9, 291, 293; and
consumption, 14, 54, 59,
188, 253; and restaurants,
160; and shopping, 187, 213,
253, 255, 256, 257; as
commercial culture, 19–20,
42–3; Disney World, 52–3,
60, 67, 76, 77; gendered,
196; in public space, 22, 29,
32, 36, 52–3, 294; inclusive,
42, 44, 50, 265, 277, 281,
293; national, 49;
negotiation of, 10, 24, 211; of
citizenship, 264; of local
identity, 37–8; of streets,
189–90; urban, 19, 34, 42–4,
190, 191, 215; vision of, 37
public space, 3, 20, 24–5, 83,
116, 138, 266, 267, 282, 286,
291, 294; access to, 22; and
culture, 113, 115, 120; and
Disney World, 49, 53, 59, 61,
65, 67, 69; and museums,
108, 119, 129, 133; and
restaurants, 160; and
shopping, 193–4, 213, 257;
commercialism of, 3–4, 19,
261–2, 293; democratization
of, 25–30; design and control
of, 2, 36, 38–9, 261, 274–6,
285, 292; multiculturalism
in, 288; of modernity, 42, 45,
259; of postmodernity, 188;
privatization of, 2, 11,
24–37, 45, 52, 275, 280;
urban, 2, 28, 39, 41, 54,
259–62 *see also* framing,
parks, restaurants, shopping
centers, shopping streets,
women

Queens Plaza, 250
Queens, New York, 162, 163,
167, 175, 179, 226 (map)

race, 62, 125, 207, 229, 235, 238, 247, 286; racial balance, 255–6; racial change, post World War II, 21, 205, 213, 215, 216, 254, 265; racial politics, 291; racial segregation, 21, 26, 41, 44, 200, 202, 231–2; racism, 263 *see also* ghettos

Reagan administration, 32

representations, 10, 14, 19, 41, 46, 53, 83, 120, 198, 254, 271, 282, 290; ethnic, 21, 36, 119, 230, 236; museum, 69; of power, 44; of space, 69, 293; politics of, 41, 290–1; visual, 15–16, 32, 271, 274

restaurants, 1, 2, 8, 10, 13, 14, 17, 20, 22, 32, 46, 65, 70, 80, 84, 110, 112, 133, 138, 144, 153–84, 203, 207, 245, 259, 267, 270, 273, 275, 281–2, 283, 284, 292, 294; as transnational institutions, 157–9, 180, 181; customers, 155, 156, 157–8, 163–5, 167, 177–80; design, 156, 163–5; divisions of labor in, 152, 156–8, 168–71, 171–75, 182, 183; employees, 156–8, 159, 165–8, 168–71; growth of, 161; hiring, 154, 156, 160, 163, 171–2, 181, 182; owners, 163–4, 175–80, 165, 167; waiters, 70, 133, 152, 154, 155, 156, 165, 166, 167, 168, 169, 171, 172, 174, 175, 207, 208, 208–9, 211–3, 294

riots, urban, 2; 1960s, 207, 230–1, 234, 235, 236; 1992, 9, 43, 45, 72, 211n, 237

Rockefeller Center, 116, 121, 133, 135

Rockefeller Foundation, 116

Rosenzweig, Roy, 29

Santa Fe, New Mexico, 20, 21

Scotto, Salvatore, 281–2

security, 24, 27, 28, 30, 36, 42, 52, 67, 211, 261, 294; desire for, 55, 259; guards, 28, 30, 31, 33, 34, 35, 39–41, 46, 54, 65, 209, 227, 228, 250, 266, 285, 291; industry, 39–41, 42 *see also* civility, fear of crime

service economy, 9, 52, 63, 73, 112, 115, 268, 273 *see also* Disney World

service sector, 160, 268; growth in, 159–60; industries, 12, 69–74, 111; jobs, 62, 86, 106, 166, 269, 272

Seurat, Georges, 276, 287, 292

Segal, Martin, 110

shopping, 187–257; as public culture, 190, 217, 253–4, 256; spaces, 59, 240, 247–8, 250, 253, 255, 256, 257, 262

shopping centers, 19, 22, 44, 64, 89, 208, 212, 236–9, 245, 248, 250, 252, 262; suburban, 19, 22, 33, 36, 37, 38, 44, 54, 55, 64, 129, 134, 139, 188, 190, 191, 194, 196, 207, 208, 209, 213, 215, 246, 248, 252, 254, 255; urban, 19 *see also* ghetto shopping centers

shopping malls, *see* shopping centers

shopping streets, 46, 193–4, 199, 203, 217, 230, 242, 247, 252, 254, 255–6, 267, 268, 284, 292; ethnic, 190, 197, 206–7, 212, 293–4; neighborhood, 34, 187n, 190–1, 192–4, 196–8, 200–7, 248, 249, 250, 252, 255, 256, 281 *see also* 11th Street

Simmel, Georg, 189

Simon, Kate, 197, 199–200, 203–4, 247

simulation, 53, 69

social class, 155, 193, 196, 197–8, 200, 202, 211, 245,

248, 250, 254, 255, 264, 268, 284, 291; and neighborhood revitalization, 124–5, 239, 246, 255; and race, 235, 238–9, 244, 247; class boundaries, 64, 65, 115, 116, 256; culture, 264–5; in public space, 19, 25, 31, 191, 264

Sony Corporation, 13

Sony Plaza, 3, 36, 259, 260, 261, 262, 293, 294

Sorkin, Michael, 54

space, 13, 253, 260; and social control, 19, 48, 54, 55, 57, 64, 65, 66, 77, 261, 286, 293 *see also espaces conçus, espaces vécus*, public space

special assessment districts, 33 *see also* business improvement districts

street vendors, 210, 212–3, 223, 228, 230, 233, 239–46, 248, 255, 256, 275, 283; complaints about, 241–2; protests, 242–5 *see also* African Market

Strong, Curtis, 206

suburbs: businesses' movement to, 12, 36, 207, 208, 255; residents' movement to, 36, 43, 214, 216, 254

Suttles, Gerald, 41, 194n

symbolic economy, 3, 7, 8, 10, 11, 14, 17, 23, 49, 55, 65, 79, 80, 102, 106, 107, 110, 114, 115, 119, 120, 122, 129, 139, 142, 144, 147, 151, 153, 155, 156, 159, 161, 162, 180, 182, 213, 260, 266, 270, 278, 288, 294; and Disney World, 46, 49, 52, 55, 74–7; definitions of, 3, 7–10, 23–4, 46; examples of, 3–7, 14; growth of, 8; occupational stratification in, 75, 161; production of space and symbols, 2, 10, 19, 23–4, 119, 265

Tanglewood, 88, 96, 105

Taos, New Mexico, 20

television, 46, 49, 54, 67, 75, 76, 77, 86, 112, 114, 115, 145, 146, 153

theater, *see* Broadway theaters

theme parks, 9, 50–1, 53, 54, 55, 83, 259, 263, 294 *see also* Disney World, Euro Disney

34th Street, 67, 275

34th Street Partnership, 34, 35–6, 67, 68

Times Square, 9, 10, 44, 46, 66, 116, 121, 122, 133–42, 259, 267, 293; art installations, 17–9; redevelopment, 17–9, 37, 133–42, 224, 271 *see also* Broadway, 42nd Street, Times Square BID

Times Square BID, 37–8, 66, 133, 139–42; community court, 37–8

tourism, 2, 50, 58, 63, 79, 82, 92, 103, 105, 110, 113, 155, 180, 191, 202, 247, 271, 273, 277, 279, 280; cultural, 77, 78, 80, 81, 82, 83, 88, 285; ethno–, 277; tourist economy, 14, 61, 88, 102; tourist industry, 20, 79, 84, 107, 111, 273; tourists, 19, 56, 58, 98, 135, 244, 247, 259, 268, 272

urban design, 270, 275, 285

urban planning, 54, 55, 116, 122, 254

urban redevelopment, 1, 16, 22, 216, 290 *see also* Harlem, economic redevelopment

urban renewal, 54, 81, 89, 116, 121, 128, 207, 215, 217, 254, 267, 288

urban studies, 268–9, 289–94

Van Gogh, Vincent, 15, 16, 292

Venturi, Robert, 190

vernacular culture, 46
vision, 10, 28, 31, 36, 37, 53, 65,
   67, 80, 107, 150, 151, 253,
   257, 261, 265, 266, 275,
   278–89
visual: aesthetics, 274, 282;
   coherence, 67, 70, 77, 138,
   286; consumption, 28, 36,
   271; culture, 113, 150, 151,
   212, 265, 269, 282; display,
   9, 68, 249, 251; framing,
   292; identity of cities, 287,
   289; images, 54, 93, 98, 101,
   269, 278, 287; order, 48, 274,
   275, 276; representation,
   15–16, 23, 24; strategies, 11,
   64, 69, 107, 275, 277, 278–9,
   286–7 *see also* framing

Wallace, Mike, 53
Weinstein, Richard, 131
West Indian–American Day
   Carnival Parade, 20, 160
whites: as customers, 206, 207,
   229, 230, 251; as employees,
41, 171, 174; as storeowners,
   200, 207, 234, 236, 237, 241;
   ethnic culture, 237, 254,
   256; in North Adams, 83; in
   Orlando, 62; in public space,
   31; neighborhoods, 43, 192,
   201, 202, 210, 250, 251
Whyte, William H., 27, 30
Wideman, John Edgar, 205, 206
Wilkinson, John, 41
Williams College, 84, 86, 89; and
   art world, 89–90; Museum of
   Art, 84, 89–90; Theater
   Festival, 88
Wilson, Alex, 53,
Wilson, David, 41
women: and shopping streets,
   187, 188, 190, 194–5, 199,
   205, 223, 246; in public
   space, 28, 38, 189, 204
working class, 264; as
   consumers, 67, 230; culture,
   44, 154; identity, 103; jobs,
   214; neighborhoods, 43, 191,
   206, 211, 249, 274, 281

Breinigsville, PA USA
19 August 2010
243798BV00006B/34/P